MYSTICISM AND SYMBOLISM IN AITAREYA AND TAITTIRĪYA ĀRAṆYAKAS

Mysticism and Symbolism in Aitareya and Taittiriya Āraṇyakas

DR. B.D. DHAWAN
[*Formerly a member of the Punjab Civil Service*]

Gian Publishing House
29/6 SHAKTI NAGAR • DELHI-110007 • INDIA

GIAN PUBLISHING HOUSE
29/6, Shakti Nagar, Delhi-110007

ISBN 81-212-0094-6

PRINTED IN INDIA

Published by Mrs. Gayatri Garg for Gian Publishing House, Delhi (India) and printed by B.N. Printers at Mohan Printing Corp., Padam Nagar, Delhi.

Dedicated to the Sacred Memory of
My Parents

Mātṛdevo Bhava
Pitṛdevo Bhava } *TĀ*, VII.11.2.

Venas tat paśyan nihitaṁ guhā sat.........

VS, XXXII.8.

Only a wise person can see that Eternal Absolute Supreme Being who is shrouded in mystery.

Trīṇi padāni nihitā guhāsya.................

VS, XXXII.9.

Three-fourth of the Supreme Being remains enshrouded in mystery.

Foreword

The word "Veda" means "the knowledge par excellence", that is, "the sacred, the religious knowledge". It does not mean one single literary work, but a whole great literature, which arose in the course of many centuries and was handed down from generation to generation by a galaxy of enlightened sages through verbal transmission, till finally it was declared at some prehistoric period to be "devine revelation", on account of the supremely sublime nature of its contents. The belief in the "sacredness" of this literature arose as it were, spontaneously, and was seldom seriously disputed.

However, the "Vedic Literature" consists of four different classes of literary works. The third of these classes is called the Āraṇyakas ("forest texts") each of which is joined to one of the four Saṁhitās or the Vedas. The Aitareya and Taittiriya Āraṇyakas belong to schools of thought of the Ṛgveda and Yajur Veda, respectively. The first "Philosophic Treatises" of hoary past have mostly remained unexplored as compared to the supervening Vedic literature called the Upanishads. It is, therefore, both a pleasure and privilege to introduce this work to the academic world. Dr. B.D Dhawan's book on "Mysticism and Symbolism in Aitareya and Taittirīya Āraṇyakas" is rather a pioneer work in this field of the Forest Texts.

The author has not only given a brief sketch of the two Āraṇyakas, but the subject of mysticism and metaphysical contents thereof has been diligently explored and systematically presented in the book. It is a matter of great satisfaction and pride to note that even in that remote past, the philosophic thoughts of India had reached its pinnacle of glory and the basic concepts about God and the human soul were clearly known and lucidly brought out. Dr. Dhawan has taken pains to explore the hidden depths of these ancient works and this book contains a warehouse of knowledge about this specific, but a little known, branch of Vedic literature. It is, therefore, a pleasure to preface these few lines to his meticulous account of the fundamental principles of Indian epistemology or philosophic thought. The reader will quickly sense that he (an administrator turned scholar) is a thorough and pains-taking researcher. It is a matter of great satisfaction to have known such a person who constitutes a rare example of so much dedication to explore and suitably present the subtlities of uniquely sublime "Vedic Literature".

December 9, 1986

BHAWANI LAL BHARTIYA
Prof. and Head,
Dayanand Chair for Vedic Studies,
Punjab University,
Chandigarh.

Preface

This book, by and large, constituted my thesis which culminated in the award of the Degree of Doctor of Philosophy to me by the Punjab University, Chandigarh (India) in the year 1981. In fact, the thesis owed its origin and emergence to my revered guide and teacher, Dr. J.D. Vidyālaṅkāra, M.A., Ph.D. (London), presently Professor in the Department of Sanskrit, Pali and Prakrit, Maharshi Dayānanda University, Rohtak, Haryana. Besides, very perseveringly and affectionately helping me in the prosecution of my studies for M.A. in Sanskrit during the years 1975-77, it was he, who induced me to the study of Vedic literature. It was once again he, who guided my deep-seated lure to unravel the mysteries of the Supernatural that the present voyage into almost unknown and unexplored sea of the ancient Āraṇyakas or the Hermit texts was undertaken in the first half of the year 1978. With God's grace, my insignificant (but persistent) efforts ultimately fructified in the consummation of this work. During all these three years or so, Dr. Vidyālaṅkāra always steered me clear of all the difficulties and very willingly, diligently and ably explained to me even the most intricate metaphysical and mystical intricacies of the Aitareya and Taittirīya Āraṇyakas which primarily constitute the basic subject-matter of this study. *Ipso facto*, my mind is overwhelmed with intense emotions in sheer thankfulness and gratitude towards Dr. Vidyālaṅkāra.

I am also greatly obliged to the erudite and saintly Dr. Ram Nath Vedālaṅkāra, previously professor of Dayānanda Chair for Vedic Studies, Punjab University, Chandigarh and who was also one of my guides. That great living Vedic scholar so many times very affectionately and lucidly explained to me certain difficult passages and stanzas of the books of my study. He also gave me all the books that were available with him in the library. What impressed me most was that he used to work on his books even at odd hours even in inclement and unfriendly season. I always took inspiration from him in becoming a *karma-yogī* in life.

I will be failing in my duty if I do not heartily offer my thanks for the occasional guidance and assistance (through books) which Dr. Ram Gopal, the then Professor of Kāli Dāsa Chair and Dr. Bhawānī Lal Bhāratīya, presently Professor of Dayānanda Chair for Vedic Studies, Punjab University, Chandigarh have been giving me. My heartfelt thanks are also due to Dr. Veena Kapur wife of Dr. O.N. Kapur for helping me in diverse ways.

My immense thanks and gratitude are also due to my wife who perseveringly and very affectionately reared me all these years of more than a decade in the prosecution of my studies, *ab initio*, in Sanskrit language. Left to herself, she would not personally like my devoting so much time and energies to the study of a subject which would not, ordinarily, add to our economic well-being; but looking to my perseverence and determination, she has always been gracefully extending all love and affection to me and willingly tolerated my confinement for long hours, either in the Punjab University Library or some other solitary cell.

My thanks are also due to Dr. Jagdish S. Sharma, the previous Librarian, Punjab University Library, Chandigarh and Mr. R.S. Dang, the then First Library Assistant in the same library for making me comfortable in the library and helping me in so many other diverse ways. I must also express my thanks to Mr. Ram Nath Goyal and Mr. Jogendar Paul Singh, my friends and stenographers who always willingly and gladly typed so many pages of my hand-written notes. They also took dictation of certain chapters from me and gave me back fairly typed material. Thanks are also due to Mr. P. C. Ahuja, stenographer for typing the original sources in Sanskrit in Devanāgarī script.

In the end, I would sincerely pray that this work may, even in some insignificant way, serve as a means of bringing about a wider knowledge of the contents and sublimacies of these venerated texts and a discriminating appreciation of their sublime teachings.

Chandigarh B.D. DHAWAN
September, 1987

Transliteration of Sanskrit Words and References

The transliteration of Sanskrit words follows the current usage of Western Oriental scholars. However, the anglicized spellings have been used in respect of such Sanskrit words which find mention in the dictionaries of English Language. No diacritical marks have been given on such words.

In addition to the footnotes supplied in the body of the book, certain original texts in Sanskrit, which are necessary to elucidate the topic under discussion, have been given in the form of references at the end of the chapter concerned and indicated by source numbers, e.g. S.1, S.2 etc. These sources have been quoted from the Aitareya and Taittirīya Āraṇyakas published by Anandāśrama Sanskrit Series. References of the Aitareya Āraṇyaka specify the number of the Book, Chapter and Section (Āraṇyaka, Adhyāya and Khaṇḍa, respectively) of each verse. Similar references of the Taittirīya Āraṇyaka specify the number of the Book and Chapter (prapāthaka and Anuvāka respectively) of each stanza.

SCHEME OF TRANSLITERATION

Vowels	a ā i ī u ṛ ḷ e ai o au
anusvāra	ṁ
visarga	ḥ
Consonants	
gutturals	k kh g gh ṅ
palatals	c ch j jh ñ
cerebrals	ṭ ṭh ḍ ḍh ṇ
dentals	t th d dh n
labials	p ph b bh m
semi-vowels	y r l v
sibilants	s as in *sun*
	ś palatal sibilant pronounced like the soft *s* of Russian
	ṣ cerebral sibilant as in *shun*
aspirate	h

List of Abbreviations

Alphabetic list of abbreviations of the titles of the cited texts :

AA	: Aitareya Āraṇyaka.
Bṛh U	: Bṛhadāraṇyaka Upanishad.
Ch U	: Chhāndogya Upanishad.
Kaiv U	: Kaivalya Upanishad.
KS	: Kāṭhaka Saṁhitā.
KU	: Kaṭha Upanishad.
MS	: Matrāyaṇī Saṁhitā.
Manu	: Manu-Smṛti.
MU	: Mahā-Nārāyaṇa Upanishad.
Muṇḍ U	: Muṇḍaka Upanishad.
RV	: Ṛgveda Saṁhitā.
Śat Br	: Śatapatha Brāhmaṇa.
Śvet U	: Śvetaśvetara Upanishad.
TA	: Taittirīya Āraṇyaka.
TS	: Taittirīya Saṁhitā.
VS	: Vājasaneyi Mādhyandina-Śukla-Yajurveda-Saṁhitā.

CONTENTS

Introduction

Broadly speaking, the entire Vedic literature can be divided into the following four parts :

(*i*) The Vedic Saṁhitās;
(*ii*) The Brāhmaṇas;
(*iii*) The Āraṇyakas; and
(*iv*) The Upanishads.

The Ṛgveda, Yajurveda (both of white and black schools) Sāmaveda and the Atharvaveda with their various branches constitute the Vedic-saṁhitās. The traditional Indian Thought believes the Vedas to be "*Apauruṣeya*" or "Revelation of God", but to the modern Indian mind, they are the outcome of spiritual experiences and inspirations of the great ancient seers who existed during various periods. The Vedas are not the outcome of a single omniscient mind; but collection of divine inspirations of a galaxy of really merited seers; their heirs and followers over a period of centuries.

Nature of Contents of the Saṁhitās

A glance through the Ṛgveda reveals that its hymns are an outright pouring of the heart of the devotees to the gods (who were, in general, personifications of natural forces) with the belief that the latter were kind and sympathetic and would in turn bestow worldly prosperity, heroic sons etc. on the devotees. It is essentially a book of prayers. The ancient Aryan had firm faith in the benevolence of the gods and the efficacy of his prayers to them to elicit their full protection and kindness in his mundane existence. However, with the passage of time and development of sacrificial cult, the Ṛgvedic verses came to be considered to be imbued with secret power and were used in the various rituals so as to rather compel the gods to bestow the desired boons or gifts on the sacrificer. The supremacy of the Ṛgvedic gods underwent a basic change at the stage of collection of the Yajurveda and the Sāmaveda. Majority of the mantras of the Yajurveda and all the stanzas of the Sāmaveda except 72 to 75 verses were taken from the Ṛgveda. Thus, though the basic mantras in both of these Vedas remained the same; yet the purpose of their application underwent a basic change or transformation. The same mantras when enshrined in the Ṛgveda conveyed the spontaneous prayer and out-pouring of the heart of the devotee supplicating to the Supreme Existence of the universe for help and succour in his worldly life. These very verses, when recited from the later two above quoted Vedas with the accompaniment of subsequently elaborated ritualism, came to be regarded as imbued with the secret power. Thus, with the advance of times and concomitant evolution of priestly ritualism, mere transplantation of the same mantras in the succeeding two Vedas meant a vital and rather greatly significant metamorphosis. The verses which once constituted the simple and devoted prayers of the hotṛ priests of the Ṛgveda became surcharged with the capacity of rather compelling the supplicated gods to bestow the avowed mundane boons when recited with the concomitant ceremonialism by the Adhvaryu and Udgātṛ priests of the Yajur and Sāma Vedas respectively. Things did not end there. The seers who, in the course of time, contributed to constitute the collection known as the Atharvaveda rather gleaned the social customs, magical formulae, incantations etc. then prevailing in the lower strata of the Aryans. Thus, the so-called black magic came to acquire the strength of moral sanctity when embodied in the form of Atharvaveda. All this transformation from the Book of Prayers (i.e. The Ṛgveda) to the subsequent Vedas were, by and large, attributable to the resurgence of the Brāhmaṇical sacrificial liturgy. Thus, ipso-facto, the supremacy of the Ṛgvedic gods underwent a basic change with the evolution of the sacrificial cult.

Nature of contents of the Brāhmaṇas

During the succeeding stage of the emergence of Brāhmaṇical

literature, the once all powerful but essentially benevolent, Ṛgvedic gods became subservient to and were ipso-facto, obliged to bestow the desired worldly gifts on the sacrificer when the sacrifice was performed strictly in accordance with the detailed and cumbersome procedure harnessed into operation by the fertile mind of the priestly class, A huge liturgy involving immense expense of time and money was developed and the performance of Śrauta Yajñas like Vājapeya, Aśvamedha etc. could only be a practical feasibility for the ruling, fuedal or well-to-do sections of the society. Laying out of the sacrificial campus and collection of various kinds of essential material, bricks of the fire altar etc. was really a huge and costly affair. Besides, the performance of the various rituals necessitated a sizable band of priests with their inevitable and exacting fees etc. Still, above all, the fear of a curse befalling on the sacrificer was persistently there in case even a minor lapse took place in the performance of a ceremony against the prescribed ritual (S. 1, 2).

Nature of contents of the Āraṇyakas

All this, ipso-facto, had inevitable reaction and rather abhorrence on the public mind and the rational section of the priestly class. This culminated in the emergence of the third category of Vedic literature known by the name of Āraṇyakas (The Hermit-Texts or The Forest Text-Books). In majority of the cases, these Hermit texts and the subsequent literature known by the name of Upanishads (The Philosophical Treatises) form a part and parcel of the Brāhmaṇas or are appendices thereto. It is, therefore, but natural that the language and style of these Hermit Texts and Older Upanishads may be quite prosaic; but all the same, they are richer in the mystic and symbolical content as compared to the Brāhmaṇas proper which are basically and intrinsically liturgical both in their matter as well as in details. The Hermit texts do not deal with the details regarding the actual performance of various sacrificial ceremonies and primarily devote themselves to the exposition of the philosophy behind the ritualism. Some of these texts also contain the Upanishad bearing the same name or title.

What is an Āraṇyaka ?

There is some uncertainty as to the exact meaning of the word

Āraṇyaka. Sāyaṇa gives two somewhat different interpretations of it :

1. In the preface to the Aitareya Brāhmaṇa (Aufrecht's edition,[1] p. iii), he described it as :

"The Brāhmaṇa in which rules have been laid down for observance of the vows to be performed in the forests (S. 3)."

2. In the preface to the Āraṇyaka itself he says :

(*a*) "In the Aitareya Brāhmaṇa, there is a separate part called Āraṇyaka. It is called Āraṇyaka because of being taught in the jungle" (S. 4).

and

(*b*) "In the portion dealing with the explanation of the sattras, it has been laid down that the Āraṇyaka is meant to be studied in a jungle. In this, an analysis is given of the duties to be performed by the hotṛ priest in the performance of the ceremony of Mahāvrata" (S. 5).

The latter view is energetically supported by Oldenberg and is accepted by Macdonell. Deussen feels that the name is given because, on account of its mysterious character, it should be imparted to the student not in the village; but outside it. The contents of the Āraṇyakas perhaps favour rather the latter conception so far as they consist mainly of all kinds of explanations of the ritual and allegorical speculations contained therein. The aim of the Āraṇyakas was to supply a substitute for the sacrificial rites to be used by vānaprasthas (Hermits). Keith feels that this view is far fetched. The Āraṇyakas seem originally to have existed to give secret explanation of the ritual and to have pre-supposed that the ritual was still in use and was known. However, the tendency was for the secret explanation to grow independent of the ritual until the stage was reached when the Āraṇyakas passed into the form of Upanishads.

Etymologically, the word Āraṇyaka is interpreted as :—*Araṇye Bhavaḥ* (*Araṇya+Vuñ*). The suffix '*Vuñ*' has the meaning of the state of being.

Relationship of Āraṇyakas with Earlier Literature

The Āraṇyakas as well as the older Upanishads belong to the

various Vedic schools. In fact, they form only component parts of the Brāhmaṇas. Brief particulars of some of the important Āraṇyakas may pertinently be given below :

Sr. No.	*Particulars of the Āraṇyaka*	*Name of the Veda to which it belongs*	*Name of the Brāhmaṇa of which it is part or appendix*
1.	The Aitareya Āraṇyaka	Ṛgveda	The Aitareya Brāhmaṇa
	The Aitareya Upanishad also forms its part.		
2.	The Kauṣītaki Āraṇyaka	Ṛgveda	The Kauṣītaki Brāhmaṇa
3.	The Taittirīya Āraṇyaka	Black Yajurveda	The Taittirīya Brāhmaṇa
	The Taittirīya Upanishad also forms its part.		
4.	Bṛhad Āraṇyaka	White Yajurveda	Śatapatha Brāhmaṇa
	The most important Upanishad, Bṛhadāraṇyaka Upanishad, also forms its part.		
5.	Ist section of Chāndogya Upanishad	Sāmaveda	Tāṇḍya Mahā Brāhmaṇa
6.	Jaiminīya Upanishad Brāhmaṇa	Jaiminīya or Talavakāṛa school of the Sāmaveda	—

Difference in the nature of contents of Āraṇyakas and Upanishads

Though the Hermit-Texts or the Āraṇyakas basically dealt with metaphysics; but all the same, there is a self-evident and conspicuous influence of the immediately preceding liturgical cult of the Brāhmaṇic period. The Āraṇyakas seem to have their origin at a time when the efficacy of performance of various public and private sacrifices according to detailed and rigid procedure (worked out even upto minor details) had taken a full sway over the life of the then Aryans. Naturally, the majority of the then tradition-ridden Aryans would rather shirk to listen to anything which would even remotely deprecate the poular sacrificial religion. Hence, the handful of saner seers of the Āraṇyakas had really a very difficult and sensitive role to play. Thus, retaining the language, style and main contents of the liturgical cult, these seers gave a metaphysical interpretation to the performance of various acts of the different sacrifices. However, the metaphysical content of the Āraṇyakas constitutes rather a less significant portion as compared to plethora of ritualistic details from which, perhaps, on account of the peculiar social and religious circumstances then prevailing, they could not possibly extricate themselves. Thus, it remained for the supervening literature known by the name of Upanishads to completely give up the details of the liturgical contents and primarily bring forth and espouse the mystical and philosophical aspects both in the cosmic and microcosmic fields. It was primarily on account of these reasons that Paul Deussen[2] opines as follows :

> "In the Upanishad texts, we may hope for a deeper insight into the rise of one of the most remarkable and prolific creations of thought that the world possesses."

Reasons for selecting only two Āraṇyakas for study

A glance through the above list of the extant Āraṇyakas shows that the Aitareya Āraṇyaka is the more important Hermit text that pertains to the Ṛgvedic school of thought. In the entire Vedic literature, the Ṛgveda has its most prominent place to adore. Hence, the justification for taking up the Aitareya Āraṇyaka for a detailed study in this work. The second work taken up for analysis in this book is, "The Taittirīya Āraṇyaka" which, undoubtedly is the most important Forest Text-Book pertaining to the Yajurveda. This Vedic Saṁhitā has its own unique importance in the then highly developed field of liturgical cult. In fact, every verse of this Veda is sacrifice-oriented. Above all, this Āraṇyaka is the most voluminous of all available hermit texts so much so that one of the most important Upanishads called Taittirīya Upanishad also forms its part and parcel. Any study of this type would have been rather miserably incomplete in case this most important Āraṇyaka had not fallen within its ambit. Detailed study of Symbolism and Mysticism alongwith certain subsidiary issues found in the Aitareya and Taittirīya Āraṇyakas has furnished adequate material to constitute this book. Besides, efforts have also been made to succinctly and clearly bring out the important aspects of the entire literature falling under the caption of Āraṇyakas in the study particularly in respect of its distinctive features vis-a-vis the preceding and succeeding Vedic literature. Hence, the justification to include only these two Āraṇyakas within the compass of this work.

NOTES AND REFERENCES

1. Original not seen, *cf.* Keith, AA. p. 15.
2. The Philosophy of the Upanishads, p. 53.

SOURCES

१. विधिहीनस्य यज्ञस्य सद्यो कर्ता विनश्यति ।

२. अवज्ञया कृतं हन्याद् दातारं नात्र संशयः ।

३. अरण्यव्रतरूपं ब्राह्मणम् ।

४. ऐतरेयब्राह्मणेऽस्ति काण्डम् आरण्यकाभिधम् ।
अरण्य एव पाठ्यत्वाद् आरण्यकम् इतीर्यते ॥

५. सत्त्रप्रकरणेऽनुक्तिर् अरण्याध्ययनाय हि ।
महाव्रतस्य तस्यात्र हौत्रं कर्म विविच्यते ॥

CHAPTER

ONE

A Broad Spectrum of the Aitareya Āraṇyaka and a Brief Sketch of its Contents

The subject-matter of the Aitareya Āraṇyaka has been spread over a span of five Books, each of which has been called as an Āraṇyaka. Each of these five Āraṇyakas has been subdivided into one or more Adhyāyas or chapters. Each Adhyāya has again been further subdivided into one or more khaṇḍas or sections.

The Forest-texts, though later in the evolution of thought, more philosophical and less ritualistic in their essential nature; yet they constitute a part and parcel of the Brāhmaṇical literature. Thus, despite the absence of any detailed analysis of the actual performance of any ritual in the Aitareya Āraṇyaka, it has neither been possible for it to completely liberate itself from the characteristically archaic language of the parent literature nor from the plethora of illogical and at times rather really amusing and funny reasoning of the Brāhmaṇas.

The Aitareya Āraṇyaka characteristically suffers from a lack of continuity of thought so as to develop a particular concept or an abstract philosophic idea or a ritual, *ab-initio*, to its natural and rational climax. In fact, a glance through various parts of the aforesaid Forest text shows that the various sections have a lot of marked and distinctive incoherence. The subject-matter seems to jump over from one concept to another altogether unconnected one. There is a characteristic lack of continuity of thought. So many sections are rather curiously studded with abstract statements in between a mass of verses written by different seers about various deities. These are rather irresistible observations which shall find full corroboration from some of the instances quoted from some parts of the Āraṇyaka in Appendix I.

A BRIEF DESCRIPTION OF THE CONTENTS OF THE ĀRAṆYAKA

The first Book consists of an explanation of the Mahāvrata from a ritualistic and allegorical point of view. It describes the different Śastras of the morning, midday and evening libations of the Mahāvrata day of the Gavāmayana.

The second Book consists of two distinct parts. The first (comprising Adhyāyas 1-3 and 7) deals with the allegorical signification of Uktha, importance of speech in human life, creative powers of puruṣa as material and efficient cause of creation, importance of prāṇa in life, creative powers of God, plethora of psuedo-mysticism, concepts of the ātman/Brahman, freedom of the latter from the limitations of name, form, gender etc. The second part comprises of Adhyāyas 4-6, and is the Upanishad par excellence.

The third Book treats of the mystic meaning of the various forms of the text of the Saṁhitā, the Nirbhuja, pratṛṇṇa and ubhayamantra, of the vowels, semivowels etc., the Saṁhitā, pada and krama pāṭhas of the Saṁhitā and importance of prāṇa in human body. It also details out so many superstitious ill-omens.

The fourth Book consists solely of the Mahānāmnī verses. The presence of these verses is explained by Sāyaṇa on the ground that they must be studied in the forest.

The fifth Book consists of a description in a Sūtra style of the Mahāvrata ceremony. In the first Book, the description of this very ceremony is in Brāhmaṇa style. Sāyaṇa feels that the description in this Book is divine while that in the fifth Book is by diverse Rishis. Stotras and Śastras used in the performance of the Mahāvrata ceremony as detailed out in this Āraṇyaka have been catalogued in Appendix II.

With the above general background, a broad spectrum of the main contents of the Aitareya Āraṇyaka is given as per supervening details :

(i) *Pseudo-mysticism*

To an average reader lacking the requisite faith in the spiritual sublimacy of the Vedic literature in general, the Aitareya Āraṇyaka makes quite a dismal reading and but for the brief upanishadic portion, the reader's entire faith in the oft-repeated high philosophy of this category of literature is very rudely shaken if not entirely taken off. Barring again the upanishad proper, almost every page of the Āraṇyaka is despoiled of much needed sanity and rationalism. The common reader finds himself grossly enmeshed in the rigmarole of priestly authoritative pronouncements—from which he does not see any sane means of escape. To a modern mind of the scientific age with due amount of intelligence, the Āraṇyaka in general (except the upanishadic portion and certain other really lofty stanzas/passages) has hardly any elevating and much less unitive influence towards the Supernatural. No doubt, spiritualistic sublimacies of the book are definitely there in a good measure; but all the same, they are greatly over-shadowed by a plethora of irrational priestly dogmatism.[1] Inevitably, the book, therefore, makes quite an uninteresting reading.

(ii) *Unusual significance attached to Mahāvrata*

The ceremony of Mahāvrata has been eulogised to an unduly high degree. The very inception of the ceremony has been connected with a Ṛgvedic parable regarding Indra's becoming great after killing his mighty foe called Vṛtra. It was on account of this greatness showered on Indra that the great festival of Mahāvrata came to be celebrated.[2] The Mahāvrata has been identified with Brahman and it is through performance of this rite that the Imperishable One is attained.[3] Performance of this ritual in accordance with the devised procedure is surcharged with the concomitant competence of bestowing the entire worldly wherewithal, health, long life, fame etc. on the sacrificer and his family.

(iii) *Dominance of priestly class*

At the time of the Saṁhitās, the deities were supreme but kind beings. They bestowed diverse worldly wherewithal on the singers of their praise. However, with the advance of times and development of ritualistic intricacies during the period of evolution of Brāhmaṇical literature; the gods became subservient to correct procedural performance of a particular rite and they were rather, thereafter, obliged to part with the avowed mundane objectives. All this contributed to the augmentation of the priestly class as such and assigned them a unique status/position in the society. It was because of this reason that the priests came to enjoy so many immunities and privileges. As for example, in case a non-brahmin found fault with the method of pronunciation of Vedic verses, it could result even in his death; but if the fault-finder happened to be a brahmin; then instead of cursing him, the reciter is required to wish him well and increasing prosperity only.[4] Brahmins were also required to be heartily fed gratis in a sizable number for warding off the ill-effects of omens.[5]

(iv) *Social conditions*

As is evident from the above, the priestly class was, in general, held in high esteem in the society. The Āraṇyaka also laid stress on practice of truthfulness, moral uprighteousness and charity in life. A significant prayer[6] declares the firm determination of the speaker to speak only of what is right and true. Niggardliness has been deprecated in the strongest terms and it has been said that a miser earns for himself ill-fame and thereby, ipso-facto, renders himself like a living-dead person. Speaking of untruth has also been condemned in strongest terms and a liar has been said to dry up right from his very roots like a tree and perish. The house-holder has been required to nourish his wife and children and also be kind and affectionate towards them. Likewise, the sons have also been required to be upright in their dealings and do only praise-worthy deeds. Similarly the property of the father and son(s) has unequivocally been stated to be joint and common. It was not owned by them individually and severally.[7]

The society was also then plagued by a number of ill-omens which were considered ominous for the well being, longevity, prosperity, health etc. of the experiencer thereof. As atonement[8] thereof some religious observances, cooking of meals, milk, free feeding of Brahmins, recitation of certain prescribed verses etc. were considered essential by the observers of these ill-omens. Subjugation of the enemies, the evil-minded and haters has also been duly stressed upon.

(v) *Mystic and metaphysical beliefs*

Briefly speaking, it may be stated that the Āraṇyaka[9] clearly brings forth the concepts of Brahman, Ātman, their mutual identity, omnipresence of the former, its having no inherent gender, permeation of the ātman throughout the body right from the nails of the feet upto the ends of the hairs of the head. The Ātman is the sole subject or knower in this world. Though invisible, it is the raison d'etre of a living creature. Doctrines of transmigration of the soul and salvation had also been fully developed by then. Significance of OM has also been briefly hinted at though not in a clear and forceful manner. One prominent feature of the metaphysical contents of the Āraṇyaka is the detailed account of the evolution of the universe from the Primeval Ātman.

A BRIEF SKETCH OF THE CONTENTS OF THE AITAREYA ĀRAṆYAKA

First Book

The first Book though gives sufficient details about the procedure and the rites/verses to be used in performance of the ceremony of Mahāvrata; yet it does not navigate into the actual enactment thereof. It no doubt details out the broad details of this ceremony; but also, inter-alia, lays more stress on the use of particular metres like Triṣṭubh, Gāyatrī etc. in the various verses to be recited, prefixation of the ṛks with vyāhṛtis, re-arrangement of verses by joining the first quarter of a pada with second quarter of the second pada and the like extension of verses by prefixation of a mystic word like him or *hiñkāra*, extension of certain verses by interpolation of parts of other verses like '*Nadam Va Odatīnām*; *Puruṣaḥ* etc. so that the verses may be converted into certain particular metres which were avowedly more effective in bestowing wordly gains like children, cattle, prosperity, food, fortune, wed-lock, honour, long life, strength, glory, health, control over the three worlds etc. Similarly recitation of certain hymns like Bhardwāja, Kayāśubhīya, Sajanīya, Tārkṣya etc was considered instrumental in driving away evil, bestowing harmony, long life, children, cattle and welfare.

Full two sections (Khaṇḍas—I.2. 3-4) have been devoted to the need of a swing in the ceremony, the wood and number of planks to be used, material and number of its ropes, fixation of its height from the ground, the manner of ascent to and descent from it so that the essentially accruing results be off-spring, prosperity, food etc.

The Brāhmaṇical concept that the fire altar should have a

bird-like shape has also been adhered to and the verses have also been detailed out so as to represent important limbs of the śastra-bird. Some amount of philosophizing has also been done—as for example :

(*i*) Sūdadohas (verse) is breath and by breath, he joins together all the joints;

(*ii*) Just as tail is the support of all birds, similarly of all the stomas, the *ekaviṁśa* is the support.

Despite plethora of ritualistic details and apparently superficial philosophizing, the first Āraṇyaka is not devoid of the philosophic or mystic content. The Gāyatrī has been stated to be Brahman, lightness and splendour. Speech unites with Brahman. There is strong correlation between mind and speech, by speech names are made, speech is denoted by rich in prayer, wherever there is vāc, there is Brahman. Similarly the first Āraṇyaka is studded with certain abstract statements like :

(*a*) *Brahma Vai Vasukraḥ*;

(*b*) *Brahma Vai Hiṁkāraḥ*; and

(*c*) *Nada* indeed is Man.

The Māhavrata day has also been identified with Brahman as it leads to its achievement. Coming over to real metaphysics, section I.3.8 clearly states that there is a ruling deity over each of our five sense organs and the soul prevails wholly in all the limbs upto hair and nails. In fact, all beings down to ants are born thus pervaded. Thus, Brahman duly existed as a principle of unity at the time of this Āraṇyaka alongwith the doctrine of the Ātman (S. 1).

Second Book

II.1.1-2. In contrast to the ritualistic details contained in the first Book, the second Book, though not entirely shorn of the liturgical references and semblances, is primarily philosophical in its subject-matter and thought. Besides, being studded at places with ethical teachings and moralising, the Book brings out that the Brahman alone is the Sole Creator of the world. He is the Supreme Entity, is Omnipotent and pervades in all the creatures and other forms of existence. There is identity between the

Ātman and Paramātman. Theory of karma, transmigration of soul, life in heaven, concept of immortality etc. have also been clearly brought out so much so that the very starting section of this Book says : "This is the path; this is the sacrifice, this is brahman; this is truth. Therefore, let no man diverge from it." The aim of human existence is happiness in this life and attainment of liberation after death. The above statement contains a formula for attainment of both.

The connotation of 'Uktha' has been invoked to illustrate certain cosmic and microcosmic forces and their respective primary functionaries, as for example, the earth and fire, the sky and air, heaven and sun, the mouth and speech, the nostrils and breath, the forehead and the eye. The Earth has been stated to be both food for the creatures that live on it and feeder thereof in the ultimate analysis of things. On this very analogy, the man has also been stated to be both feeder and food. A deep note of mysticism has been struck when it has been stated that the man is great and Prajāpati (S.2).

II.1.3. Coming over to the origin of seed, it has been said that the process of evolution of the world originates from Prajāpati through gods, rain, herbs, food, creatures etc. The man has also been defined as the 'abode of brahman'.

II.1.4. A detailed description about the entry of brahman or the ātman in the bodies of the various creatures through the tips of the feet, hoofs or claws and its subsequent upward ascent into remaining parts of the body has been given. Further more, the parable of leaving the human body and re-entry into it, one by one, in turn by speech, eye, ear, mind and finally the prāṇa has been quoted to prove that the body cannot exist without the vital airs. It is on this account that the prāṇa has been given the epithet of 'uktham.'

II.1.5. The so-called 'uktha' has been assigned the role of creating the day and nights. In fact, this uktha is nothing short of Prajāpati himself who, intrinsically speaking, is alone the regulator of time in this universe. It has further been asserted that different cosmic forces like fire, sun, moon and the quarters are represented in the body by speech, sight, mind and hearing respectively. The uktha has also been stated to be truth because in the ultimate analysis, the uktha is nothing, but Prajāpati himself.

II.1.6. Divulging out the importance of speech in life, it has been spelled out that the entire creation in this universe is cognised through a specific name. These names are like various knots in the continuous rope of speech. It is through the process of giving names that all things (animate or inanimate) are identified and described. Then the diverse powers of uktha have been detailed out.

II.1.7. Dilating on the creative powers of Puruṣa, he has been delineated both as efficient and material cause of the creation of the world. Full details have been given in chapter V infra.

II.1.8. The material cause of the world has been given out as water and the entire creation as the off-shoot. Complete identity between man and the gods constitutes a key note of this Āraṇyaka. Thereafter, the immense importance of prāṇa has been brought out as per fuller details in chapter V infra.

II.2.1-4. In these four sections, creative powers of prāṇa, its all pervasive nature, importance of recitation of one thousand bṛhatīs and identity between the soul and God have been brought out as per details in chapter V of this work.

II.3.1. *Creative powers of God*

In this section, the creative powers of the Self, the five fold hymn have been brought out as per fuller details in chapter V infra.

II.3.2. In this section, a determined effort has been made to explain the different stages of conscious life as per greater details given in chapter V of this work.

II.3.3. The Cosmic Man or Puruṣa has been stated to be as vast as the sea. It has also been stated to be omnipresent.

II.3.4-5. In both of these sections, lot of irrational philosophization has been indulged in so as to bring out significance of the great litany (Mahaduktham) and recitation of 1000 bṛhatīs as per fuller details in chapter III infra.

II.3.6. In this section, importance of syllable OM, charity and leading of a truthful and morally upright life has been brought out. Fuller details thereof have been given in chapter V infra.

II.3.7. In this section, completion of the great litany has been equated to god Indra and has been said to be instrumental to attainment of glory and salvation. The sacrificer acquires status of Indra and shines in those worlds. The remaining portion of the section advocates procreation for prolongation of the human race.

II.3.8. This long section brings forth the concepts of the Ātman/Brahman, freedom of the latter from the limitations of name, form, gender and identity between Self and the Absolute. It also asserts the God to be inducer of good deeds. Fuller details thereof have been given in chapter III infra.

II.4.1-3. In these three sections, creation of the universe from the Primeval Ātman, evolution of the man with various faculties, creation of food, entry of the soul into the body have been detailed out. Man has also been declared as replica of God. Fuller details thereof have been given in supervening chapter V.

II.5.1. In this section, the doctrine of transmigration of soul has been clearly elucidated. It refers to three births of man, concepts of heaven and ultimate attainment of immortality. This section also details out the moral and social duties of the man to caressingly support and nourish his wife and progeny. The son, when grown up, is also enjoined upon to perform good deeds in his life.

II.6.1. This section clearly brings out that Ātman is the sole sentient being in the human body and knowledge is its pre-eminent characteristic. Hence, it is the soul alone which is the doer of everything. Identity between the Ātman and brahman and omnipresence of the former have also been fully brought out.

II.7.1. In this section, the importance of mind and speech in acquiring learning has been stressed and these two have been asserted as the two pins for understanding the Veda, the supreme source of knowledge. It is followed by a prayer that the knowledge acquired by me may not forsake me and I may work day and night to attain that knowledge. The second Book closes with a very significant prayer that I and my teacher speak about the real and the true (Ṛtam and Satyam)—an extremely difficult task and therefore, 'Ṛtam and Satyam' themselves may afford us much needed protection in this world.

The Third Book

III 1.1-2. The first two sections of the first chapter deal with the philosophy underneath the basic union or saṁhitā in the cosmic and microcosmic forces in the world. The opening few sentences detail out a broad spectrum of the universal forces or the deities. Earth and heaven have been delineated as the two halves and air or ether is the uniting medium between them. In man, this union consists of mind, speech and breath. Rain, through the agency of god Parjanya, has been taken to be the uniting medium between earth and sky by another class of Vedic seers. Earth represents lower half and heaven, the upper half and breath, the ether in the human body. Just as the Sun, lightning and fire are the three lights in the macrocosm, so are eyes, heart and seed (Retas) in the human frame. Thus, broadly speaking, there is parallelism in the basic and broad structure of the universe as well as the human physical frame.

III.1.3-4. Lot of philosophization has been done about the results accruing from the recitation of Vedic verses in Nirbhuja, Pratṛṇṇa and Ubhayamantra forms. They represent the saṁhitā, pada-pāṭha and krama-paṭha respectively of the Vedic stanzas. Fault can be found with the pronunciation of the Ṛks in the first two forms; but no defects can possibly be found in the ubhayamantra form or krama-paṭha because accentuation of the various vowels in the saṁhitā and pada-pāṭha is retained in full in the ubhayamantra. Recitation of the verses in the Nirbhuja and Pratṛṇṇa results in the attainment of food and heaven respectively while both are attained by recitation of Ubhayamantra. No one should find fault with the pronunciation of reciters of the Vedic verses; because the curse given, if any, by the reciter in retaliation shall come out true. However, the Āraṇyaka rather authoritatively asserts that if the person finding fault with the pronunciation of the verses happens to be a brahmin, then the reciter should wish him well and increasing prosperity only. This provides a guarantee to the Brahmins against any insult as well as injury of any kind. Continuing the subject of curses or imprecations, it has been stated that a curse from a reciter of the Vedic verses can even result in death of the fault-finder.

III.1.5. The reciters of the Nirbhuja believe that the former syllable is the first half, the latter the second half and the space between the two is the union. This space not only creates union between the two syllables, but also enables distinction of the accented syllables from the unaccented ones and separation of the mora and what is not. All this knowledge bestows on the reciters prosperity, fame, long life and ultimately heaven after death.

III.1.6. In this section, relationship between speech and prāṇa has been brought out as per fuller details given in chapter V infra. Delineating the importance of speech, it has been said that by speech are the Vedas and metres composed. By speech, friends and all beings are befriended. Besides, there is great correlation between speech and breath.

Speaking about Prajāpati-Saṁhitā, it has been said that son is the result of union between husband and wife. The act of union is the begetting. This union is Aditi. Aditi is all whatever there is—so much so it is father, mother, child and begetting. He, who knows this union, obtains children, wealth, fame, glory, heaven and long life. All this is obviously pseudo-mysticism.

III.2.1. This chapter opens with a sentence bringing out the importance of breath in the human body. The breath has been equated to the principal beam on which a house rests. Likewise, it has been said that the eye, the ear, the mind, the speech, the senses, the body, the whole self rest on breath. The prāṇa, bones, marrow, flesh and blood of the human body have been likened to the sibilants, mutes, vowels and semi-vowels respectively in the field of words. There are seven hundred and twenty of bones, marrow and joints in the human body. This number is equivalent to count of days and nights in a year. The Ātman which consists of sight, hearing, metre, mind and speech is like the days in number. He who knows this similarity between the Ātman consisting of the constituents like sight, hearing etc. and the number of days in a year obtains union, likeness and nearness to the days, becomes rich in sons and cattle and lives a long life.

III.2.2. According to another seer called Kauṇṭharavya, there is a similarity between above quoted Ātman consisting of sight, hearing, mind etc. and the syllables (instead of days according to the earlier view) both in macrocosmic as well as microcosmic existences. The syllables when referred to the gods are actually bones with reference to the human body. There are one thousand and eighty bones, marrow and joints in the human body. So many are the rays of the Sun. They make the Bṛhatī verses and the Mahāvrata day. One who knows similarity between the Ātman and the syllables is blessed with sons, cattle and long life. All this, though given outward semblance of deep-seated philosophy, is actually nothing other than what may be termed as pseudo-mysticism.

III.2.3. Another seer called Bādhva felt that there are four so-called persons — person of the body, person of the metres, person of the Veda and the Great Person. The last mentioned

Great Person is omnipresent throughout the length and breadth of this universe and is known by the name of Brahman.

III.2.4. One who recites the Veda to another (with the exception of father and teacher), the Vedas yield him no milk or wisdom. He forgets what his teacher has taught him and becomes oblivious of the path of virtue. So, a man who knows this should neither lay the fire for another nor act as a priest in a sacrifice for another nor sing the sāmans or other śastras of Mahāvrata for another.

A major part of this section has been devoted to the delineation of Vedic superstitions or omens as to the duration of life. The various omens have been divided into two categories--first those pertaining to the awakening state and the second to the state of dreams. It appears quite pertinent to quote a few of such omens. A person should perceive that the days of his life are numbered if he sees one of the following omens of each of the above-mentioned two categories :

(i) *Omens of Awakening State*

- (*a*) when the sun is seen by the person concerned like the moon and its rays do not manifest themselves;
- (*b*) when the sky is seen red like a madder;
- (*c*) when his head smells like a raven's nest;
- (*d*) when he sees himself in a mirror or in the water with a crooked head or without a head or when his pupils are seen inverted or crooked;
- (*e*) when the fire appears blue like the neck of a peacock.

(ii) *Omens of Dreaming State*

- (*a*) when he sees a black man with black teeth; he kills him or a boar kills him;
- (*b*) when he sees a monkey jumps on him;
- (*c*) when he drives with a team of asses and boars;
- (*d*) when wearing a wreath of red flowers, he drives a black cow with a black calf towards the south.

With a view to ward off the ill-effects of the omens of the awakening state, the Āraṇyaka recommends recitation of fifteen verses of the Ṛgveda[10] and also doing of what the person concerned considers necessary. Similarly, when he sees any of the specified omnious dreams, he should fast and cook a pot of milk and offer it, reciting a verse of Rātri hymn (RV.X 127, 16) to each oblation and having fed the Brahmins with other food, himself eat the oblation. Let him know that the person within all beings who is not heard, not reached, not thought, not subdued, not seen, not understood, not classified, but hears, thinks, sees, classifies, understands and knows is his own Self.

III.2.5. Discussing the upanishad or secret of whole speech, the mutes, sibilants and vowels have been stated to represent the various elements or functionaries in the cosmos, three Vedas, sense organs and the three breaths. The human body is an imitation of the cosmos. The description may briefly be elucidated as follows in the form of a chart :

Concerned syllables of speech	*Details of what these syllables of speech represent in the field of* :		
	Cosmos	*Vedas*	*Human body*
(*a*) Mutes	Earth and fire	Ṛgveda	Eye and prāṇa
(*b*) Sibilants	Sky and air	Yajurveda	Ear and apāna
(*c*) Vowels	Heaven and sun	Sāmaveda	Mind and Vyāna

Then follows a comparison between the divine and human lutes. Both Sāyaṇa and Keith interpret the divine lute so as to represent the human body. Of course, the human lute does mean the usual musical instrument made of wood. Thus, the comparison between the two types of lutes, actually lands itself into that between human body and the usual wooden lute. Both have been said to have head, stomach, tongue, fingers, vowels/tones, consonants/touches, sound and hairy skin. He, who knows this divine lute, is heard when he speaks, his fame fills the earth and whereever they speak Aryan tongues, there is he known. In other words, it means that a man learned in letters becomes well-known and is heard with reverence among civilised people. In the end, has been quoted a recipe for being an effective speaker. A verse signifying the essence of speech has been quoted. If this verse is recited before giving a discourse, then the orator shall be heard with all attention, appreciation and reverence.

III.2.6. Speaking about the Brāhmaṇa pertaining to speech (*vāg brāhmaṇam*), the importance of ṇakāra (cerebral nasal) and ṣakara (cerebral sibilant) in the saṁhitā recitation of the Vedic verses has been brought into lime light. The former has been termed as strength and the latter as the prāṇa or self of the saṁhitā-pāṭha. In case there be doubt, if the verses are to be recited with or without ṇakāra or ṣakāra, then they should be recited with them rather than without. These saṁhitās should not be told to anybody who is not a resident pupil nor has been with the teacher for less than a year and neither to one who is himself not to become a teacher. All this is merely priestly dogmatism.

The Fourth Book

General : This Āraṇyaka delineates the Mahānāmnī verses. A brief account of these verses is contained in the chronologically supervening literature known by the name of Āśvalāyana Śrauta Sūtras (VII.12.10). On the fifth day of the pṛṣṭhya six day ceremony, at the midday pressing of the soma, corresponding to the Niṣkevalya Śastra, the Udgātṛs sing sometimes the Śākvara Sāman as one of the Pṛṣṭha Stotras and then use the Mahānāmnī verses as the basis of the Sāman. These number nine, but for the purpose of the Sāman, they are made into three, each consisting of three verses. These verses are recited adhyardhakāram, that is first one and a half verses are recited, then comes a pause, then the remaining one and a half, followed by the syllable OM. Then are recited the nine purīṣapadāni, additional verses. These may either be recited simply straight on as they stand in the text or the first five may be made into two sets of five syllables each.

All the nine Mahānāmnī verses are in praise of god Indra. Multiple epithets have been used for him. He has been addressed as most generous, lord of mights/wealth, wise, strong, most powerful, bearer of bolt, most powerful of heroes, most generous of givers, conqueror and unconquered. He is strength, resolve, mighty order, capable of bestowing favours, ancient, bright one with extolling rewards, lord of men, slayer of vṛtra, kind and guileless friend.

Various prayers have been made in these verses to god Indra. He has been requested to guide us on to the right path or mode of life, for bestowing on us glory, strength, wisdom, wealth, heroic sons, victory over foes, his favours and extolling rewards.

In the supervening purīṣapadāni or additional verses, the important gods like Agni, Vishnu, Pūṣan and all other gods have been invited to witness that Indra is strong and can wield any amount of strength according to his will. Consequently, a prayer has been made to the omniscient and all-sustaining Indra to be always near us for affording instantaneous protection.

The Fifth Book

General: The Mahāvrata ceremony has been described both in the first and fifth Āraṇyakas. In the former, the description is in Brāhmaṇa style while in the latter, the delineation of the ceremony is in sūtra form. Sāyaṇa feels that the description in the first Book is divine or '*apauruṣeya*' while that in the fifth Book is by diverse seers. He further says that in this Book, the special application of the Mahāvrata ceremony has been brought out and there is also difference in the verses to be recited in the ceremony because of the difference in their usage by diverse branches of the ritualistic cult. Keith, however, asserts that the fifth Book consists mainly of a description in a sūtra style of the Niṣkevalya Śastra of the midday libation of the Mahāvrata. It forms a sort of complement to Book I. A reading through this Book does not bring home the fact that it deals with the Niṣkevalya Śastra only. It deals with the performance of entire Mahāvrata ceremony though in the sūtra form.

V.1.1-4. Unlike the first Book, performance of Mahāvrata ceremony is initiated by recitation of Sāmidheni verses which accompany the kindling of the fire. A bull is offered to Viśvakarman accompanied by muttering of certain specified verses. This is followed by recitation of various Śastras like Ājya, Prauga etc. followed by three oblations in the Agnīdhrīya fire. Then are offered ten oblations by the Hotṛ on the mārjālīya altar followed by worship of the Sun and three rounds of dance by the maidservants carrying pitchers full of water around the mārjālīya altar. Thereafter, the fire altar is worshipped in its simplest bird shape by offering oblations to the Gāyatra, Rathantara etc. sāmans. Subsequently, the Hotṛ returns to his seat as he went. Then, the swing is got ready in certain position as per fuller details in the first Book. Thereafter, the Hotṛ strikes the swing with a lute of udumbara wood having hundred strings. Different notes corresponding to various metres are produced. After following the prescribed procedure, the Hotṛ then mounts the swing gradually in the prescribed manner while reciting specified verses so that gods like Vasus, Rudras etc. may first mount the swing. One foot of the Hotṛ must continue touching the ground from the swing. The other priests also perch themselves in the manner as per specified directions. Demounting from and remounting to the swing is also to be done in the specified manner.

V.1.5-6. Then, the Prastotṛ priest proclaims the first Pratihāra of the pañcaviṁsa stoma followed by six other mantras. Prayers are put forth for the greatness, glory, good fortune etc. of the consecrated person followed by reciting of certain other Śastras. Sacrificer should give much food on this day. A prince pierces a skin. Drums are beaten and wives of the sacrificers play on lutes. There is intercourse of creatures and a conversation between a student and a courtesan accompanied by singing of various sāmans of the Niṣkevalya Śastra which are intertwined with another specified verse.

V.2.1-5. Then have been detailed out the verses pertaining to the neck, head and vertibrae verses of the Śastra bird. These verses are recited in a specified manner by interpolation of OM. The verses of the right wing are connected with Rathantara sāman. After their recitation, the prescribed verses/hymns including saṁpāta hymn, paṅkti verses etc. are recited. Verses of the left wing are connected with Bṛhat Sāman. There are 101 and 102 verses respectively in both of these right and left wings. Then, follow 80 tristichs in Gāyatrī, Bṛhatī and Uṣṇiḥ metres.

V.3.1-2. Then are recited the thigh verses. Nividis are also inserted in a particular hymn. Various verses are transformed into Bṛhatīs. As many decades of such verses are inserted, so many years a man shall live beyond the normal life at the rate of 10 verses for a year. Then, are recited the prescribed verses after converting them into anuṣṭubhs followed by muttering of certain other verses. Thereafter, the Adhvaryu brings up the vessel containing the libation and three atighrāya bowls. The Hotṛ descends from the swing and it is tied up towards the west so that it may not slay the reciter when about to eat. The third pressing in this rite is taken over from the last day of Abhipalava rite. This completes the Mahāvrata and the Agniṣṭoma. At the proper time, the swing should be left near water and the seats of grass are burnt.

V.3.3. This section catalogues the principles to be followed in the recitation of the Mahāvrata. It has been laid down that none who has not been initiated should recite Mahāvrata nor should it be recited when there is no altar, nor should one recite it for another nor if it does not last for a year. One may, however, recite it for a father or a teacher.

Recitation of Mahāvrata should not be taught to one who is not a regular pupil and has not been so for atleast a year, nor to one who is not a brahmacārin and does not belong to the same school nor to one who has not come to the place where the teacher lives. Performance of Mahāvrata should not be taught to a child or an old man. It should only be taught by sitting in an erect posture on the ground. It should not be learnt after eating meat or seeing a dead body. The student should not shave himself or bathe or put on a wreath or have sexual intercourse. While learning this, the student should not learn anything else. He should never forget this in life. He who knows the Mahāvrata should not communicate nor dine nor amuse himself with one who does not know this. Coming over to the rules of study, it has been stated that it should not be studied in dry season like the months of January and February. It should not be studied before sun-rise and after sun-set, nor when a thick cloud has risen. When rain falls out of season, study of the Veda should be suspended for three nights. During the course of learning the Mahāvrata, no other worldly talk should be indulged in. Study of Mahāvrata leads on to the knowledge and attainment of Brahman.

NOTES AND REFERENCES

1. See part B of chaptei III infra.
2. AA., I. 1.1.
3. AA., V. 3.3.
4. AA., III. 1.4.
5. *Ibid.*, III. 2.4.
6. AA., II. 7.1.
7. AA., II. 1.8.
8. *Ibid.*, III. 2.4.
9. See part A of Chapters III and V infra.
10. RV., IX. 67.21-27; VIII. 6.30; IX. 113.6-11; I. 50.10,

SOURCES I

ऐतरेयारण्यकम्

१. अयं त्रिष्टः पुरुषः सोऽत्राऽऽलोमभ्य आ नखेभ्यः सर्वः साङ्ग आप्यते तस्मात्सर्वाणि भूतान्यापिपीलिकाभ्य आप्तान्येव जायन्ते । (१.३ ८)

२. पुरुष एवोक्थमयमेव महान्प्रजापतिरहमुक्थमस्मीति विद्यात् । (२.१.२)

CHAPTER
TWO

A Broad Spectrum of the Taittirīya Āraṇyaka and a Brief Sketch of its Contents

In the Black Yajurveda School, the Taittirīya Āraṇyaka[1] is only a continuation of the Taittirīya Brahmaṇa and the conclusion of the Āraṇyaka is formed by the Taittirīya Upanishad and the Mahānārāyaṇa Upanishad.[2] The contents[3] of the Āraṇyaka have been catalogued as follows :

Book No.	*S. No. of the section(s)*	*Nature of passages*	*Brief subject-matter*
1	2	3	4
I	1-32	Mantra with Brāhmaṇa	The Āruṇaketuka fire-piling.
II	1, 2	Brāhmaṇa	Vedic study.
	3-6	Mantra	Repentance (Kūṣmāṇḍa Homa).
	7, 8	Brāhmaṇa	—do—
	9	,,	Vedic study.
	10-13	Brāhmaṇa	Five daily sacrifices.
	14, 15	,,	Interruption of study.
	16-18	,,	Repentance.
	19, 20	Mantra (with Brāhmaṇa in 19)	Brahmopasthānas.
III	1-11	Mantra	The Hotāraḥ (verses for the cāturhotra fire-piling).

1	2	3	4
	12	Mantra	Verses of Puruṣa hymn of Ṛgveda for fire-piling.
	13	,,	Verses for the human sacrifice.
	14	,,	Verses for the animal sacrifice.
	15-21	,,	Verses for the Brahmamedhan
IV	1-42	,,	The Pravargya.
V	1-12	Brāhmaṇa	—do—
VI	1-12	Mantra	The cremation verses.
VII-IX	Whole	Mantra and Brāhmaṇa	Taittirīya Upanishad.
X	1-64	—do—	Mahānārāyaṇa Upanishad.

There is no doubt that the Taittirīya Āraṇyaka is a mere agglomeration of material. Various verses and Brāhmaṇical passages have been taken from the different Saṁhitās, certain inextant Śākhās and Brāhmaṇas. The above brief survey of the contents of the Āraṇyaka shows that the first six Books or prapāṭhakas are characteristically ritualistic and constitute Volume I of the book published in the Ānandāśrama Sanskrit Series. Keith[4] has observed that the Pravargya sections and the cremation verses are later additions to the Āraṇyaka. Volume II ibid. consisting of Books VII to X constitutes the Taittirīya and Nārāyaṇa Upanishads. The latter Upanishad is universally admitted as 'Khila' or supplementary to this Hermit-text. Heterogeneous nature of its contents also abundantly proves the same. Eulogisation of Nārāyaṇa as the supreme Godhead is unmistakably a development much later to the Saṁhitās. This lavish praise of Nārāyaṇa has, therefore, very justifiably, been potent reason to give this chapter the title of Nārāyaṇa Upanishad. A particular verse[5] does also unequivocally request a particular deity to retire from the ritualistic ceremony. This is definitely a much later development in the liturgical science. With the above general background, a broad spectrum of the main contents of this book may, very pertinently, be given as per below mentioned details :

(a) *Beautiful Prayers*

The Āraṇyaka significantly appeals to any rational mind by the various types of prayers to the Almighty which are studded almost in the entire book right from the beginning to the end. The very opening stanza (S. 16) of the Āraṇyaka contains a beautiful prayer which, if properly perceived, lands the reciter in the conviction that he must make God his Supreme-Resort in case he is desirous to lead a healthy and happy life. It is also a characteristic feature of this book that each chapter opens and ends with an identical prayer. Succinctly speaking, the various prayers contain solicitations to God for bestowing on us good health, physical strength, lustre, fame, divine glory, wealth, long life, prosperity, off-springs, cattle, cultured behaviour, bravery, peaceful life and for harmonious as well as comforting action of all macrocosmic forces towards us including protection of our lives, off-springs and cattle. Quite a sizeable of them are from the different Vedas. Six of such prayers that are representative of these beautiful supplications have very pertinently been quoted at the end of this chapter (S. 1-6).

(b) *Morally Exalted Life*

Leading of morally exalted life has been repeatedly stressed. Purity of means of our earnings, thought, word and deed, sweetness of behaviour, upright dealings, removal of sins, truthfulness, healthy-mindedness, virtue, study of Vedas, amiable behaviour, respect for parents, teachers, guests, adoption of only those earlier precedents of conduct which are blameless/virtuous, charity, respect for the learned people, giving up of bad qualities like anger, control of sense organs, tranquility of mind, performance of Agnihotra/sacrifice, renunciation, universal brotherhood, etc. have been catalogued as diverse qualities for adoption in life. Three verses quoted at the end will, in a representative manner bear out the above (S. 7-9). Just as waters automatically flow down the slopes, similarly all sins may flow off from our lives. A laudable verse[6] lays down that the Earth and Aditi are our mother, the middle regions our brother, the sin is our enemy and the heaven is our father.

Theft, killing of a learned Brahmin, indulgence in sodomy, killing of an embryo, incurring of debt and gambling have been catalogued[7] as the principal vices.

Despite the stress on adoption of high ethics in life; certain verses[8] of Book VI do clearly establish that the Aryans believed in the leading of very long (S. 10) and active lives wherein dance, laughter had their due place so much so that they had also developed the deep-seated psychology of even resisting the onslaught of premature death (S. 27).

(c) *Significance of Study of Scriptures and Real Nature of Austerity*

A number of sections[9] (Anuvākas) of this Hermit-text lay immense stress on the regular prosecution of study of the Vedas and teaching thereof every day throughout life. In liturgical parlance, this is called Svādhyāya Yajña. This study can be carried out at any time of the day and night, in any posture (may be even lying on a bed or walking), at any place irrespective of its being a cosy home or an unwelcoming forest, loudly or in low tone and in any weather (calm or otherwise). Besides, adoption of virtues like perfect purity of heart, truthfulness, austerity, self-control, tranquility, humanism, charity, performance of daily sacrifices; repeated stress has been laid down on the punctilious and dutiful carrying on of study of the Vedas and teaching thereof in life.[10] It has unequivocally been stated that study and teaching alone constitute real austerity in life. Besides realisation of the self, the study also bestows long life, sharpness, strength, prosperity, eminence, divine glory, foodgrains, brilliance, heaven etc. on the performer. The modern way of accepted worship of sitting in a particular posture early in the morning as well as in the evening, muttering the name of a particular deity or a set of them, contemplation and so-called formal meditation do not find their reverberations in this Hermit-text. It stresses more on taking of life to a higher moral pedestal as the means for self-realisation rather than the present day concept of more frequent and prolonged participation in religious congregations.

(d) *Mystic and Metaphysical Beliefs*

Briefly speaking, it may be stated that immanence and supremacy of a single Godhead, evolution of the entire macrocosm and microcosm from Him, presence of the identical individual soul in each creature, identity between the Universal Soul and the Individual Soul constituted the firm mystical idealogy of the then Aryans. The symbol Om was held in great reverence and a potent medium for self-realisation. Despite the multiplicity of various deities, it was firmly believed that they all had their origin and originality in the One who, in scriptural parlance, is called as Brahman.

(e) *Social Conceptions*

No doubt, the then Aryans felt deeply concerned on the death of a kith and kin; but they never believed in prolonged grief and a sort of at least mental death with the dead one. They believed in living a vigorous, active and purposeful life and never gave way to unnecessary worries. They disapproved of the custom of self-immolation of the widow with her deceased husband; but required her to live a life of lustre and strength with her second husband. The social aims of life were hard work in various productive channels and earning of wealth profusely by adopting above-board means. They also believed in recreational activities of life.

(f) *Attitude Towards Enemies*

The Vedic Aryans fully believed in the crude law of the Nature called, "Survival of the Fittest." Hence, they always kept themselves fully fit for this mundane existence and had no mercy for their foes and all evil forces. The entire Āraṇyaka is abundantly studded with so many passages and stanzas wherein complete annihilation of all those who hate us and whom we hate has been repeatedly sought for. Some of the verses do require the enemy to be completely pounded out of existence and their faces may never be seen near us. Five Ṛgvedic verses[11] quoted in X.20 aim at the destruction of all demonical forces, malevolent foes protection from calumniator, burning of an enemy like a piece of dry wood and obliteration of all those who are hostile to us (S. 11-15).

Besides the above broad features of the Āraṇyaka, it may be stated that certain verses/passages do contain black magic,[12] prayers to various gods, cosmogonic evolution of the universe, etc. In fact, study of the Upanishadic portion brings home the fact that the development of philosophy had reached almost its pinnacle which is, partly out of sheer ignorance, admitted to have been attained at the stage of chronologically supervening Upanishads. The importance given to fun and frolic, dance and laughter, happiness and rejoicing in the lives of the then Aryans much belies the subsequent supreme importance to renunciation in the Vedantic philosophy. In fact, the Aryans constituted a nation that was very much up and doing in all walks of life.

A BRIEF SKETCH OF THE CONTENTS OF TAITTIRĪYA ĀRAṆYAKA

First Book

I.1. The Āraṇyaka opens with a beautiful Ṛgvedic prayer invoking the blessings of God, the Almighty that we may see and hear only good or auspicious things of life. We may have strong limbs, well-contented self and may also lead a full span of life leased out to us. May God bestow well-being and happiness on us and keep off misfortunes or calamities (S. 16).

Then follow prayers to the goddess who has been given the epithets of Bhuvana-Sūvarī, Parjanya-Sūvarī and Deva-Sūvarī (Creatress of the entire world including gods and maker of rain). Broadly speaking, she has been addressed to be gifted with extreme greatness and is worthy of reverential worship. Prayers have, therefore, been made to her that waters, fire, air and Sun may promote our well-being and we may be gifted with sons. Then, follow prayers for our protection from floods, demons, disease, disability and invincible foes. Oh God ! the waters and the entire vegetation may be for uplift and alleviation of our troubles. Oh Sarasvati ! like the atmosphere, you also be very compassionate or gracious to us.

I.2. In this section, the importance of time, its all-controlling characteristic and supreme control of the Almighty have been evolved As a stream after originating from its source gains in volume through the confluence of so many diverse rivulets and flows as a big river, likewise the various counts of time like moments, seconds, days, months etc., go to constitute the bigger measure of time called year. God has been given the epithets like Varuṇa, Pūṣan, Svadhāvan (Self-supporter). In the ultimate analysis, time alone is most instrumental in the evolution of the visible creation.

I.3. In the next section, a broad survey about the distinctive characteristics of the spring, rainy and summer seasons has been given. It has been stated that the Sun has seven rays. The seventh ray alone was its own kind and the remaining six rays were produced by the Sun itself. A significant observation has been made that a person who leaves a real friend is highly undependable.

Coming over to the distinctive characteristics of the various seasons, it has been stated that the spring season is the best, most vivid and has congenial climatic conditions. The next following summer season is very hot and the entire Earth virtually burns under its tremendous heat. With the advent of rainy season, there is abundance of vegetational/agricultural growth and people attain prosperity. Animals feel happy and procreate. During this season, people lay the foundation of their plentifulness for the year.

I.4. Detailing out the characteristic features of the next following winter season, it has been stated that the atmosphere in this season is very clear and free from mist. People should take nourishing diet and also massage the body with oil. During the succeeding 'Hemanta season', cold winds blow and people have to put on warm clothes and head-gears. In the next following season of acute winter, there is deficiency of water, harsh winds blow and there are also occasional onslaughts of lightening.

I.5. In the supervening section, terrifying character of gods like Indra and Rudra has been portrayed. This is followed by a parable regarding bows of the All-gods, Indra, Rudra and Saṁyu being very vast and invincible. Indra disguised himself as an ant and cut off the heavenly end of the bow of the All-gods. The heavenly end of the bow cut off the head of Rudra[13] and pounded it. The head so pounded became 'Pravargya'.[14] Hence, Rudra does no harm to a person who performs the sacrifice with 'pravargya'.

I.6. The next section describes the climatic conditions and the inevitable effects of the intense cold season. As a Brahmin with an upright life is universally respected, similarly a person who knows the distinctive features of all the seasons is able to bear them well, despite their extremities. A hard working person has usually plentifulness for his (and his family's) consumption and also for offering to God. With abundance of rain, there is lot of vegetational growth. People feel happy and carry on their studies without any ill-will between the tutor and the taught.

I.7. There are seven Suns by the names of Āroga, Bharāja etc. There is an 8th Sun called 'Kaśyapa' which continuously shines over the mountain called Meru. This Sun is extremely luminous and powerful. All the seven Suns derive their luminosity from Kaśyapa. All these seven Suns illuminate and provide energy in all directions and they are also instrumental to the creation of cyclic change of seasons. Though seers have put forth that there are eight Suns; yet only one is visible in this world. This finds corroboration from the Ṛgvedic verse (I. 115.1) that the Sun is the very source of life of all animate as well as inanimate creatures.

I.8. In this section, the importance of time and the process of evaporation resulting in the falling of the rain has been described. Vishṇu has been stated to be the Imperishable Creator, Sustainer of heaven and Earth and the Last-Resort of all creatures. He has been addressed as 'Tripāda'. This section also details out the process of transmigration and the concepts of heaven and hell.

I.9. The next section catalogues eight types of fires and eleven names each of air and Gandharvas and six types of winds. Goddess 'Gauri' has been stated to have all-pervasive influence. The Imperishable One created all the creatures and great seers like Jamadagni. Such seers (through their divine inspirations) wrote hymns in praise of God. These hymns give solace to human mind and intellect and are conducive to their alround happiness and welfare. The section ends with a beautiful prayer beseeching for our welfare and that of our animals and also alleviation of all our ailments.

I.10. This section describes the functioning of heaven and earth as great benefactors and suppliers of all food materials like the true aśvins who maintain moral order in this universe. The earth and sky are conducive to procreation and instrumental to the coming off of the cycle of days and nights. There are prayers that men may have plentifulness in their lives and may sing songs in the praise of Almighty in thankfulness. Thus, various natural forces act in unison so as to ensure prosperity and happiness in this world.

I.11. The next section opens with two verses which purport to say that certain persons desirous of purification started making a sacrifice to Brahmā (Pratna) for obtaining food. They offered well-cooked Puroḍās (ground rice pounded into a cake) as an oblation. The seven seers including Atri, Agastya induced the unmanifest to become manifest. These seers adorn the sky as stars. These are seen at night; but are invisible during the day on account of excessive brilliance of the Sun. However, the Moon does not render other satellites invisible. Then, follows the prayer contained in the widely known Gāyatrī Mantra (RV., III. 62.10) for giving us brilliance and also to rightly guide our intellects. It is followed by an equally well-known Ṛgvedic prayer contained in V.82.1.

I.12-13. Sections 12 and 13 contain verses in praise of Indra for abundance of rain and consequential growth of life-sustaining vegetation. Similarly prayers are there to other gods. It has been stated that the earth, sky and heaven have eight sons and eight husbands. Goddess Aditi has been stated as the mother, father and son of all the gods so much so that she is herself the creator of all the deities as well as the entire creation. Then, the names of all her so-called eight sons have been mentioned.

I.14. Section 14 brings out the supreme importance and never ending passage of time. A prayer has been made for the longevity of the reciter's life and that of his offsprings and cattle.

I.15-20. The next six sections contain prayers to various gods like Sun, Rudra etc. for bestowing brilliance on the reciter and saving him from the various types of hells. Then, follows an invocation to certain deities to fulfil our desires.

I.21. In the next section, majority of the verses already quoted and cursorily reviewed above in section 1, have been repeated with the addition of certain new groups of seers.

I.22-27,32. To start with, the basic importance of water in the macrocosm has been brought out. Thereafter, the procedure to be adopted for kindling the Āruṇketuka fire, the sacrifices in which it is to be kindled, the names of seven other fires, objectives achieved through the kindling of the Āruṇketuka fire, restraints and observances to be kept while kindling this fire etc. have been delineated upto section 27 and in section 32. A detailed note on Āruṇketuka fire has been added as Appendix III at the end of this work.

Section 27 preponderates with so many prayers to gods like Indra, All-gods, Āditya etc. to bestow prosperity, health, off-springs and protection on us. There is description of transmigration of the soul and concept of salvation. The human body has been described as the abode of gods/happiness and also beset with a light, namely, the Ātman. This section also brings out identity between the individual and universal souls. All these aspects have been dealt with separately in the chapters pertaining to metaphysics and mysticism.

I.28. It is a very brief section which contains prayers to Agni (the resplendent Brahma) that the goddess of death and corruption and another demoness called vācyāyā may be destroyed alongwith their omnious and variegated evil forces. All the evil motives like jealousy, hatred, anger, betwitchment including various demons be annihilated.

I.29. The next section opens with the counsel that let us worship the divine god of rain for bestowing on us rain and food-grains. Our prayers may enter the very heart of brilliant 'Parjanya'. Let the winds and certain specified deities (who live among all men and are kind to them) be comforting to us. The entire vegetation may profusely fructify and be satisfying to the gods by being offered as oblations. Let the rain god who impregnates all the vegetation/plantation, animals and human-beings, be comforting to us.

I.30. This section contains prayers for re-invigoration of our body and lost strength/vigour of our various organs and capacities. The prayer starts with the supplication that the various organs of the reciter be re-invigorated so that he may regain youth, strength, divine glory and profuse prosperity. Whatever semen has been wasted by him in different wrongful channels may be reproduced so that he may attain longevity and divine lustre. Whatever semen has been fruitfully expended by the reciter, that be restored. He may be made comfortable by his sons and be also gifted with further linear progeny.

I.31. This section contains prayers to god Vaiśravaṇas (Kubera) for inviting him to the sarifice and bestowing wealth, removing misery, affording protection and partaking share in the oblations being offered after kindling of the Āruṇketuka fire. Then, hundred oblations are offered to Rudra after all the people have gone to sleep. The brother of Vaiśravaṇas has also been prayed not to obstruct the inflow of economic gains to us. Besides other prayers, the section ends with the prayer that waters and vegetation may be for our uplift and removal of our troubles.

I.32. Broad sketch of this section has already been given above in the paragraph pertaining to sections I.22-27.

Second Book

II.1. The second Book characteristically opens with a beautiful prayer to the various god-heads including Brahman, Earth, Agni, Vegetation, Vāk and Vishṇu. The remaining portion contains a parable regarding competitive efforts of the gods and demons to attain heaven and importance of wearing the sacred cord. This portion has been fully detailed in Chapter VII.

II.2. The next section also opens with another short narrative which has been fully described in Chapter VII infra. This section advocates worship of sun which has been stated to culminate in attainment of Supreme Brahman.

II.3-8. Verses contained in sections II.3-8 pertain to Kūṣmāṇḍa sacrifice. These sections do exhibit a very high degree of morality and a sincere desire permeates them that our lives may be very much above-board and free from sins. There are plethora of prayers to various deities like Tvaṣṭā, Agni etc. for wiping off our different sins. Truthfulness, healthy-mindedness, charity, worship of gods, performance of Yajña, amiable behaviour, righteous deeds and universal brotherhood have been stated to be chief and the desired virtues of our lives. A laudable verse puts forth that the Earth and Aditi are our mother, the middle regions our brother, the sin is our enemy and the heaven is our father. They promote our well-being and we may not attain those low worlds to which go the persons who die issueless (S.17). Theft, killing of a learned Brahmin, indulgence in sodomy, killing of an embryo, incurring of debt and gambling have been catalogued as the principal vices. Prayers are galore for complete annihilation of our enemies, weakening of their soldiers and that they be completely powdered out of existence. Repeated supplications have been made to the deities to bestow on us longevity, prosperity, sound health, divine glory, bodily strength, valour, off-springs, cattle and mighty warriors. Likewise, there are prayers for alleviation of our calamities, disease and saving us from sudden or accidental death. The supreme objective of life has been put forth as attainment of the Supreme Brahman. Some restraints and observances have also been catalogued for observance during the performance of this sacrifice. Details thereof as well as the ethical teachings of these sections have separately been dealt with in Chapter V infra.

II.9. This section is purely Brāhmaṇical in its exposition and presentation. The sole thought sought to be communicated is that by performance of Yajña and self-study of scriptures like Vedas, Purāṇas, Gāthās etc.; one can attain God and consequential salvation as well.

II.10. According to this section, Deva, Pitṛ, Bhūta, Manuṣya and Brahma Yajñas are five sacrifices to be performed every day. These sacrifices are respectively to be consummated by offering oblations in fire, by offering water with svadhā, by offering grain, rice etc. to birds, feeding the Brahmins and self-study that may be of even one verse from Ṛg, Yajur or Sāma Veda. Self-study of the various Vedas, Purāṇas, Kalpas, Gāthās, etc. propitiates the gods who in return bless the propitiator with long life, sharpness, strength, prosperity, eminence, divine glory, food-grains etc.

II.11. In this section, details have been given as to how the Brahma-Yajña is to be performed. The preliminary verses require the performer to go out of his village in north-eastern direction, sit on Darbha grass after spreading proper cloth etc. at the time of sun-rise, wash his various limbs with water, sit in a particular posture and loudly recite the syllable OM. Giving out the importance of syllable OM, it has been said that all the ṛks as well as gods are subservient to it. A person who does not know this significance, he will gain no benefit from study of Ṛgveda. Those who know its importance, gain eminence and prosperity. Thereafter, the three Vyāhṛtis are to be recited followed by recitation of the Gāyatrī mantra and certain other verses.

II.12. The succeeding section gives details of alternative methods of doing the self-study. In case, the consecrated person is somehow unable to go out of the village and undertake self-study, then the alternatives spelt out in this section permit him to do so within the place of his abode, by day or night and that too quietly. This can also be by just reading out (of course with application of mind) by sitting or even walking or even lying down. By doing so, the reciter shall be purified. The section closes with cataloguing of obeisances to Brahman and certain gods.

II.13. This section gives out that if the self-study is done loudly at mid-day, then the reciter attains the intense brilliance of the Sun. With a view to support this assertion, Ṛgvedic verse (I. 115.1) has been quoted which, inter-alia, says that the Sun is the Ātmā of the entire animate and inanimate world. This svādhyāya Yajña begins in the morning and ends in the evening. Then, the closing verse containing obeisances is to be recited three times. The self-study is to be formally brought to a close by giving a fee to the priest and the quantum thereof is as per option or choice of the reciter.

II.14. Coming over to the timing of the aforesaid self-study, this section lays down that it can be started even if it be cloudy weather, may be raining, the lightening may be falling, clouds may be thundering or even a storm may be blowing or even if it may be the day of Amāvasyā (night when Sun and Moon dwell together). In fact, he who does this self-study during such inclement weather, he does a veritable penance. A person who completes such self-study, he attains high social status, prosperity, cuts off the cycle of deaths and births, overcomes accidental or sudden death, attains heaven and salvation.

II.15. This section begins with the assertion that there are only two situations in which self-study should not be prosecuted. These are becoming impure of the person concerned himself or the place of recitation being impure or dirty. In the doing of self-study, no external material is needed. God Himself is its sole wherewithal. Hence, if a person performs this self-study by getting up early in the morning, he is successful in this world and also wins the yonder worlds. He can do this study while walking, while sitting, while lying down, in the jungle or within the village of his abode according to his capacity. In this way, he is also freed from the debts that he owes to the preceptors, gods and ancestors. He becomes free from these obligations in all the three worlds and lays out for himself the path of gods as well as that of the Pitṛs. Soon after its birth, the Agni was held by sin and that sin was annihilated by offering oblations by the gods. Whatever imperfections or sins are there in the Agni, Yajña, reciters and verses themselves, they are removed by the oblations, by performance of the Yajña itself, by payment of fees, by recitation of verses and by self-study respectively. Thus, svādhyāya is purifying even for the gods. He who gives it up, gains little knowledge of the scriptures (of true knowledge) and also loses the seat for himself in heaven. This conclusion has been supported by quoting some verse bearing on the importance of self-study. One who gives up a friend well versed in the scriptures, he loses any share in the speech. He also, intrinsically speaking, does not know the real path of goodness. Hence, self-study is a must in life. One who does self-study with determination, he acquires mastery over the same and also attains salvation. It has been said that in case a person criticises the present and pristine learned Vedic scholars, he invites on himself the wrath of all important gods like Sun, Agni etc. Hence, it has been laid down rather authoritatively that all the gods reside in a Brahmin who is well versed in knowledge of Vedas. Ipso-facto, such scholars should be paid obeisances every day. Nothing insulting should ever be said to them. In this way, all the gods are pleased.

II.16. This small section lays down atonements for the wrongs done by a person. It opens with the advice that in case a person has been performing sacrifices for harming others or for the sake of satisfying his greed alone, then he is shorn of all fame in this world as well as in the yonder world. As an atonement of his such misdeeds, he should complete study of the Veda three times by observing complete fast. As an alternative, he should recite the Gāyatrī mantra for three nights continuously without taking any food. A good cow should also be given to a noble Brahmin as a gift. It is by this gift that he pleases the latter. In fact, just like a noble Brahmin, the Ātman is also the noblest. Hence, the justification for gifting of a 'vara' (good cow) to a 'vara' (noble Brahmin) for satisfaction of another 'vara' called Ātmā.

II.17. Continuing the elaboration of the atonements in this section, it has been said that in case a person performs a sacrifice for an ignoble or at least undesirable person, then he renders fruitless all the Vedic knowledge acquired earlier by him. Hence, such a priest should retire to a jungle, make himself seated on some neat and clean place in healthy environments and do self-study. He is not to pay any pecuniary fee; but observance of fast by him shall constitute his fee. The very place shall be the upasada (a ceremony preceding Sutyā), the seat the Sutyā, his speech the Juhu (a curved wooden laddle), his mind the upabhṛt, his resolution the dhruva, his prāṇa the oblation, the verses of Sāma Veda as Adhvaryu priest, the atoner himself the Yajña, breathing last by him, the gift or donation. Hence, such a Svādhyāya Yajña is very successful.

II.18. In this section, the procedure as to how a Brahmacāri who has somehow broken his vow of celebacy is to atone for the same. He is required to offer two oblations in sacrificial fire on the night of Amāvasyā with clarified butter by reciting the prescribed verse. After having offered these oblations, he should fold both of his hands, stand on one side and recite two prescribed mantras thrice each as the gods are called trebly truthful—in thought, word and deed. Both of these verses are prayers to gods like Maruts, Indra, Bṛhaspati and Agni for restoration of fertility, long life, strength, divine glory and perfect functioning of all the limbs of the body. This very procedure of atonement should be followed by a person who feels himself to be impure or sinful. As laid down in section II.16, a good cow should be given to a noble Brahmin as a gift.

II.19. The first verse contains prayers for attainment of the three worlds, Brahman, gods, the abode of the gods etc. Thereafter, it has been made out that the Supreme-being to whom prayers are being offered, is upholder of virtue, all-pervading and all the gods are within his control. He is divine, powerful and known by the epithet of Śiśumāra.[15] One who knows this does not fall prey to any kind of accidental or sudden death. He also does not die issueless and is also able to attain heaven. The Śiśumāra is eternal and support/lord of all the creatures. He is also supreme and all the creatures look to him for help. Hence, repeated obeisances to Him who is also called Śiśukumāra.

II.20. In the last section, obeisances have been made to the various directions and intermediate regions including the gods residing therein. Obeisances have also been made to the residents of the region in between Gaṅgā and Yamunā rivers. Similarly, obeisances have been made to the seers living in this region. The second Book comes to a close with the prayer with which it opened.

Third Book

III.1. In this Book have been given the mantras for laying the fire-altar of cātur-hotra sacrifice and the Brāhmaṇical aspect of this sacrifice has been given in the Taittirīya Brāhmaṇa. It opens with a beautiful prayer seeking for our welfare and happiness. In the body of the first section, it has been clarified that for the performance of the above-said sacrifice, no material equipment like sruk, ghee, fire-altar etc. is needed since the author of the Āraṇyaka is not dealing here with superficial ritualism; but intends to give a metaphysical interpretation to the ritual. The equipment consists of our reflecting capacity, mind, speech etc. Then follow obeisances to the all-controlling god of speech to come and partake of the Soma being offered and also bestow much-needed wealth and prosperity on us.

III.2. The Earth, the Heaven, Rudra and Bṛhaspati are respectively the Hotā, Adhvaryu, Agnīt and Upavaktā priests of the cātur-hotra sacrifice. Vācaspati and Indra are respectfully invoked to bless the sacrifice by their presence and bestow bodily strength and heaven on the sacrificer.

III.3. In this section, Agni, Aśvinas, Tvaṣṭā and Mitra have respectively been named as another set of above-said four priests.[16] It has been said that Soma creeper precedes the Soma juice, and the god Śukra precedes the shining one (viz. Soma). Then, follows an invocation to Indra to the sacrifice.

III.4. It has been said[17] that your eye, prāṇa, back, Ātmā, limbs and other parts of the body represent the Sun, air, heaven, sky, the sacrifice and the earth respectively. Oh vācaspati! guide our prayers and reverential worship (which is pleasing to the gods) to heaven.

III.5. In this section, there are seven rishis called Mahā-havi,

Satya-havi, etc. who act as priests. The latter part of the section contains prayers to Vācaspati, who is the controller of our minds and has high renown.

III.6. In this section, the hotā, sacrificer's wife, adhvaryu, abhigara (the priest who calls out approvingly to other priests), oblation and austerity have been identified with speech, consecration, air, water, mind and oblations respectively. Then, follow recitation of the three vyāhṛtis and oblations to the self-born Brahman.

III.7. This section catalogues ten Hotā priests who represent Yajña, Bhartā etc. Prayers go forth in each of these ten stanzas to each of them to bless the worshipper with off-springs, prosperity, vigour, fame, firmness, invincibility etc. in his life.

III.8. This section contains prayers of the Black Yajur-veda (Maitrāyaṇī-Saṁhitā I.9.2; I.32.1; I.9.8; I.39.7 and Kāṭhaka-Saṁhitā IX. 10) to twenty of the gods like Agni, Savitṛ, Indra, Soma, etc. to grace the sacrifice with their presence and come also well-equipped with all the material necessary for successful completion of the sacrifice. The sacrificer presents himself duly surcharged with faith. In this section, the author of the Āraṇyaka comes down to the ritualistic plain in contradistinction to the metaphysical level maintained in the earlier sections.

III.9. The verse in this section contains the names of the spouses of various gods. Senā, Dhenā, Pathyā, Vāk, Anumati have been stated to be consorts of Indra, Bṛhaspati, Pūṣan, Vāyu and Prajāpati respectively. Similarly, names of wives of many other gods have been specifically mentioned. All the four directions and equal number of intermediate regions have also been stated as the wives of certain unspecified gods.[18]

III.10. The verses of this section contain prayers to a multitude of gods like Savitṛ, Varuṇa, Prajāpati, Soma, Rudra, Brahman etc. for bestowing immortality, wealth, happiness, fulfilment of various desires including clothes, animals like cows, horses, donkeys, elephants, food-grains, chariots etc. on the sacrificer.

III.11. This section is highly mystical and also contains various prayers. The Sole Godhead of the universe is Brilliance Par-excellence, affectionate, all-pervasive, creator, and sustainer of all creatures including gods, friend of all good people, set in the heart of all creatures, embodiment of immortality, giver of all wealth, Supreme controller of the universe, Supreme abode of the Perfect Order, producer of all foods/plantations and regulator of time. Prayers have been put forth for fulfilment of even the best of our desires, bestowal of power, bodily strength, splendour, wealth, cattle, off-springs and bravery (S. 18). The Imperishable One glides gently into the hearts of all the creatures.

III.12. This section delineates the process of creation of the universe. In fact, the Puruṣa Hymn of Ṛgveda (X. 90) or a major part of Chapter 31 of the Yajurveda has been reproduced here. In addition, two other very mystical verses have also been embodied in this section. All these verses have been properly analysed in the chapters on mysticism and metaphysics.

III.13-14. These sections give further exposition of the Supreme Brahman. The Primeval Puruṣa is extremely brilliant and much beyond the ambit of ignorance. He is the seed of entire creation and is symbol of the divine procreative energy. Days, nights, satellites and the various deities are His ostensible limbs like lateral sides, mouth etc. The single Godhead permeates all creatures in diverse ways. Life comes to an end as soon as His Representative leaves the physical frame of the creature concerned. He is the Supreme controller and maintainer. Flow of waters, functioning of Agni and other gods is within His control. The same Brahman is the very life of Yajña and also pervades Soma. He is one and only one. The Un-manifest was originally instrumental to the creation of the manifest. Prayers are also there for the destruction of our enemies.

III.15. This section also deals with the Brahman who has been addressed as Lord-of-Death and given the purposeful epithet of Hari.[19] He is the best among all the deities who fully remain within his control. He is beholder of men and has been offered prayers for protection of the reciter and his off-springs and grant of longevity, prosperity etc. The God of death is a cause of fear to all and has, therefore, been requested to go to its own yonder path which is different from that of the gods. He is addressed these prayers as he is taken as having been equipped with eyes to see and ears to hear. Yama is pristine, best among men and also their lord. He is the first born of all creation.

III.16. This section[20] is in praise of sun who is remover of darkness, worth-seeing by all and immense source of light. He makes the entire world bright. He has been stated to be extremely bright and prayers for inviting him to the sacrifice have been put forth.

III.17. The single verse contained in this section is addressed to

Soma who has been given the epithet of Madintama (extremely happy). He has been requested to work for our prosperity by affording full protection from all sides.

III.18. The only verse contained in this section is in praise of goddess Ushas. It has been said that those mortals who get up early in the morning, they attain the goddess of the morning.

III.19-20. Both of these verses are recited at the time of cremation of the dead body. The verse contained in section III.19 pertains to the placing of wood on the dead body. The words used in this verse show that with adding of each piece of wood, the fire becomes severer and severer.

The verse contained in section III.20 constitutes offerings to various gods who can possibly obstruct the path of the departed soul to the Yama-loka so that they may not put any obstruction in the upward journey.

III.21. The verse contained in the last section is used in some sacrifice. The words used in accusative case pertain to particular gods and those used in the instrumental case pertain to particular parts of the body of the sacrificial animal.

Fourth Book

IV.1. Pravargya[21] is a ceremony introductory to the Soma-sacrifice at which fresh milk is poured into a heated vessel called Mahāvīra or gharma or into boiling ghee. The Pravargya is a part of Agniṣṭoma sacrifice. It is performed twice both in the morning and in the after-noon for at least three days. The first section of the fourth Book contains prayers to speech, the lord of speech, seers and many deities. Prayers are there that the heaven, earth, moon, Prajapati etc. may be instrumental to our happiness/prosperity and to those of our children and cattle. The prāṇa and apāna have been requested to save the reciter and the sacrificer from the clutches of death. Then, follows a beautiful prayer for civilized behaviour, sweet speech etc. and for seeking blessings/protection of the deities and for the satisfaction of the ancestors.

IV.2-8. Verses contained in sections 2 to 8 pertain to the construction and placing in position of an earthen ware vessel called Mahāvīra. This vessel[22] has a height of one span and is little contracted (like a mortar) in the middle. It has a rim or belt about three fingers lower down from the top of this large and deep bowl. It has at the end a hole or spout for pouring in liquid. It resembles three pots placed on one another.

IV.9-11. The verses used in sections 9 to 11 pertain to the performance or Pravargya-yāga including the act of its leaving the place of sacrifice. The verses used in these three sections are also to a large majority from the Maitrāyaṇī Saṁhitā (IV. 9.8-11). Some of them are also from the Ṛgveda, Vājasaneyi-Mādhyandina Śukla-Yajurveda-Saṁhitā and from some extinct Śākhās of the Saṁhitās.

IV.12-39. The verses used in sections 12 to 39 are either from Saṁhitās, Taittirīya Brāhmaṇa or from some extinct Śākhās. As for example, the mantras contained in IV. 27, IV. 30 to 32 are not locatable anywhere else. A number of verses are focussed against our enemies for their destruction, *e.g.*, IV. 22, 23, 30, 34, 37-39, IV. 42.21 etc. The verses contained in IV. 26 is a sort of magic formula for destruction of a thief. The verse contained in IV. 27 is pure black magic and has very harsh language. The verses contained in sections IV. 28, 29, 31-33, 36 etc. are for destruction of ferocious beasts and inimical insects.

IV. 40-42. Sections 40 to 42 contain beautiful prayers requesting for perennial comfort/happiness, prosperity, long life, lustre, divine glory, fame and wealth in our this life and that hereafter. Prayers are galore wherein the diverse personified natural forces like Vāyu, Āditya, sky and other gods have been repeatedly requested to bestow all the worldly wherewithal on us and to function in such a way that our entire life may be full of comfort, prosperity, health, longevity, happiness and peace. Most of these prayers are contained in the various Saṁhitās. Some of these very beautiful prayers are quoted in original at the end of this chapter (S. 19-23). Some prayers are there for calamities to fall on those who hate us and on those whom we hate, *e.g.*, IV. 42.3-4.

Fifth Book

Whole of Book V (sections 1-12) contains the Brāhmaṇical expositions[23] about the supernatural character of the ceremony of Pravargya. It gives rather a highly metaphysical colouring to the ritualistic ceremony of Pravargya. A detailed account of this ceremony and its supramental character as exhibited in Books IV and V has been given in chapter VI infra. Ipso-facto, all those details need not be elaborated in this general sketch. The very origin[24] of Pravargya has been enshrounded in mystery by invoking the parable or myth of a Soma sacrifice having been arranged by the gods, vainglorious behaviour of Vishṇu,[25] cutting of his head and its subsequent pounding so as to give birth to this ceremony. The pravargya is considered as the head of all Soma sacrifices and no such ritual can possibly fructify in bestowal of the avowed worldly objectives until and unless this ceremony is also essentially performed. Strict rules have been evolved directing the sacrificer to keep his face in another direction so that his breath may not be incident on the Mahāvīra. Similar directions are there about his standing so as not to be in between the Sun and the vessel of the Pravargya. Violation of these instructions can afflict the sacrificer with the horrible disease of leprosy. Use of various metres at the time of putting Mahāvīra in position has been considered as instrumental to bestowing of learning on the sacrificer. Actual placement of the Mahāvīra in the quadrangular mound of earth(called Khara) accompanied by recitation of verses of various metres is surcharged with the capacity of bestowing lustre and vanquishing his foes on the sacrificer. Performance of other ritualistic details also bestows children, long life, food, control of evil forces, lustre, divine glory, heaven and authority of a king on the sacrificer. It sounds quite henotheistic when the pravargya has been given epithets like '*Garbho Devānām*'; '*Matiḥ Kavīnām*' etc. After a spate of oblations to diverse gods, a pot-sherd is to be left in the northernly direction of Rudra. While doing so, the pot-sherd should not be seen by the sacrificer. If he does so, he shall be rendered blind by one eye. The person consecrated for performing the pravargya ceremony should not eat meat, should not do sexual intercourse, should not drink water in an earthen pot and the remnants of food left by him should not be eaten by his son.

Almost each step in the performance of the ceremony of pravargya has been surcharged with mystery. It has been laid down that it should be discharged in an orderly manner only in the eastern direction. It is on account of this that the Sun itself rises in the east. While so discharging the pravargya, a piece of gold is required to be placed underneath it, water should be sprinkled over it thrice and it should also be gone around reverentially six times. Besides bestowing so many mundane gains, the pravargya acts as a spell for the destruction of all those who are inimical to us or whom we despise. It is fulfiller of all our desires and washes off all sins. Orderly discharge of the pravargya in a direction in which a specified enemy of the sacrificer lives shall put the former into immense trouble. Further philosophizing in this behalf goes on to assert that discharging of pravargya on a branch of Udumbara tree can bring the sons of a particular enemy to grief and its discharge on darbha grass shall fetch rain.

Carrying further the process of metaphysical interpretation of ritualism, it has been laid down that the pravargya is called Prajāpati when it is in the state of being prepared as earthenware; samrāṭ when it is fully composed, Gharma when it has been cooked and Mahāvīra when it is being taken out for orderly discharge. It is of the nature of Sun. It is called Gharma during the day and king at night. The process of henotheistic eulogization reaches its climax when it has been asserted that the pravargya is nothing but an embodiment of Prajāpati himself. Performance of the ceremony of pravargya continuously for twelve days results in fulfilment of various desires, attainment of gods, longevity, heaven etc. In case performance of this ceremony is succeeded every day by performance of the ceremony of Upasada (a sacrificial festival preceding a Soma pressing), then the Sun, ipso-facto, shines brightly over the upper and lower worlds.

Sixth Book

Whole of this Book (sections 1 to 12) is, in fact, devoted to the funeral rites and contains much of the material of Book XVIII of the Atharvaveda. Largely these verses are also contained in the Ṛgveda. The readings of this Āraṇyaka and the Ṛgveda are wont to agree together rather than with those of the Atharvaveda. An analytical study of these verses brings to light a plethora of knowledge about the metaphysical, mystic, social and moral beliefs of the Aryans of that distant past. Important features of these diverse kinds of beliefs may very pertinently be sifted below under various heads :

(i) *Mystical Conceptions*

A glance through almost all the twelve sections of this book brings out the fact that it is only the mortal human frame which is rendered inactive and functionless by the incidence of what is known as death. The subtle existence or the Self imprisoned in the body does not at all become inactive or moribund. The Ātman alongwith the subtle body leaves the body of the deceased person and continues its upward ascent to the worlds of the evil or the righteous[26] persons, the ancestors, the Soma, warriors, seers, Sūrya, the Prajāpati, the heaven or the highest heaven[27] according to the deeds and charity, if any, practised by the deceased person during his life time. In the highest heaven, the deities can make the departing soul join God, the third light[28] and thus make it immortal.[29]

(ii) *Metaphysical Conceptions*

Clear conceptions about transmigration, re-birth, heaven and hell are also repeatedly permeating almost throughout the entire span of this Book. Prayers are also galore for the upward ascent of the soul along a happy path and the Devayāna and its happy settlement in the worlds of the Fathers[30] and Prajāpati or the highest heaven,[31] where it may also get a spouse and live together happily. Various obstructing demonical forces, dogs of Yama, trees etc. have also been solicited not to hinder in the upward ascent of the soul along the auspicious path.[32]

(iii) *Theory of Karma or Actions*

The departing soul finds an abode for itself according to the extent or quantum of good deeds done and charity practised during mundane life. The messengers of Yama do exercise due discrimination in giving suitable abode while taking off from this world the truthful, the untruthful,[33] the worshippers of God and benevolent persons. The vicious and righteous persons definitely go to different worlds after death. The departing soul attains the world of the ancestors, the highest heaven, becomes immortal and even comes back to this world for re-birth according to its deeds.

(iv) *Ethical Conceptions*

Leading of a morally exalted life has been greatly stressed in this Book. Agni has been requested to wash off our sins and also to purify our means of livelihood (S. 24). Life was not a mere drudgery and much less a dead weight with the Aryans of that remote age. People aimed at and prayed for living upto a ripe age which should be full of dance and laughter (S. 25-26). In the attainment of this objective, there prevailed a firm and positive will that the onslaught of death can be kept off for leading a very purposeful and long life. We may prosper financially, have pure means of livelihood, be performers of Yajña and be also gifted with children (S. 27). Great stress has been laid down on wiping off the sins from our lives and earnings. Prayers have also been made for even the revile and evil-minded to become devotees of God and for ultimate attainment of salvation. As waters automatically flow down from the slopes and higher levels, similarly sins may flow off from our lives.

(v) *Social Conceptions*

No doubt, the verses of Book VI depict a great concern of the surviving relatives and friends of the deceased for the latter's settlement in heaven, salvation etc. but they also bring out a positive approach of the survivors towards life. Prayers are galore that kith and kin of the departing dead persons may be blessed with offsprings, long and healthy lives, prosperity, abundance of food, vegetation, happiness, freedom from miseries etc. There may be no sins in their lives and they may have pure means of livelihood. They may also perform Yajñas. None may die at a premature age and may live long for hundred years. The women folk may remain unwidowed with their noble husbands. They may embellish and adorn themselves with fragrant balms, lead happy lives free from any disease, be respected and live with their husbands.

About the widow, it has been said that she may be gifted with lustre, strength and divine glory after the death of her husband. Reference is there to the old custom of self-immolation by the widows on the pyre of their dead husbands; but the relevant verses do require her to get up from the pyre, not burn herself but live a purposeful life with a second husband[34] for the sake of living a life full of lustre and strength. She is also required to live back for rearing of the children of the dead person (S. 28-31).

Bravery and acquisition of learning were also considered as qualities really worth attainment in life. The social aims of life were also fun and frolic, dance and laughter, happiness and rejoicing.

Seventh Book

VII.1. Books VII to IX of Taittirīya Āraṇyaka contain what has subsequently come to be known as Taittirīya Upanishad. These three Books are now-a-days known as Sikṣāvalli, Brahmānanda-valli and Bhṛguvalli respectively. However, no such nomenclature is evident from the body of the original text of the Āraṇyaka. The seventh Book opens with an invocation, adoration and supplication to God to remove all the obstacles in the way of attainment of spiritual wisdom The prayer also speaks of the determination of the writer to speak the right and truth.

VII.2. The next section puts forth that we will expound pronunciation, letters or sounds, pitch, quantity, force or stress, articulation and combination. It is essential that one must learn to recite the text of the scriptures correctly. Hence, the need for a lesson on pronunciation.

VII.3. Then follows a lesson regarding the significance of combinations. To start with, the Master and the disciple pray that the light of sacred knowledge may illumine them both and that they both may attain the glory of wisdom Next follows exposition regarding combinations under the below noted five heads :

(*i*) Adhilokam (with regard to the world).

(*ii*) Adhijyautiṣam (with regard to the luminaries).

(*iii*) Adhividyam (with regard to knowledge).

(*iv*) Adhiprajam (with regard to progeny).

(*v*) Adhyātmam (with regard to Self).

Earth and heaven with the connecting links of ether and air go to form the world. Fire and Sun with the connecting links of water and lightening are important with regard to the luminaries. The teacher and pupil through the medium of knowledge and instruction are important with regard to knowledge. The mother and father through the process of procreation and the junction of progeny are important with regard to progeny. The lower and upper jaws through the medium of speech and the organ of speech are important with regard to self. One who knows these great combinations is gifted with off-springs, cattle, divine glory, food and heaven.

VII.4. This section contains prayers of a religious preceptor and depicts his longings to have good disciples in largest number all the year round so that he may be able to disseminate knowledge to the largest number. Some of the stanzas contain prayers to the Almighty that he may be blessed with intelligence, be possessor of knowledge and a vigorous body with the various organs in perfect working order. The teacher may also be gifted with abundant clothes, cattle, food and prosperity. Just as waters run downward and months roll into years, likewise students of sacred knowledge who are well-equipped, disciplined and peaceful may converge to the preceptor from all sides. There is also a longing of the religious teacher that he may become famous among men and be more renowned than the rich. Finally is delineated the faith of the preceptor that God is his final refuge and the latter may shine forth to him.

VII.5. This section details out the fourfold mystic utterances called Vyāhṛtis. They are Bhūḥ, Bhuvaḥ, Suvaḥ and Mahaḥ. The fourth is Brahman; it is the Self and other gods are its limbs. Vyāhṛtis are so-called because they are uttered in various rituals. Bhūḥ, Bhuvaḥ, Suvaḥ and Mahaḥ are this world, atmosphere, yonder world and the Sun respectively. By the Sun indeed do all worlds become great. These four utterances are Agni, Vāyu, Āditya and Moon respectively. By moon, indeed, do all the luminaries become great. These four utterances are Ṛg verses, Sāman chants, Yajus formulas and Brahman respectively. By Brahman indeed, do all the Vedas become great. In the fourth combination, they are prāṇa, apāna, vyāna and food respectively. By food, indeed, do all the vital breaths become great. These utterances are four and these are fourfold combinations. One who knows these, knows Brahman. To him, all the gods pay tribute.

VII.6. The next section explains rather in a cryptic style as to the way in which the soul in the heart moves by a passage through the bones of the palate right upto the skull where the hairs are made to part, and on the way greets the Brahman who is his Lord and Master. The body of this Brahman is space, his soul is the real, his delight is life, his mind is bliss, abounding in tranquility and immortal—Thus, O Prācīnayogya (Man of Ancient Yoga) worship.

VII.7. This section elucidates the fivefold nature of the world and of the individual. Following is the fivefold division with regard to the world or all material existence :

(*i*)	Earth,	atmosphere,	heaven,	the (main) quarters,	intermediate quarters.
(*ii*)	Fire,	wind,	sun,	moon,	stars.
(*iii*)	Water,	medicinal plants,	vegetation,	space,	one's body.

Now follow details with regard to oneself.

(*i*)	Prāṇa,	vyāna,	apāna,	udāna,	samāna;
(*ii*)	Sight,	hearing,	mind.	speech,	touch;
(*iii*)	Skin,	flesh,	muscle,	bone,	marrow;

VII.8. The next section lays down that OM is Brahman and it is all this. It is on account of this basic reason that the various prayers and rituals are started with the recitation of OM. Any recitation started with the recitation of AUM fructifies in the attainment of Brahman.

VII.9. The succeeding section catalogues the most important observances that are essential for leading a happy life. For achievement of this objective, perfect purity of heart, truthfulness, austerity, self-control, tranquility, humanism, performance of house-hold sacrifices, hospitality, procreation, doing of self-study and teaching are essential.

VII.10. This section contains details of rare and happy experiences of a sage called Triśaṅku after self-realisation. The details of such experiences have duly been sifted in Chapter V of this work.

VII.11. In this section, the Ācārya, addresses the pupils after they have completed the course and become 'snātakas', which corresponds to graduates in a modern university. It is almost like a modern convocation-address containing direct moral advice to the departing pupil. He is asked to respect the law, to speak the truth, to study the Vedas, to offer ceremonial as well as daily oblations to the fire, to respect parents and the teacher, to receive guests with hospitality, to practice humanity, to increase and multiply, to perform only faultless actions, to respect the learned persons, be charitable and offer obeisances/money to the Preceptor.

VII.12. The last section closes this Book with the prayer with which it opened.

Eighth Book

VIII.1. Book VIII opens with an invocation that God may protect and be pleased with both the teacher and the disciple. Both of them may work together with vigour and their study may make them illumined. May there be no disliking between them (S.32).

The second part of this section elucidates the nature of Brahman, its place in the human heart and fulfilment of all desires as a result of its realisation. It is from the primeval Ātman that the five gross elements like space, air etc. and subsequent evolution of the universe took place. Speaking about the nature of man, it has been said that he is inherently the essence of food. Various organs of the human body are also developed and maintained by food.

VIII.2. Continuing the importance of food in the lives of all creatures, this section lays down that all living creatures are produced, developed, sustained by, and ultimately resolve into food. Food indeed is the eldest born of all things and thus the healing herb of all. Food should be worshipped as veritable Brahman. Food is eaten and it also eats things. It devours the creatures that feed upon it. Therefore, it is called food from the eating. Those who worship the Eternal as food, attain the mastery of food to the uttermost. Thus, food has supreme importance in the life of man from his birth till death. He has already been stated to be the essence of food. It is called the first of the five sheaths or 'bodies of man' in which the Self is manifested as the ego. The first of them consists of food.

VIII.3-5. Continuing the elaboration of these sheaths or bodies of the soul, sections 3 to 5 of this Book describe them to be the physical, the astral, mental, intuitional and beatific 'bodies' of man. Every internal body is enclosed within an external one and all of these bodies have the shape of man.

VIII.6. This section, at the very outset, lays stress that in case revelation of God is to be attained, then the seeker must develop the unflinching and deep-seated faith that God is. On the contrary, a non-believer loses the very faith in the existence of God. Then follow questions regarding the worlds to which the wise and ignorant respectively go after death. Thereafter, a brief account has been given of the emanation of the universe from the Supreme Creator which also clearly lays down that God is omnipresent and is present even in contradictories like this and that, the defined and the undefined etc.

VIII.7. The next section first of all states that before coming into existence of this universe, there was mere non-existence. From this state of the Unmanifest, God himself evolved the entire manifested existence. The creation so made was simply beautiful. The essential nature of Brahman is bliss and it is on account of universal permeation of this highest blessedness that every creature breathes and lives. In fact, the bliss of God is the sustaining force underneath all existence, both sentient and insentient. Even the least doubt in the all-pervasive nature of God and feeling of otherness gives rise to fear.

VIII.8. In this section, it has first of all been stated that all cosmic activity like blowing of wind, rising of Sun etc. takes place under the fear of the Supreme-Being. It is followed by an interesting account of the gradation of blisses right from a measure of a unit of human bliss to that of the bliss of Brahman. Then, supervenes an unequivocal statement regarding identity between the Self and the Absolute followed by details as to how a knowledgeable soul reaches the Supreme Bliss after death.

VIII.9. This section reiterates the belief of the seer of the Āraṇyaka that through the agency of human mind and speech, one cannot attain the Brahman. A knower of Braman does not at all feel afraid of any body at any time. Furthermore, stress has indirectly been laid on leading of a morally upright life for ensuring Self-realisation.

Ninth Book

IX.1-6. The first six sections of this Book detail out the dialogue between Bhṛgu and his erudite father—Varuṇa when the latter was approached by the son for making him understand the real nature of Brahman. The father asked him to perform penance and explore the truth for himself. After performing repeated penance, the revelation dawned on the son that it was none out of food, prāṇa, mind and knowledge which possessed the prescribed qualifications of Brahman; but Bliss alone fulfilled these requisite qualifications. The knowledge so imparted has great mystical significance and is known as *Bhārgavī Vāruṇī Vidyā.*

IX.7-10. In the next three sections and the initial part of section 10, the vital and basic importance/role of food in our life has been rather perseveringly brought out. It has been given out that the following instructions be strictly adopted as a rule or solemn vow in life :

(*i*) One should not talk ill of food (S. 33).

(*ii*) One should not despise food (S. 34).

(*iii*) One should make for himself much food (S. 35).

(*iv*) In any way whatsoever, one should acquire much food (S. 36).

After giving out the above-quoted fundamental importance of food in life; great mutual interdependence of food, vital air, the human body, water, light (a species of fire), ether and the earth has been given great stress. In fact, these mantras do argue on the basic premise that all food is produced from earth and there is an unbreakable and essential link among the five gross elements called space, air, fire, water and earth in the process of evolution of the universe from the Imperishable One. It has also repeatedly been said that a knower of all the above is gifted with abundance of food, becomes a good eater thereof and is also blessed with prosperity, progeny, divine glory and great fame.

The remaining portion of section IX.10 details out importance of hospitality, meditation on Brahman in different forms and raptures of mystic ecstasy.

Tenth Book

General : The tenth Book of the Taittirīya Āraṇyaka published in the Ānandāśrama Sanskrit Series contains what has been named as Nārāyaṇopanishad. Both Bhaṭṭabhāskara and Sāyaṇa have admitted that it is a 'Khila' or supplementary. The supplementary nature of this Book is also clear from its structural organization. In the collection of One-hundred-and-eight Upanishads, published from Bombay and other places, two works are included with the title Nārāyaṇopanishad. Of these, the longer one is generally distinguished by the designation Mahānārāyaṇopanishad. The same Upanishad is also known as Yajñiki Upanishad. Col. G.A. Jacob[35] has stated as follows :

"The Mahānārāyaṇa Upanishad comprised in the Tenth Book of the Taittirīya Āraṇyaka is well-known to scholars, and has been published both in Calcutta and in Bombay...A large portion of the Upanishad consists of extracts from various Saṃhitās."

It is an assemblage of passages used in various ritualistic contexts and there is the general lack of unity in the treatment of the subject-matter. This Upanishad has been printed as per below noted details :

1. Taittirīya Āraṇyaka with Bhaṭṭabhāskara's commentary, published from Mysore in Bibliotheca Sanskrit Series;
2. Taittirīya Āraṇyaka with commentary of Sāyaṇa in two parts, published in the Ānandāśrama Sanskrit Series;
3. The Mahānārāyaṇa Upanishad, published in the Bombay Sanskrit Series, edited by Col. G.A. Jacob;
4. Yajñikyupanishad brought out in the Adyar Library Series,

5. The Nārāyaṇopanishad included in the One-hundred-and-eight Upanishads published from Bombay.

The text presented in all these books is not precisely the same. Apart from the difference in the length of the text, differences of reading, additions and omissions of passages and transposition of textual units are also there. Sāyaṇa has written commentary on the Drāviḍa recension with sixty-four sections. The Ānandāśrama edition also contains an appendix reproducing the tenth Book under the sub-title of Nārāyaṇopanishad with eighty sections. This is known as Andhra recension. Sāyaṇa has also made reference to recensions of Karṇāṭaka and another one with seventy-four and eighty-nine sections respectively. About this Upanishad, Sāyaṇa has further observed as follows :

"Whatever was left over to be mentioned in respect of karma, upāsanā and jñāna after recital of the Saṁhitā and Brāhmaṇa is brought together in this miscellaneous work."[36]

X.1. With the above general background, it may be stated that the first section contains a diverse collection of first eighteen verses from different Saṁhitās and some of the principal Upanishads with a view to sublimate the supreme qualities of a single Godhead in Prajāpati. It also contains the philosophic surmise that 'I am Brahma', besides a brief account regarding the evolution of the macrocosm from the Supreme Imperishable Being. There are quite a sizeable number of verses to various gods, goddesses and personifications of certain birds and grass wherein prayers have been put forth for granting us long life of hundred years, prosperity, protection of our lives including those of our cattle and children, removal of our various troubles, increasing happiness, bestowing good fortunes, wiping off all our sins, vanquishment and destruction of all our enemies etc. Prayers are also there for grant of heaven to the righteous ones after death and to take the sinners to hellish worlds.

X.2-5. Sāyaṇa[37] has said that after the first eighteen verses of the first section of the tenth Book, the remaining part of the Upanishad mostly deals with holy utterances prescribed for facilitating meditation and other religious acts connected with worship intended to lead an aspirant to the Divine Reality. Accordingly, sections 2 to 5 ibid. contain prayers to various deities like Agni, Earth, Air, Heaven, Sun, Manes etc. to bestow food on us. Oblations are also accordingly offered to them including Brahman (Mahat) followed by supplications for keeping us off the sins and for preserving our sacrificial acts and protect us to attain full knowledge by wiping off our ignorance. A prayer has been put forth to that Śatakratu to preserve everything that belongs to us.

X.6-7. The next two sections contain salutations to Brahman who is manifold and the best in the Vedas. He is attainable by the good. Salutations have also been offered to the various deities and seers along with a prayer that the reciter may not forget whatever sacred knowledge has been heard by him.

X.8-9. In the eighth section, it has been laid down that righteousness, truth, hearing of Vedas, control of organs etc. constitute penance. The succeeding section dilates on high ethical values and brings out the importance of adoption of righteousness in life and shunning of evil.

X.10. The next section has a collection of twenty four verses which are, intrinsically speaking, of a heterogeneous character and in no way present a development and much less evolution of a single thought or subject. A few verses dilate on the nature of the soul and indispensable need of grace of God for attaining self-realisation. Another set of two verses lays emphasis on moral exaltation of life and the element of renunciation as conditions precedent for attainment of salvation. Another set of five verses clearly states the Brahman to be the sole origin of the entire microcosmic and macrocosmic existence. He is also all-permeating. Another well-known verse, on the contrary, puts forth the Supreme Godhead as a mere spectator in the process of cosmogony leaving the task of creation as a joint enterprise of the Prakṛti and the individual soul. The last verse extols the importance of Brahman. A number of Ṛgvedic verses[38] quoted in this section contain beautiful prayers for bestowing on us above-board life, prosperity, off-springs and that the entire cosmic phenomena may be sweetening in our lives. Remaining verses[39] taken from the Ṛgveda are just ritualistic and mere eulogies for Agni and ghee.

X.11. The succeeding section brings out rather henotheistic qualities of Nārāyaṇa in an exhaustive manner. It is equally exhaustive in cataloguing the nature, size, location in the body and other qualities of the individual soul. The closing verse fully establishes the identity between the individual and universal souls,

X.12-13. The 12th section contains obeisances to Brahman, the creator of the universe. The succeeding section unequivocally states that the Sun is verily the Brahman. The hymns, formulae and chants of Ṛg, Yajur and Sāma Vedas respectively find their origin, collection and abodes in the Sun. Thus, it is not the Sun; but the triple knowledge (of the above three Vedas) that shines and enlightens the world. The Golden Person (or Brahman) is within the Sun. Thus, this prose passage clearly states that the splendour of the Sun really belongs to the Absolute.

X.14. The next following section catalogues various attributes, powers and qualities of the Supreme Person identified with the all-encompassing Sun for the purpose of worship and meditation. The Sun has been stated to be energy, splendour, strength, renown, sight, hearing, soul, mind, anger, various deities like Death, Mitra etc. wind, ether, prāṇa, the Rulers of the worlds, Prajāpati, regions, happiness, immortality etc. This gives a henotheistic account of the Sun and meditation on him results in union with the Absolute and co-residence with Him.

X.15. The fifteenth section lays down that the Sun is giver of light and water. The Āditya is OM. The gods worship him as Austerity and truth and make other offerings. That form of the Sun is Brahman. He is really worth attainment. He represents water, fire, flavour, ambrosia, all the three Vyāhṛtis and OM.

X.16-20. The next supervening five sections[40] contain verses which are obeisances to Rudra who has been identified with the supreme Godhead. The Rudra has been depicted to be all-permeating and responsible for all the diverse creation. He has heen stated to be praise-worthy, wise, the most beautiful and mighty. Prayers offered to him fulfil the desired aims This set of prayers obeisances come to a close with five mantras[41] from the Ṛgveda. These five verses to Agni contain prayers for destruction of all demonical forces, malevolent foes, protection of the devotees from caluminators, burning of an enemy like a piece of dry wood and annihilation of all those who are hostile, whether kindred or unallied. All these stanzas depict Rudra as a beneficient deity as against the scholiastic belief that he makes others weep and puts them in trouble.

X.21. This section declares that Aditi or Mother Earth is the common mother of all celestial and terrestrial creatures including manes. She is very fertile, extensive, great, defied mother, praise-worthy, support of all, rich in crops, broad, possessing a wealth of objects, universal, ensuring well-being, exceedingly blissful, transformed into the bodies of the creatures, bountiful, virtuous and immortal.

X.22-30. Briefly sifting sections X. 22-30, it may be said that the verses contained therein eulogise water as the supreme deity and contain prayers for our moral uprighteousness in life. It has been repeatedly said that we may be purified of all misdeeds including those committed by eating of prohibited foods, acceptance of gifts from vicious persons, sins committed by thought, word, hands, feet, stomach and the procreative organ. They are offered as an oblation in the Self-luminous Truth, the source of Immortality. Prayers eulogising Gāyatrī metre rather in henotheistic terms and invoking its presence have also been put forth. One stanza repeats all the seven Vyāhṛtis preceded by OM and then the well-known Gāyatrī mantra.[42] The 30th section contains a verse which speaks of a later development of the ritualistic cult unequivocally requesting the invited deity to retire.

X.31-38. The next eight sections contain various stanzas utilised in different types of oblations. The first clearly brings out the unity of single Godhead despite diverse epithets having been given to Him. All other verses except one are ritualistic and are recited at the time of offering oblations to all the five types of human-breaths. These verses also pray for full and proper digestion of the consumed food and realisation of the Supreme-being for attainment of immortality. The last verse in this group is deeply mystic and brings out the basic identity between Brahman and the Ātman which permeates the entire body and is also of the size of a mere thumb.

X.39-42. The next four sections glorify the deity presiding over the power of intelligence and contain prayers to her. Briefly speaking, these verses depict the goddess of intellect as all-pervasive, beneficient, healthy-minded, strong, friendly, very pleasantly disposed and very beautiful. Prayers go forth to her that we may be enlightened, be capable of expressing the Supreme Truth, may acquire intelligence, be gifted with divine knowledge, be learned, may attain wealth, intelligence and mental powers of the celestial beings.

X.43-47. The next five sections contain five verses which contain salutations to Śiva. Salutations are also there to Mahādeva with His various epithets like Vāmadeva, Rudra, Sarvabhūtadamana, Sarva etc. In these verses, Rudra is addressed as benign, terrific, destructive, master of all knowledge, Lord of all creatures, the preserver of the Vedas; overlord of Hiraṇyagarbha and Brahmā. Besides being always kind, he is solicited not to subject the reciter to repeated births and lead him beyond birth into the state of bliss and liberation.

X.48-50. The next three sections contain verses that are called Suparṇa mantras. These are prayers for attainment of God-realisation and bliss. The devotee tells the Almighty that he is His (God's) own child and the latter may take-off all his ominous dreams and destroy all his sorrows. For that, the devotee offers as an oblation even his life-breath. It has been said that Brahman and Bliss are attainable through intellect. Then follow prayers[43] for being bestowed with progeny, affluence, all that is good and riddance from all sins. It has also been solicited that all the macrocosmic phenomena and the flora and fauna be beneficial and full of sweetness for us in life. Reiterating the importance of intellect in attainment of Bliss and Brahman, two verses have just been repeated from an earlier section.[44] Introducing an element of pseudo-mysticism in all these three sections, it has been said that the Suparṇa mantras may be imparted to a Brahmin even without being solicited. Recitation of these verses is surcharged with the mystic power that absolves the perpetrator even from the sin of killing a Brahmin, an embryo and a warrior. The reciters gain the fruit of the performance of Soma sacrifice and they are also gifted with the divine faculty of purifying the person who reverentially serves free meals to as many as even one thousand Brahmins at a time. It is also significant to observe that the verse eulogising the Suparṇa mantras in all these three sections ends with OM.

X.51-61. The eleven stanzas contained in these eleven sections are prayers recited for self-purification by offering oblations into the consecrated fire. Through all these verses, purification of our breaths, the sense organs, mind, sperm, intellect, intentions, aims, various limbs of the body, skin, blood, fat, bones etc., the qualities of the five sense organs, all the gross elements and all the five sheaths of the soul has been sought for. It has also been sought that the reciter may attain the Supreme Light bereft of all sins and their cause, the passions. The last four stanzas particularly and solely offer oblations to the all-pervasive God, the Supreme who is interested in his creation and AUM. One of these verses[45] makes intensified prayers to the Divine Person to bestow on the reciter added purity and knowledge. All these sections lay great significance on moral exaltation for attaining self-realisation.

X.62-63. The next two sections primarily narrate the different types of twelve penances like truthfulness, control over sense organs, nyāsa etc. which, if punctiliously followed, can be instrumental to the realisation of the Self. Comparative merits and limitations of these modes of penance have also been given therein. Renunciation has been stated to be the best and most effective of all austerities in God realisation. Supreme qualities and the highest position of the sole Godhead in the entire creation have also been clearly and effectively put forth. After self-realisation, the cycle of repeated births and deaths comes to a final stop. The symbol OM has unequivocally been stated to be most effective means of contemplation on the Supreme.

X.64. The last section very rightly, cogently and lucidly brings out the fact that a practiser of renunciation (the highest penance) does not at all need any of the usual material wherewithal or equipment for enlightenment. He need only cultivate in himself qualities like faith, longing or love for the Supreme and annihilate his basic emotions like anger as essential steps for attainment of knowledge of the Self. The various limbs of his body would serve the purpose of external instruments of worship like sacrificial post, ghee, fire, sacrificial fee, different priests etc. The practice of the penance of renunciation should continue till death of the practiser and that shall constitute the so-called completion of his sacrifice in worship of the Almighty. After delineating rather the pseudo-mystical belief that a person dying in particular phases of the itinerary of the Sun attains companionship with the Sun, the Moon or both or the manes; it has been stated that a knower of the Brahman attains His greatness.

Like all other Books of this Āraṇyaka, the tenth prāpāṭhaka also characteristically ends with the invocation with which it opened. This verse finds mention in majority of the earlier Books and contains a prayer that the teacher and taught may conjointly, happily and effectively go through whole of the courses of study.

NOTES AND REFERENCES

1. Edition with Sāyaṇa's commentary in Bibliotheca Indica and Ānandāśrama Sanskrit Series No. 36 in two volumes (Second edition, 1926).
2. In the Ānandāśrama Sanskrit Series, it has been given the title of 'Nārāyaṇa-Upanishad'.
3. Keith, A.B. The Veda of Black Yajus School (Harvard Oriental Series, Vol. 18, Second issue, 1967), p. Lxxviii.
4. The Veda of Black Yajus School (Harvard Oriental Series, Vol. 18, Second issue, 1967), p. Lxxxi.
5. T.A., X.30.
6. T.A., II.6.9.
7. *Ibid.*, II.8.
8. *Ibid.*, pp. 444, 449.
9. T.A., II.10-15; VII.9.
10. *Ibid.*, VII.9.
11. RV. IV. 4.1-5.
12. T.A., IV.27.
13. Cf., p. 45 infra.
14. Buitenen J.A.B. has discussed 'Pravargya' in his book of the same title published from Pune in 1968. Dr. Kashikar C.G., rejected the views of Buitenen in his article published in the bulletin of the Centre of Advanced Studies in Sanskrit, University of Poona, Pune, 1973.
15. Sāyaṇa calls Him as Super-Brahman.
16. Sāyaṇa has termed the verse contained in this section as pañca-hotṛ mantra. He increases the number of four priests specifically quoted in the section to five by saying that the priest Adhvaryu is always assisted by another priest called Pratiprasthātā.
17. According to Sāyaṇa, verse contained in this section has its application in animal sacrifice.
18. Sayaṇa requires a brick of the wives to be laid on the fire-altar after recitation of this verse
19. *Haraṇaśīlaḥ—prāṇa hartā.*
20. The verses contained in sections III.16 to 21 are also contained in Taittirīya Saṁhitā of Yajurveda in hymns I.4.31 to I.4.36 respectively.
21. Sanskrit-English Dictionary by M. Monier Williams. According to Sāyaṇa, verses pertaining to the ceremony of Pravargya have been given in the fourth Book. The Brāhmaṇical exposition of these verses has been given in the succeeding Book V. Majority of the verses used in the performance of

this ceremony are (with minor variations) out of those regarding Pravargya in the Maitrāyaṇī-Saṁhitā (IV. 9.1-11). Some of them are also found in the Ṛgveda, Saṁhitās of the white and black Yajurveda.

22. Kane, P.V., The History of Dharam Śāstras, Vol. II, Part II, p. 1147. Bhandarkar Oriental Research Institute, Poona, 1941 (Government Oriental Series, Class B, No. 6).

23. The word Brāhmaṇam means: 'explanation or utterance of a learned priest, of a doctor of the science of sacrifice, upon any point of the ritual. Collectively, it means a collection of such utterances and discussions of the priests upon the science of sacrifice'. (Winternitz M., History of Indian Literature, pp. 187-188, IInd edition, 1972).

Grammatically, Brāhmaṇam can be defined as '*Brahmaṇa idam*', where the term Brahman stands for the sacred knowledge of the Veda or a priest.

According to Sanskrit-English Dictionary by M. Monier Williams, it means Brāhmaṇical explanations of sacred knowledge in their sacrifices. It is the Brāhmaṇa portion of the Veda as distinct from its Mantra and Upanishad portions. The Brāhmaṇas contain rules for the employment of the mantras or hymns at various sacrifices, with detailed explanations of their origin, meaning and numerous legends. According to Sāyaṇa (as quoted in the above dictionary), they contain two parts : (*i*) Vidhi or rules or directions for rites; and (*ii*) Artha-vāda or explanatory remarks.

24. It has earlier been said in section 1.5 (page 32 supra) that the ceremony of Pravargya was invented on account of the pounding of the head of Rudra by the heavenly end of the bow of the All-gods; but here, it has rather been surprisingly stated that this ritual came into being due to blowing off of the head of Vishṇu. This basic difference in the origin of Pravargya has remained unexplained in the text of Taittirīya Āraṇyaka. However, in his commentary, Sāyaṇa explains in the former section that here Rudra, in fact, signifies nothing but 'Āruṇketuka Fire.'

25. Cf. p. 32 supra.
26. T.A., VI. 1.
27. T.A., VI. 3., VI. 4.
28. T.A., VI. 4.
29. T.A., VI. 6.
30. T.A., VI. 1.
31. T.A., VI. 4.
32. T.A., VI. 3.
33. T.A., VI. 5.
34. T.A., VI. 1.
35. Preface of Mahānārāyaṇa Upanishad published in the Bombay Sanskrit Series.
36. Ānandāśrama Sanskrit Series, (p. 689), published in 1981.
37. *Ibid.*
38. RV. V. 82.4-5, I. 90.6-8.

39. RV. II. 3.11 and IV. 58.1-4.
40. T.A. X.16-20. The verse in section 17 is primarily from RV. I.43.1.
41. RV. IV. 4.1-5.
42. RV. III. 62.10.
43. Verses 2 and 3 and 4 to 6 of section X.49 are contained in RV. V.82.4-5 and I.90.6-8 respectively.
44. T.A. X. 10.4, 6.
45. T.A. X. 60.

SOURCES II

तैत्तिरीयारण्यकम्

१. अग्ने नय सुपथा राये अस्मान् । विश्वानि देव
वयुनानि विद्वान् । युयोध्यस्मज्जुहुराणमेनः ।
भूयिष्ठां ते नम उक्तिं विधेमेति । (१.८)

२. तत् सवितुर् वृणीमहे । वयं देवस्य भोजनम् ।
श्रेष्ठँ सर्वधातमम् । तुरं भगस्य धीमहि । (१.११)

३. मधु मनिष्ये मधु जनिष्ये मधु वक्ष्यामि मधु वदिष्यामि,
मधुमतीं देवेभ्यो वाचम् उद्यासम्ँ शुश्रूषेण्यां मनुष्येभ्यस्तं,
मा देवा अवन्तु शोभायै पितरोऽनुमदन्तु । (४.१)

४. शं नो मित्रः शं वरुणः । शं नो भवत्वर्यमा । शं न इन्द्रो
बृहस्पतिः । शं नो विष्णुरुरुक्रमः । नमो ब्रह्मणे । नमस्ते वायो ।
त्वमेव प्रत्यक्षं ब्रह्मासि । त्वमेव प्रत्यक्षं ब्रह्म ।
वदिष्यामि । ऋतं वदिष्यामि । सत्यं वदिष्यामि । तन्मामवतु
तद् वक्तारमवतु । अवतु माम् । अवतु वक्तारम् ॥ (७.१)

५. शरीरं मे विचर्षणम् । जिह्वा मे मधुमत्तमा । कर्णाभ्यां
भूरि विश्रुवम् । ब्रह्मणः कोशोऽसि मेध्याऽपिहितः ।
श्रुतं मे गोपाय । (७.४)

६. मधु वाता ऋतायते मधु क्षरन्ति सिन्धवः । माध्वीर्नः
सन्त्वोषधीः । मधु नक्तमुतोषसि मधुमत्पार्थिवँ् रजः ।
मधु द्यौरस्तु नः पिता ॥ मधुमान्नो वनस्पतिर्मधुमाँ्
अस्तु सूर्यः । माध्वीर्गावो भवन्तु नः । (१० १०)

७. स नः सिन्धुमिव नावयाऽतिपर्षा,
स्वस्तये । अप नः शोशुचदघम् । (६.११)

८. अग्निश्च मा मन्युश्च मन्युपतयश्च मन्युकृतेभ्यः पापेभ्यो
रक्षन्ताम् । यदह्ना पापमकार्षम् । मनसा वाचा हस्ताभ्याम् ।
पद्भ्यामुदरेण शिश्ना । अहस्तदवलुम्पतु । यत् किंच दुरितं मयि ।
इदमहं माममृतयोनौ । सत्ये ज्योतिषि जुहोमि स्वाहा ।
(१०.२४)

९. वाङ्मनश्चक्षुः श्रोत्रजिह्वाघ्राणरेतो बुद्ध्याकूतिः संकल्पा मे
शुध्यन्तां ज्योतिरहं विरजा बिपाप्मा भूयासँ् स्वाहा । (१०.५२)

१०. इमं जीवेभ्यः परिधिं दधामि । मानोऽनुगादपरो
अर्धमेतम् । शतं जीवन्तु शरदः पुरूचीस्तिरो
मृत्युं दद्महे पर्वतेन । (६.१०)

११. यो मां द्वेष्टि जातवेदो यं चाहं द्वेष्मि यश्च माम् ।
सर्वाँ् स्तानग्ने संदह याँ् श्चाहं द्वेष्मि वेच माम् । (२.५)

१२. सुमित्रा न आप ओषाधयः सन्तु । दुर्मित्रास्तस्मै
भूयासुः । योऽस्मान्द्वेष्टि । यं च वयं द्विष्मः । (४.११)

१३. यदेतद् वृकसो भूत्वा । वाग्देव्यभिरायसि । द्विषन्तं मेऽ
भिराय तं मृत्यो मृत्यवे नय । स आर्त्याऽऽर्तिमार्च्छतु । (४.३०)

१४. द्विषो नो विश्वतो मुखाऽति नावेव पारय ।
अप नः शोशुचदघम् । (६.११)

१५. उदग्ने तिष्ठ प्रत्या तनुष्व, न्यमित्राँ ओषतात् तिग्महेते ।
यो नो अरातिं समिधान चक्रे, नीचा तं धक्ष्यतसं न शुष्कम् ॥
(ऋग्वेद ४.४४)

१६. भद्रं कर्णेभिः शृणुयाम देवाः । भद्रं पश्येमाक्षभिर्यजत्राः ।
स्थिरैरङ्गैस्तुष्टुवा ँ सस्तनूभिः । व्यशेम देवहितं यदायुः ॥
स्वस्ति न इन्द्रो वृद्धश्रवाः । स्वस्ति न पूषा विश्ववेदाः । (१.१)
स्वस्ति नस्तार्क्ष्यो अरिष्टनेमिः । स्वस्ति नो बृहस्पतिर्दधातु ।
ॐ शान्तिः शान्तिः शान्तिः ।

तैत्तिरीयारण्यकम्

१७. भूमिमाताऽदितिनो जनित्र भ्राताऽन्तरिक्षमभिशस्त
एनः । द्यौर्नः पिता पितृयाच्छं भवासि जामि-
मित्वा मा विवित्सि लोकात् । (२.६)

१८. ये ग्राम्याः पशवो विश्वरूपाः । विरूपाः सन्तो
बहुधेकरूपाः । तेषा ँ सप्तानामिह रन्तिरस्तु ।
रायस्पोषाय सुप्रजास्त्वाय सुवीर्याय । (३.११)

१९. शं नो वातः पवतां मातरिश्वा शं नस्तपतु सूर्यः ।
अहानि शं भवन्तु नः शँ रात्रिः प्रतिधीयताम् । (४.४२)

२०. शं यो देवीरभिष्टय । आपो भवन्तु
पीतये । शं योरभिस्रवन्तु नः । (४.४२)

२१. अन्तरिक्षँ शान्तं तद्वायुना शान्तं तन्मे
शान्त ँ शुच ँ शमयतु । द्यौः शान्ता साऽऽदित्येन ।
शान्ता सा मे शान्ता शुच ँ शमयतु । (४.४२)

२२. पृथिवी शान्तिरन्तरिक्ष ँ शान्तिर्द्यौः शान्तिर्दिशः
शान्तिरवान्तरदिशाः शान्तिरग्निः शान्तिर्वायुः
शान्तिरादित्यः शान्तिश्चन्द्रमाः शान्तिर्नक्षत्राणि
शान्तिरापः शान्तिरोषधयः शान्तिर्वनस्पतयः

शान्तिर्गौः शान्तिरजा शान्तिरश्वः शान्तिः
पुरुषः शान्तिर्ब्रह्म शान्तिर्ब्राह्मणः शान्तिः
शान्तिरेव शान्तिः शान्तिर्मे अस्तु शान्तिः । (४.४२)

२३. तच्चक्षुर्देवहितं पुरस्ताच्छुक्रमुच्चरत् । पश्येम शरदः
शतं जीवेम शरदः शतं नन्दाम शरदः शतं मोदाम शरदः शतं
भवाम शरदः शत ँ शृणवाम शरदः शतं प्रब्रवाम शरदः
शतमजीताः स्याम शरदः शतं ज्योक्च सूर्यं दृशे । (४.४२)

२४. अप न शोशुचदघमग्ने शुशुध्या रयिम् । अप नः
शोशुचदघं मृत्यवे स्वाहा । (६.१०)

२५. प्रांजोऽगामा नृतये हसाय
द्राघीय आयुः प्रतरां दधानाः । (६.१०)

२६. आनन्दाय प्रमोदाय पुनरागा ँ स्वान्गृहान् ।
अप नः शोशुचदघम् । (६.११)

२७. मृत्योः पदं योपयन्तो यदैम द्राघीय आयुः
प्रतरां दधानाः । आप्यायमानाः प्रजया धनेन
शुद्धाः पूता भवथ यज्ञियासः । (६.१०)

२८. इयं नारी पतिलोकं वृणांना नियधेत
उप त्वा मर्त्य प्रेतम् । विश्वं पुराणमनुपालयन्ती
तस्यै प्रजां द्रविणं चेह धेहि । (६.१)

२९. उदीर्ष्वं नार्यभि जीवलोकमितासुमेतमुपशेष एहि ।
हस्तग्राभस्य दिधिषोस्त्वमेतत्पत्युर्जनित्वमभिसंबभूव । (६.१)

३०. सुवर्ण ँ हस्तादाददाना मृतस्य श्रियै ब्रह्मणे
तेजसे बलाय । अत्रैव त्वमिह वय ँ
सुशेवा विश्वा स्पृधो अभिमातीर्जयेम । (६.१)

३१. धनुर्हस्तादाददाना मृतस्य श्रियै क्षत्रायौजसे बलायं । अत्रैव त्वमिह
वय ँ् सुशेवा विश्वा स्पृधो अभिमातीर्जयेम ।मणि ँ् हस्तादाददाना
मृतस्य श्रियै विशे पुष्ट्यै बलाय । अत्रैव त्वमिह वय ँ्
सुशेवा विश्वा स्पृधो अभिमातीर्जयेम । (६.१)

३२. सह नाववतु । सह नौ भुनक्तु । सह वीर्यं
करवावहै । तेजस्वि नावधीतमस्तु मा विद्विषावहै ।
ॐ शान्तिः शान्तिः शान्तिः । (८.१)

३३. अन्नं न निन्द्यात् । तद् व्रतम् । (९.७)

३४. अन्नं नपरिचक्षीत । तद् व्रतम् । (९.८)

३५. अन्नं बहु कुर्वीत । तद् व्रतम् । (९.९)

३६. यया कया विधया बह्वन्नं प्राप्नुयात् । (९.१०)

CHAPTER
THREE

Mysticism : Its Nature, Origin, its Relationship with Sacrificial Ritual and Details thereof in Aitareya and Taittirīya Āraṇyakas

Mysticism in common speech-usage is a word of very uncertain connotation. It has in recent times been used an equivalent for two characteristically different German words :

(*i*) *Mystizismus* : stands for the cult of the supernatural, for theosophical pursuits and for a spiritualistic exploitation of physical research.

(*ii*) *Mystik* : stands for immediate experience of a divine-human intercourse and relationship.

The word 'mysticism' has further more been commonly used to cover both :

(*a*) the first-hand experience of direct intercourse with God, and

(*b*) the theologic—metaphysical doctrine of the soul's possible union with the Absolute Reality, *i.e.* with God.

It would be conducive to clarity to restrict the word 'mysticism' to the latter significance, viz., as an equivalent for the German word Mystik and as designating the historic doctrine of relationship and potential union of the human soul with ultimate Reality and to use the term :—'mystical experience' for direct intercourse with God.

Origin and Nature of Mysticism

Mystical experience is primarily a psychological question and the doctrine of mysticism is essentially a metaphysical problem. Mystical experience is as old as humanity, is undoubtedly one of the original grounds of personal religion, and does not stand or fall with the truth or falsity of the metaphysically formulated doctrine of mysticism. Mystical experience is marked by the emergence of a type of consciousness which is not sharply focalized or clearly differentiated into a subject-object state. The subject and object are fused into an undivided one. Whatever is seen, heard or felt in these moments is flooded with inrush from the abysses (spiritual profundity) of the inner life. Deep-lying powers, not ordinarily put into play, seem suddenly liberated. The usual insulations which sunder our inner life into something like compartments, seem shot through. The whole being in an integral and undivided experience finds itself. Not only so, but transcendent energies from beyond the margin appear to invade the individual self, a larger, environing consciousness, an enfolding presence, makes itself felt. Lofty appreciation of beauty or sublimity, absorbed enjoyment of music, serene companionship with nature, sudden insight into the meaning of a truth, the awakening of love, moral exaltation of life in the pursuit of duty, illustrate some types of experience which immensely transcend 'knowledge'—experiences in which subject and object are fused into an undifferentiated one, in which self is identified with object.

'Mysticism', on the other hand, in its narrow and exact historical significance is a doctrine of union with the Absolute. It implies a certain metaphysical conception of God and of the soul, and it implies further, 'a mystic way' of attaining union with the Absolute. God, according to Vedānta, is Absolute Reality, Pure Being, Perfect Form with no admixture of 'matter', *i.e.* with no potentiality or possibility of change. God is that which absolutely is, one permanent, immutable and free of every thing that implies process or becoming. However, there is something in the human soul which is unsundered from the Absolute. It is called 'pure reason', 'recollective faculty', 'apex of mind', 'inward light' etc.

This intellectual formulation necessarily involves a via negative. The Absolute Reality, the God with whom the soul seeks to be united, is above and beyond all that is concrete and finite. We can preserve the finite oneness and wholeness of His being only by eliminating all that is finite in our account of Him. He is not this. He is not this (Neti, Neti). The soul that would reach the goal of bliss in union with Him must, therefore, rise above states and processes, emotions and thoughts, aspiration and deeds.

Modern Mysticism

It echoes in the following writing of Vivekānanda :

> "Where is there any more misery for him who sees this oneness in the universe ?......this oneness of life, oneness of everything."

This is just a broad translation of verse XL. 7 of White Yajurveda.

Mysticism as Found in the Āraṇyakas

As has already been stated in the 'Introduction' to this work, the Āraṇyakas or the 'Forest-Texts', by and large, followed the ritualistic texts called Brāhmaṇas. The mystical interpretations thereof were, therefore, naturally bound to be closely related to the ritualistic cult. The Brāhmaṇas had already expounded the identity of the Yajamāna (sacrificer) with the Yajña (sacrifice) which was ultimately identical with parjāpati (The Lord of Creatures) and also identified with Brahman, the Absolute Principle of this universe. Ipso-facto, the mysticism of the Āraṇyakas presents itself in a triangular form. Though ultimately, it is the identity of the Ātman with the Brahman which has been established; yet this has invariably and rather inextricably been inferred through the medium of Yajña. This qualifying clause shall have to be constantly borne in mind while deciphering the mystic contents of the Aitareya and Taittirīya Āraṇyakas and the same are detailed hereafter :

A. MYSTICISM IN AITAREYA ĀRAṆYAKA

Concept of Brahman

The supreme concept of Brahman did exist as a principle of unity at the time of the Aitareya Āraṇyaka as should be clear from the following precedents out of the first Āraṇyaka :

(*i*) The Gāyatri is Brahman, brightness and splendour (I. 1.3)

(*ii*) Speech unites with Brahman (I. 1.1). Wherever, there is vāk, there is Brahman (I. 3.8)

(*iii*) Vasukra[1] is Brahman (I. 2.2)

(*iv*) Hiṅkāra is Brahman (I. 3.1)

(*v*) The Mahāvrata day has been identified with Brahman and leads to its achievement (I. 1.3, I. 2.2 and I. 3.1).

Permeation of Brahman in All Creatures

It has been stated in section 8 of Chapter 3 of the first Āraṇyaka that the Puruṣa or Ātman permeates the body right upto hair and nails of all the creatures including insignificant insects like ants. In another section,[2] a detailed description about the entry of Brahman or Ātman into the physical frames of all the creatures through the tips of the feet, hoofs or claws has been given. The upward rise of Brahman has been shown through the thighs, stomach and chest upto the head. It has also been stated that the descendants of particular dynasties of seers believe the stomach and heart respectively to be the abode of Brahman in the physical frame of the various creatures.

How an extremely subtle existence like the Ātman entered the body is a highly difficult question. Obviously the tips of the feet have no hole and much less an entrance to permit even an extremely subtle existence to enter. Besides, even if admitted that the Ātman entered through the tips of the feet, it could not possibly be a continuous flow upwards into all the limbs of the body like the liquid or serum of an injection through the agency of the circulating blood. All this rather pictorial description regarding entry and subsequent ascent of Brahman into all the limbs of the body, therefore, appears to be mere imaginary despite the almost universally accepted omniscience of the seers of the Vedic literature. It is not because of any ignorance on the part of the Rishis that such a crude form of description regarding entry of the soul into the body has been given; but even a cursory glance through the preceding part of the Aitareya Āraṇyaka would reveal that the seers were well-aware that the soul permeates every limb of the bodies of all the creatures; but all the same, they used this mode of its entry and subsequent ascent into the body rather metaphysically on the basis of the universal analogy of the rise of the life-giving sap from the roots in the entire vegetation world. Analogy has great institutional value and as such, the universal factum of upward flow of the life-sustaining sap in all the botanical growths has been used as a base for making the common man understand the all-pervasive character of the Ātman in the bodies of all living creatures.

In the next section,[3] it has, inter-alia, been said that speech is fire, sight yonder sun, mind the moon, hearing the quarters; this is the union of those sent forth. These deities are such in the body; but they openly appear among the deities. This is mere corroboration of the fact stated in an earlier section,[4] that behind each of our psychic faculties, there is a deity who not only regulates their functioning; but is primarily responsible therefor. All the gods originate[5] from the Prajāpati. Hence, in the ultimate analysis, it is the Prajāpati himself who permeates the bodies of all the living creatures. This view has further been fortified by quoting the saying of a seer known as Hiraṇyadant Vaida in which he asserted that the gods give him whatever is owned by him. Prajāpati or the Supreme being is the over-lord of everything—animate or inanimate. His presence in the body, ipso-facto, gives the man a capacity to have a command over everything.

In a subsequent section,[6] Puruṣaḥ (or Man) has unequivocally been stated to be the sea. It does not in any way signify any physical identity between Puruṣaḥ and the immense store house of water called sea. It simply signifies that the Man in his inherent nature is as extensive as the sea. Not only that, whatever he attains, he wants to be beyond that. If he gains the sky world, he desires to be beyond it. If he were to gain the yonder world, he would desire to be beyond it. Sāyaṇa[7] has interpreted it that the sea is typical of all unsatisfied desires. Keith[8] has also followed him. The language of the text does not say anything about the desires of the physical embodiment called man and their being unlimited. It speaks of the Cosmic Man. This view is further fortified from the next sentence of this very section which states that the Puruṣaḥ is five-fold. What is hot in him is fire, the apertures are the ether, blood, mucus and seed are water, the body is earth and breath is air. Further description of the text gives fivefold classification of the breath into prāṇa, apāna etc. The puruṣaḥ described here is not the physical frame of flesh and blood with its concomitant desires; but is the Cosmic Man which the Āraṇyaka[9] has earlier termed as 'Puruṣa evoktham eyam eva mahān Prajāpatiḥ'.

A seer called Bādhva[10] felt that there are four persons—the person of the body, the person of the metres, the person of the Veda and the Great Person. The person of the body is the corporeal self. Its essence is the incorporeal conscious self. The person of the metres is the collection of letters and the letter 'a' is its essence. The person of the Veda consists of all the four Vedas and Brahmā priest is its essence. The fourth person called Mahāpuruṣa is the year which causes somethings to fall together and others to grow up. Its essence is sun. The incorporeal conscious self and the sun are the same. This surmise is supported by the Ṛgvedic verse (I.115.1) which says that:—"The bright face of the gods hath arisen, the eye of Mitra, Varuṇa and Agni. It hath filled heaven, earth and the sky. The sun is the self of all that stands and moves." The Bahvṛcas consider the incorporeal conscious self to be in the great hymn, the Adhvaryus in the fire, the chandogās in the Mahāvrata rite. They see him in this earth, in heaven, in the air, in the ether, in the waters, in plants, trees, moon, constellations and in all the beings. Him they call Brahman (S.1). This unmistakably brings out the all permeating character of the Supreme-Being.

Brahman Free from the Limitations of Name, form and Gender

It has been rather unequivocally stated[11] that laying aside the bonds of names (in this world), the wise found their quest and rejoiced in the revealed (S.2). The word nāmā used in the fourth verse does not mean nāmāyattāḥ as construed by Sāyana; but it actually signifies definiteness in so much so that the wise definitely rejoiced in the revelation of the formless and shapeless Brahman because of whose presence in the body, all the organs function in perfect unison with each other. The seer of the Āraṇyaka does not stop here; but goes on to assert that with the revelation of Brahman, all the evils are cast off and the knower thereof rises to the world of heaven. Thus, these verses not only bring out the fact that Brahman is bliss; but that its knowledge is also ultimately instrumental to the attainment of heaven which Sāyaṇa takes as the abode of Hiraṇyagarbha or in other words, the knowledge of the Supreme-self.

Further elucidation about the characteristics of Brahman has been given in the fifth verse. It unequivocally asserts that he has neither feminine, nor masculine nor neutral gender. Both Keith and Sāyaṇa attribute this genderless quality to Prāṇa; but there is no direct or indirect indication to that effect in the verse itself. In fact, the preceding verse and the succeeding sentence in prose do talk of Brahman in clear-cut terms. The unity of thought that Brahman is nameless and formless as made out in the preceding two verses has also been sustained in this verse by saying that the same Brahman is also free from the attributes of gender. This conclusion is further corroborated from the fact that Sāyaṇa quotes a verse from Śvetāśvatara Upanishad[12] to elaborate his view point that this verse pertains to the qualities of Prāṇa. A glance through this verse of the Śvetāśvatara Upanishad reveals that it refers to the individual soul and not to Prāṇa. After saying that it is genderless, the verse lays down that whatever body the Ātman takes to itself, by that it is held. The first two verses of this section of the Āraṇyaka bring out the essential unity between the 'Self' and 'Brahman'. Consequently, it can be asserted without any sense of doubt that the genderless description given in this verse is of the Brahman and not of Praṇa.

Prajāpati as Sole Creator

Section II. 1.3 not only elucidates; but rather analyses the system of entire creation in this universe. It clearly states that the seed of Prajāpati are gods. From the gods, comes rain; from rain, entire vegetation and food, from food, creatures, thence their heart, mind, speech and action. The man is moulded by his deeds and is in the ultimate analysis, abode of Brahman (S.3). Thus, indubitably Prajāpati is the sole creator of this world.

Prajāpati as Ultimate Truth

The closing part of section II. 1.5. of the Aitareya Āraṇyaka rather authoritatively asserts 'Tat Sattyam' (That is truth). The word 'tat' unambiguously refers to uktha which represents Prāṇa and ultimately the Prajāpati. This assertion, therefore, clearly means that God alone is the ultimate truth. One who has realised this truth even his false statements assume the characteristic of being true. This apparently is a contradiction in terms. A false statement even by a fully liberated soul shall remain false and mere knowledge of Brahman by such a person shall not convert such assertion to be true. Yes, this is so and shall always remain to be so. Ipso-facto, their is nothing on this earth that can convert a lie into a truth. On the basis of this argument, the above assertion of the omniscient seers of the Āraṇyaka shall fall to the ground. However, this cannot ordinarily be. The above saying of the Rishis is obviously based on the inevitable fact that a person who has realised the importance of that truth, shall by dint of that very fact, become incapable of telling any lies as he comes to know why truth is Sattya. Such far reaching and permanent is the effect of realization of Braham on the individual concerned.

Concept of Ātmā and Brahman

The Aitareya Āraṇyaka[13] says that the Imperishable One enters the fivefold body which is carried to and fro by the harnessed steeds or by the organs of action. In the second half of each of the first two stanzas, it has been reiterated that in this body is yoked that is termed as trueness of the true and in that all the gods are in one combined. The so-called truth of truth (*Satyasya Satyam*) is nothing but what is now known as Ātmā and the gods combined in the body are just the so-called organs of perception which are the principle guides of the body in its various movements and actions (S.4). Keith admits that 'truth of the truth' may signify Brahman as per later interpretations and this concept may be as early as this Āraṇyaka; but all the same, it might be enough to take it merely as 'the essence of truth'. In fact, it is mere jugglary of words. The essence of truth cannot, by any stretch of imagination, be something, other than Truth itself. Both the essence of truth and truth itself are, ipso-facto, of the same species. Hence, here it means that in the physical frames of the creatures is a true representative of the Brahman and it subsequently came to be known as '*Ayam Ātmā Brahma*'.

Sāyaṇa feels that 'the truth of truth' in this context means Prāṇa and with a view to corroborate his interpretation, he quotes Bṛhadāraṇyaka Upanishad II. 3.6(S.5). For the identification of Brahman in the body with Prāṇa, Sāyaṇa further cites Praśna Upanishad, VI.3. Sāyaṇa seems to have travailed to draw this meaning so as to be in line with his mode of interpretation of whole of the second Āraṇyaka; but the fact remains that in the above-quoted passage of the Bṛhadāraṇyaka Upanishad, Prāṇa has specifically been stated as satyam; whereas it is not so in this Āraṇyaka. Hence, the realistic interpretation is that it is the Ātman (true representative of the Ultimate Truth) that enters the body.

As regards the union of all the gods in the body, Keith invites attention to Bṛhadāraṇyaka Upanishad (I.4.7); wherein it has, inter-alia, been stated that the Self entered the body even upto the tips of the nails. Him they see not for (as seen) he is incomplete, when breathing, he is called the vital force; when speaking, the voice; when seeing, the eye; when hearing, the ear; when thinking, the mind. He who meditates on one another of these aspects, he does not know for he is incomplete, with one or another of these characteristics. The Self is to be meditated upon for in it all these become one (S. 6). Thus, it is self-evident that it is one account of the presence of the Ātman that all the sense organs function individually as well as in unison with each other.

The second verse says the undying one joins the body after coming from the undying (S. 7). Thus, indubitably, the intrinsic source or origin of the Self is the Brahman itself and nothing else.

In the closing part of this section,[14] the body has been stated to be a chariot of the gods gifted with speech as its seat, its two sides are ears, the horses as the eyes, the driver as the mind and the breath also mounts upon it. The body has been defined as a divine chariot because the various Devas or the senses reside therein. It is not clear why the human physical frame has been given the epithet of destroyer of desires (Anakāmamārah̤). Sāyaṇa explains it that after attainment of Hiraṇyagarbha, the man does not desire to attain any other world. Apparently, the above epithet is of the human body called the divine-chariot; but this physical frame cannot be 'destroyer of desires'. Its own basic desires of eating, sleeping etc. cannot ordinarily be wiped off. If done, the body would normally disintegrate and perish. Hence, in all fairness, this epithet is actually the attribute of the Ātman whose entry into the body has been prayed for by quoting parts of two verses from Ṛgveda (X.39.12 and VIII. 73.2). It is this Ātman which is summum bonum of the human body and as true representative of the Absolute therein, is quicker than the mind and the winking of an eye. The Self alone in the man (and not his physical frame) has no desires and thus the Ātman can only possibly be given the epithet of 'Anakāmamārah̤'.

Identity Between the Self and Brahman

The Āraṇyaka[15] unequivocally states that the man is moulded by his deeds and is, in the ultimate analysis abode of Brahman. This clearly brings out the identity of the man and the Brahman because the former cannot be the abode of Brahman unless and until the Brahman lives with him and there is complete identity between the two.

In another section,[16] it has been laid down that "Brahman is called 'a' (akāra) and the 'I' is there contained." Keith says that it must be taken as a clear assertion that Brahman includes the individual self. Representation of Brahman by the syllable 'a' is purely symbolical description. Inclusion of the "Self" in the concept of Brahman was subsequently more vividly elucidated in Bṛhadāraṇyaka Upanishad.[17] A glance through the same reveals that we must experience that we are really the very self and that we are neither the bodily nor the sensuous nor the intellectual nor the emotional vestures; that we are in our essential nature entirely identical with the Pure Self.

Identity Between the Ātman and Brahman and Omnipresence of the Former

The Āraṇyaka[18] goes on to add that the self is Brahman, Indra, Prajāpati, all the gods, the five great elements, seeds of various kinds, born of eggs, born from the womb, born from heat, born by eruption of earth, horses, cows, men, elephants and all that breathes, whether it walks or flies and what is immovable. All that is guided by knowledge and rests on knowledge. In fact, the world is guided and based on knowledge. Knowledge is Brahman. He, by his knowing self, having left this world and having obtained all delights in the world of heaven, became immortal (S. 8).

Keith feels that at this stage the question which arises is whether the above justifies an attribution to the author of the doctrine that knowledge alone exists. It is quote open to argue that we only are given the doctrine that the world is guided by knowledge, which leaves us with a final dualism. He feels that probably the author went further and intended to assert the origin of all from knowledge. If so, he represents exactly the later Bhāgavata view, perhaps that of Bādarāyaṇa, of the nature of reality. The Self, or God, is conceived as creating the material world as a reality; but the exact nature of the creation is left vague. The relation of Brahman and Ātman is likewise left vague, a mere identification such as may have been meant being of little value. But, of course, none of the questions had yet clearly presented themselves.

In fact, in this section knowledge has been accepted as the prime characteristic of the self. As the basic and subjective reality underneath all creation, it is the Ātman or prajñānam itself which is identical with the Brahman. It is also through the knowledge of the self that the heavenly world and ultimately, the immortality is attained.

All-pervasiveness of Ātman

The Aitareya Āraṇyaka[19] clearly brings out the all permeating trait of the soul or Ātman in almost as philosophical terms as the later philosophical treatises known by the name of Upanishads. Coming to state the functions of the sense organs, it has been stated that in each of these sense faculties, there is latent a deity, who in fact, is the real functionary in the diverse functions of our sense organs. This is not all. Intrinsically speaking, it is the presence of the Puruṣa or the Self in all these organs who is the sole cause of their actual functioning. This Puruṣa pervades wholly in all the limbs upto hair and nails. The first Āraṇyaka, unlike majority of its assertions, goes on rather unusually to assert that all beings down to ants are born thus pervaded (S. 9).

Further elaborating the all pervasive character of the Self, it has been asserted that it is as large as heaven and earth. Ipso-facto, it does not signify the continuous prolongation or extension of any physical frame of the so-called Self; but it, very mystically, denotes its all-permeating character throughout the entire span of this universe. This concept about the immanence of God or that the subtle Ātman is immanent in all the creatures, has been later on developed more clearly and philosophically in the Upanishads.

Ātman, the Sole Doer of Everything

This section[20] opens with the stark question : "Who is he whom we meditate on as the Self ? Which is that Self ?" The reply is neither direct nor descriptive; but inferential. All the important functions of man are performed because of the presence of the primary subject viz., the Ātman in the body. The Āraṇyaka goes on to say that it is by the Ātman that one sees, hears, smells the scents, forms speech and discriminate between sweets and sour. It is again the Ātman which is the heart and the mind, perception, injunction, understanding, knowledge, wisdom, vision, firmness, thinking, considering, helping, memory, resolution, will, breath, love and desire. All these are only names of knowledge (S. 10). This may fairly be construed that knowledge is the pre-eminent characteristic of the Ātman.

Ātman, the Sole Subject in the World

This section[21] of the Āraṇyaka, though heterogenous in the subject-matter dealt with therein, ends with a deeply philosophical note. The opening few sentences rather incoherently assert that on a certain type of person, study of the Vedas does not bestow any wisdom, he does not gain by the instructions of a teacher and he also follows not the path of virtue. A major part of this section describes the various ill-omens which, when observed in the state of awakening or dreaming, avowedly harbinger the short duration of life of the observer thereof. After description of a plethora of the then prevailing such social superstitions; the section rather out-of-context brings out a significantly deep note about the philosophic nature of the Ātman which is the sole real subject or knower in this vast universe. The Āraṇyaka declares that in all beings, there is a person who is not heard, not reached, not thought, not subdued, not seen, not understood, not classified; but who hears, thinks, sees, classifies, sounds, understands and knows is the own self of each being (S. 11).

Keith observes that this is the most advanced point in the definition of the Ātman arrived at in whole of the Āraṇyaka. The Ātman is not object, but subject only. Sāyaṇa says that the Ātman never becomes an object, though of course, it assumes the role of an enjoyer of an object. The passage in question unambiguously signifies that the Ātman being the sole knower cannot be known. Sāyaṇa cites the antaryāmi Brāhmaṇa. Bṛhadāraṇyaka Upanishad (III.7.13) and certain other similar passages from two other Upanishads. The above observation of the Āraṇyaka is the harbinger of the later importance of the Ātman in the Vedantic system of Indian Philosophy.

Attainment of Salvation

In the Aitareya Āraṇyaka,[22] completion of the Great Litany of Mahāvrata by recitation of 1000 verses in bṛhatī metre has been stated to be instrumental to the attainment of glory and salvation. It has further been laid down that the sacrificer attains the status of Indra and shines in those worlds (S. 12). A careful reading of this passage establishes the doctrine of Mukti; though of course, Keith somehow specifically and unequivocally refuses to believe that this doctrine finds mention in this Āraṇyaka.

Stages of Conscious Life

In this section,[23] a determined effort has been made to explain the different stages of conscious life. The very opening sentence says that one who has clearer conception of the Self attains fuller being. In the entire vegetational growth, only sap is seen while consciousness is there in the animals only. In fact, both consciousness and sap are seen in the animals; but consciousness is conspicuous by its absence in plants and trees. Man is most endowed with intelligence and he can reproduce what he was known or seen. He can foresee the future and knows the world and what is not the world (Lokālōkau). Sāyaṇa explains them as heaven and hell. Being thus endowed with self-consciousness, the man is desirous to attain deliverance or immortality through the agency of his mortal frame (S. 13). In contradistinction to this, hunger and thirst comprise the power of knowledge of the animals. They have no memories of what they have experienced or seen. The entire experience is confined to the sensations of hunger and thirst and nothing beyond.

Keith observes that is the most philosophical part of the whole Āraṇyaka. He further adds that the distinctive marks of man are all elements which make his consciousness into an ordered system and they imply self-consciousness, as opposed to the mere consciousness of animals in the form of their receptivity of external stimuli. Observations of Keith are not only fully acceptable, but also very apt and keen.

B. PSEUDO MYSTICISM IN THE AITAREYA ĀRAṆYAKA

Though later in the evolution of thought, more philosophical and less ritualistic in their essential nature, yet the Forest-Texts Constitute a part and parcel of the Brāhmaṇical literature. Thus, despite the absence of any detailed analysis of the various rituals in the Āraṇyakas; they have neither been able to completely liberate themselves from the characteristically archaic language of the parent literature nor from the oft-repeated illogical and at times rather funny reasoning of the Brāhmaṇas. Thus, the Forest-Texts also abound in irrational reasoning or logic (if at all, it may be termed as such). This type of circuitous or unending reasoning permeates throughout the length and breadth of the Aitareya Āraṇyaka and can easily be spotted out. Some of the examples may justifically be specifically pointed out below :

(*i*) In section I. 1.2, it is, inter-alia, stated that there are four verses in the triṣṭubh and the cattle are four-footed, so the recitation of triṣṭubh verses serves to win cattle. Similarly, it is argued that there are three verses in the Virāj metre, these are the three-fold worlds and hence the verses serve to gain these worlds. Similarly identification in the number of verses in the hymn under recitation and parts of the body has been worked out without any ostensible logic as well as purpose.

(*ii*) Section I.1.4 is rather a strange conglomeration of logic and fancy. It deals with the stoma of the 25th day of the Mahāvrata rite and clearly brings out the mutual both beneficence and munificence of man and gods to each other. The human worshippers offer oblations to various gods and the latter in reciprocity bestow fulfilment of all desires on the former. So far, it is alright and quite symptomatic of the basically kind and affectionate nature of all rational entities who live for the development of each other. Then, starts the circuitous and rather characteristically, illogical reasoning of this Āraṇyaka when, somehow apparently mystical mathematical equality is worked out between twenty-one verses of this 'Stoma' and twenty one parts of the human body. However, the author of this section seems to have at once been reminded of his earlier statement about the parts of the human body being twenty five (I. 1.2). So, he embarks upon a strange reasoning so as to work up the number of verses in this stoma to be twenty-five (by repeating each of the first and last verses thrice) and thus establishes a sort of mystical identification among the number of hymns of this stoma, parts of the human body, the Ātmā and Prajāpati and the day of Mahāvrata ceremony being the 25th day. All this inherently illogical reasoning has been put forth under the plea, that "like is brought about by like".

(*iii*) After giving details about the type of wood, number of planks to be used, material of which the ropes of the swing used in the Niṣkevalya Śastra,[24] the supervening section,[25] besides giving characteristically Brāhmaṇical details like the height of the swing above the ground, direction from which it should be mounted, procedure/direction of descent etc., also does the usual exercise of attributing philosophic significance to almost every process of the ritualistic ceremony. An apparent mysticism permeates throughout the length and breadth of this section even though the same may not stand scrutiny when tested on the touch-stone of logic. Some of the examples of this type of superficial philosophizing may briefly be tabulated below :

(*a*) The height of the swing above the ground should be one fist for by that all proper food is made and all proper food is taken.

(*b*) The Hotṛ priest should mount the swing from behind because men get into a ship from behind and the swing in this ceremony is a heaven-fairing ship.

(*c*) While mounting the swing, the priest should first touch it by his chin and rise upto it with the aid of his arms and thereby the priest (and of course through him, the sacrificer) shall attain strength and bravery like the hawk among the birds.

(*d*) Mounting of the hotṛ priest on the swing and sitting of the udgātā on the seat of udumbara wood represents union of a male and female and thereby the sacrificer gains children, cattle, food and prosperity. Similarly seating of other junior priests called Hotrakas alongwith Brahmā on the seats of grass also has mystic significance for attainment of strength, sap and proper food.

(*e*) The Hotā should descend from the swing towards east because it is in that direction only that all fertilising seed or semen of the gods is born. Hence, getting down from the swing in this direction would, ipso-facto, bestow upon the sacrificer attendance of all worldly pleasures including moral and physical strength.

(*iv*) In section I.3.1 ibid., beginning of the recitation of the mid-day śastra of the rite called Mahāvrata with the utterance of the word 'hiṅkāra' has been attached extra-ordinarily excessive mystic significance. This word like the Gāyatrī metre, the Mahāvrata day, and Vasukra has been identified with Brahman. Its recitation has also been stated to be gifted with the four-fold supernatural power of bestowing children/cattle, insight into the real nature of Brahman, fulfilment of all worldly desires and discrimination between divine and human speech on the sacrificer or on one who performs the sacrifice with such a knowledge. Thus, the word hiṅkāra has been accorded the status and importance of the well-known seven vyāhṛtis. It is a very apt example of the fact that, though the philosophy and not the ritualism, had started acquiring importance at the time of the writing of the Forest Text-Books; yet the latter had not been successful in extricating themselves from the apparently irrational assertions and interpolations of the Brāhmaṇical literature over the ṛks of the Veda. This section relegates the Vedic mantras to a secondary position and the primary importance has been attached to the pre-utterance of a word like hiṅkāra which, when analysed, has obviously no meaning and much less any mysticism. Obviously, this word has greater importance than all the verses of the Veda that constitute the mid-day śastra of the Mahāvrata rite. Even a modern scientific mind accepts that the verses of the Veda constitute the inspired experiences of a large number of seers who devoted their lives to unravel the mysteries of the Ultimate Truth of this universe; but this section rather summarily attributes to the ṛks a subsidiary role and the principal power for mystic realisation has been attributed to a rather meaningless word which, in common parlance, at the most, is capable of signifying chirping of some kind of birds. Evidently, despite high claims, the word has no reasons to concentrate in itself the avowed mystic powers.

(*v*) Certain fanciful etymologies have been worked out in sections II. 1.4-5 so as to present the reader with the mystical significance of the contents thereof :

(*a*) Entry of the soul through the tips of the feet seems to have been invoked because of the mutual rhythmical harmony between words used—Prapadābhyām Prāpadyata etc.

(*b*) Udara and urū have been identified simply on the basis of two common syllables—u and r even though there is absolutely no other relationship (etymological or otherwise) between the two words.

(*c*) The head became head (Śiras) because the Brahman reached it (aśrayata). It is because of the apparently rhythmical similarity between the above two words that the head came to be called as such.

(*d*) The body is called śarīra because it aśiryata (disintegrated) and was termed as āśāri (having disintegrated).

(*f*) Deliberate similarity of sound of the syllable 'Pra' has been ensured in the use of words like Prāṇayanta, Praṇītaḥ, etc. and that of syllable 'sam' in the words samāgāt and sāyam in section II.1.5. This form of description and use of these words seems to have been rather deliberately adopted so as to give the impression that it was the mere process of stretching of the 'uktha' that the morning came into existence and its subsequent coming to a rest resulted in coming into existence of the evening. Mere tactful use of words containing identical sounds cannot be accepted as the cause of any real philosophy lying underneath.

(*vi*) In II.1.6, it has, inter-alia, been stated that the uktha is covered with metres. Since he is covered with the metres, therefore, they call them metres (coverings). There is no relationship of meaning or otherwise between the words channa (past participle from root chad) and chandas. Mere similarity of sound of the syllable 'chan' seems to have been involved so as to impart a semblance of at least superficial mysticism to the origin of the metres.

(*vii*) In the sections II.2.1-2, one philosophic assertion has been made that the Prāṇa is creator of all the principal Vedic seers, hymns, verses, half and quarter verses, syllables and even the sounds leaving aside the fact that God (here named as Prāṇa) is the soul creator of the entire universe. The arguments put forth to establish Prāṇa as the creator are in majority of the cases hardly plausible and rather constitute that may, more justifiably, be termed as pseudo-mysticism. Some of the examples are cited below :

(*a*) Composers of the first Book of the Ṛgveda are known as Śatarcins because the Prāṇa or vital-airs stayed in the living human body for 100 years.

(*b*) The Vedic seers known by the name of Mādhyamas are so-called simply because the Prāṇa placed himself in the middle of all that is.

(*c*) Because as, up-breathing, prāṇa is the swallower and as down-breathing (apān), he is delight, he is, therefore, Gṛtsamada—the seer of second Book of the Ṛgveda.

(*d*) Because all whatsoever was the friend of Prāṇa therefore, he is Viśwamitra, the seer of the third Book of the Ṛg-veda.

(*e*) Because the gods spoke to Prāṇa that "he may be dear to all of them", so he is Vāmadeva, the seer of Book No. IV of the Ṛgveda.

(*f*) As Prāṇa protected all this from evil, hence the seers of the Book V are known as Atris.

(*g*) As Prāṇa is the bearer of off-spring or Vājaḥ, so he is known as Bharadvāja.

(*h*) The gods took the opportunity of telling the Prāṇa that "he be Vaśiṣṭha or richest of all," so the latter became Vaśiṣṭha, the seer of Book No. VI.

(*i*) Because Prāṇa went forth to all whatsoever, so he became Pragātha the seer of Book No. VIII.

(*j*) Prāṇa purified all whatsoever, hence he became Pāvamanīs, the subject matter of Book IX of the Ṛgveda. Keith and Sāyaṇa wrongly interpret Pāvamanīs as the authors of this Book.

(*k*) Prāṇa said, "Let me be everything, small and great." Hence, the kṣudra sūktas and Mahāsūktas came into existence.

(*l*) Prāṇa said, "ye have said what is well-said," and hence became the hymns.

(*m*) Because Prāṇa went to all beings, therefore, he became a ṛk or verse.

(*n*) As the Prāṇa went to all the places, he became the half-verses.

(*o*) Prāṇa is a quarter-verse for he has entered all these beings.

(*p*) Prāṇa is a syllable or Akṣara, for he pours forth gifts to all these beings.

The above plethora of arguments to create or correlate the origin of each of the Vedic seers, hymns, verses, half and quarter verses and syllables with one or other activity or characteristic of Prāṇa is merely verbose without any even apparent rationale in it.

(*viii*) Concluding the process of creation of the universe, it has been said[26] that the individual soul having entered the body of the man looked through all beings, to see whether any one wished to proclaim another self. He saw this person as the embodiment of the most extended Brahman or in other words, the Brahman is all permeating and is present in all creatures in the form of a subtle existence called the individual soul. On this deep-seated real philosophy, this section rather futilely proceeds further to philosophize that the individual soul on seeing the extended Brahman in the body proclaimed, "I have seen it." Because he has been seen, he, ipso-facto, bears the name of Idandra. This funny name is nothing but a deliberate gymnastic at mystification. The word Idandra seems to have been made out by the process of elimination of some syllables and substitution of one identical sound from the sentence; "Idam adarśam itī 3" (Idandra). The Āraṇyaka further goes on to assert that he is Indeed Idandra by name. Him who is Idandra, they call Indra mysteriously. The argument has been further fortified by invoking a well known saying that the gods, by their very nature, love mystery (S. 14). All this argumentation and apparently mysterious nomenclature of Idandra for the widely and clearly understood name of Indra for the Individual soul is nothing short of what may genuinely be termed as psuedo-mysticism.

(*ix*) In the last section[27] of this Āraṇyaka have been delineated the principles that should be followed in the recitation/study of Mahāvrata. In the closing sentence, it has been stated that the Mahāvrata is the name of this great being and one who knows thus 'this' as the name of Mahāvrata, becomes Brahman.

The priests of the Brāhmaṇical cult felt that performance of particular rites in accordance with the devised procedure had the efficacy of compelling the worshipped deities to bestow the avowed worldly objectives. This part of the Āraṇyaka rather constitutes the climax so as to gift the recitation of the Mahāvrata even with the revelation of the Absolute Brahman. Yajña and Prajāpati have been identified in the Brāhmaṇical literature and prolongation of this very belief seems to be the raison-detre for the above assertion even though it may not be possible to bring it home rationally.[28]

C. MYSTICISM IN THE TAITTIRĪYA ĀRAṆYAKA

Concept of Supreme-being

In the Taittirīya Āraṇyaka[29] the Imperishable One has been stated to be the last resort of one and all. The Supreme Lord has also been given the epithet of 'Tripada'. Vishnu derives his brightness or excellence from Him. The former acts as controller and support of the vast span of earth and the heavens.

Sole Supreme Godhead

It has been said[30] that the Supreme-Being is not only self-illuminating; but also illuminates others. He is very affectionate (venam) and manifests himself in multi-forms. At the time of origin of this world that Brahman found Dasa-hotā in the sea. He created the universe and Himself entered in every creature. All the satellites, Vedas, hotṛ-priests find their ultimate resort in Him alone. He resides hidden in the hearts of all human beings, and is their mainstay or supreme controller. The apparent vividness and multiplicity of entire creation finds ultimate unity in Him (S. 15). Brahman is self-sustaining and is also the ultimate support of the gods and the entire world. He is also the mainstay of all the rituals and directions. He is the essence of all prayers and was realised (by Prajāpati) by brooding over him. The wise know Him as all-permeating, wise-doer of all actions and creator of multifarious creatures. He is friend of all good people and is set in the hearts of all the beings. He is embodiment of immortality and is omnipresent, soul of Indra, exhibits Himself in multifarious forms and is bestower of all treasures. He is bestower of immortality on gods and controller of life-span of all other creatures. The wise have always found him all-pervading among the supernatural beings like Indra, Savitā, Air and the Sun. In fact, the learned have always looked upon Him as the Supreme abode of Perfect order. He is Sustainer and ultimate Destructor of the Universe. In fact, I am myself fully enveloped by that Immortal Being (S. 16). That God is store house of golden hue and is all enveloped by brilliance. He makes all the seasons. Though God is present as Ātman in all creatures and is also all-pervasive, yet even the gods are unaware of His all-permeating character (S. 17). God is the maker of rain and thus rears the universe by outgrowth of diverse vegetation and plants. He also bestows on us prosperity, wealth and animals. He is capable of wiping off our sins, is the inexhaustible source of wealth and is the golden mountain or nourisher. Acting as Regulator of Time, it has been said that all the worlds are held or supported by Him. After so many prayers to God for grant of animals, wealth, off-springs, bravery etc., the penultimate verse of this section brings out the revelation that the gods ultimately found the Imperishable One gliding gently like clarified butter into the hearts of all animate and inanimate creatures. This significantly brings forth all-pervasiveness of the Ātman (S. 18).

Concept of Single Godhead and Salvation

The well-known Puruṣa-hymn of Ṛgveda (X.90) has been reproduced in full in section III. 12 of this Hermit-text to explain the process of creation of the universe. In addition, two other very mystical verses have been given here which very pertinently and significantly bring out the concept of Supreme Godhead and attainment of salvation by knowing Him. The 16th verse[31] forthrightly puts forth the belief that I know that greatest puruṣa who has extreme brilliance like the Sun and is much beyond the periphery of darkness or ignorance. A wise person after proper investigation or discernment lives in this life by showing proper respect for the diverse names and forms of the same Primeval puruṣa (S. 19). For him, in the ultimate analysis, everything in this universe is nothing but the God manifesting Himself in various forms and shapes.

The powerful or mighty one (Virāṭ Puruṣaḥ) whom the Creator set up before Himself was knower of all the four regions. It is only by attaining the knowledge of that Creator that anybody can attain immortality. There is no other method or path for attaining immortality (S. 20).

Thus, this remote text establishes the fact that philosophy was as much developed in that hoary past as in the modern age of fully developed Vedanta which unambiguously declares that salvation cannot come around the corner except through attainment of knowledge of the Supreme Brahman.

Continuing the exposition of the sole Godhead, it has been said that one who was born from the waters and the liquid essence of the earth (possibly tortoise as expounded in section I. 23) originated from Viśva-karman. Tvaṣṭā exists as the creator of the material or visible aspect of the world. At the stage of first origin, the Viśva-karman created everything of the world headed by the Primordial Puruṣa. Then follows the important verse quoted in the preceding section also that "I know that greatest Puruṣa who has the brilliance and hue of the Sun and who is much beyond the ambit of ignorance. Only a knower of That (Puruṣa) becomes immortal. There is no other method to attain salvation."

The Prajāpati exists in the womb as the primeval seed of all future creation. Though Himself bodiless, He procreates multifold. The wise know Him as the symbol of the divine procreative energy. The virtuous want to attain the status of Prajāpati. One who radiates heat or energy to the deities, who is their priest, who came into existence earlier than them, obeisances be to sucl lustrous Brahman (S. 21).

As supporter,[32] the Lord supports or maintains. He is the single Godhead who permeates in diverse ways. He alone is the controller of death and immortality. He alone is known as the Lord and protector. He alone is the sustainer and continues to sustain the entire sustenance (S. 22).

This God (as Ātman) leaves the bodies of those who are just born. In certain cases, it does not depart even upto old age. Thus, the God acting as Ātman is never lazy. God is supreme and maintainer/preserver of mankind. All the deities respond to His call or directions He is one and only one; but enters innumerable bodies. The manifested (world) obtained its origin from the Unmanifest. God alone is the sole protector of whatever has been created. As soon as, He decides not to maintain any body, the life comes to a close (S. 23).

Nature of Brahman

Elucidating the nature of Brahman, it has been said[33] that 'He who knows Brahma, attains the highest'. A verse declares that Brahma is the real, knowledge and infinite. It is set down in the secret place (of the heart) and in the highest heaven. A knower of the same obtains all desires together with the intelligent Brahma (S. 24). The basic characteristics of the Supreme Being have clearly been brought out here. Brahman is not only the ultimate reality; but it is also the supreme knower. It is limitless and illimitable. This verse also brings out an identity between the individual self and the universal self when it says that the latter is set in the secret place of the heart of each creature. As soon as the desire to realise the self is fulfilled; then no worldly desire remains to be satisfied. It is because after the revelation of the true nature of the self; all other mundane desires are either rendered insignificant or purposeless or the knower is completely absorbed in the matchless brilliance and bliss of the Brahman that he becomes oblivious of everything else. Evidently, all his other physical desires are fulfilled by his very thought of them. So marvellous is the experience of realisation of the Brahman.

Psychological Reflection about the Nature of Brahman

The seers of the Hermit-texts were among the foremost in their age in philosophical reflection in general and psychological reflection in particular. Great stress has been laid in certain passages of the Upanishadic portions of these texts on 'Thought power.' The flight of this thought power is very aptly depicted in section VIII. 6 which lays down : "He who meditates on Brahman as Not-Being, shall himself cease to exist. On the other hand, if one knows that Brahman is, then is he known as the real in existence (S. 25). This, obviously, means that whoever envisages the Brahman as the Existence becomes that existence and whoever envisages it as the Non-Existence, becomes that non-existence. Similarly it has been said[34] as follows in respect of meditation of God in different forms :

(*i*) In respect of human recognitions, Brahman may be recognised as preservation in speech, as acquisition and preservation in prāṇa and apāna, as work in hands, as movement in the feet, as evacuation in the anus;

(*ii*) In respect of the deities, Brahman may be cognised as satisfaction in rain, as force in the lightning, as splendour in cattle, as light in the stars, as procreation, immortality and bliss in the generative organ, as the all in space;

(*iii*) If one meditates on Brahman as support, he himself will find support; if as greatness, he himself will become great; if as mind, he himself will become possessed of mindfulness; if as adortation, he himself shall receive honour; if as the Supreme, he himself shall be possessed of the

> Supreme; if as parimara (destructive agent) of Brahman; round about him shall die all the hateful rivals as also those rivals whom he does not like (S. 26).

Above are plenty of precedents that one becomes what he conceives. The aspirant who seeks and strives to become one with the Reality in its status of Becoming, manifests and renders in his own being that truth of Brahman in the measure of his realisation. It is the essential and the pragmatic truth of the Godhead. It is something beyond us which is indeed already within us. It is, therefore, for us to reveal It (the Brahman) in our conscious nature. We can grow into it and reveal in ourselves individually the Godhead. Thus, growth into its universality and transcendance is our spiritual destiny.

God, the Soul of Nature (or Immanence of God)

How is God, the Soul of Nature and all pervasive? The Taittirīya Āraṇyaka[35] tells us that God, besides being the creator, is the Antaryāmin of the universe. It has been said that "at the time of creation, God entered everything that he created, and after having entered, became both the This and the That, the Defined and the Undefined, the Supported and Supportless, Knowledge and not-Knowledge, Reality and Unreality—yea, he became the Reality; it is for this reason that all this is verily called the Real". This passage also declares the immanence of God in all things whatsoever, even in contradictories and tells us that what thus comes to exist is the Real. The whole of Nature, therefore, which is God's handiwork, as well as God's garment, is filled and inspired by God who is its inner controller and soul.

Brahman is Bliss

It has been stated[36] that at the time of origin of the universe, the entire phenomenon was Non-Existent and Unmanifest. From this, manifest existence came into being. The Being shaped itself of its own accord. It was well and beautifully made. "Verily this so well-made is the essence or bliss of existence. On getting this essence, the man becomes blissful. Nobody could indeed breathe and live if there was not this bliss in space. It is He (Brahman) who bestows Bliss. Truly when a man finds fearlessness as support in Him who is invisible, bodiless, undefined, non-based, then he has passed beyond the reach of fear" (S. 27). Thus, when a man finds this bliss (the characteristic ingredient of Brahman) as the ingrained and inherent nature of his self, then he embraces all as so many currents of the ocean of Brahmānanda. He finds the Supreme-Being as all permeating and all other fellow beings including other creatures as projections of his own real self which consists of nothing else except Bliss. Life itself also becomes something worth-living and scope for misery, hatred etc. is also minimised, if not completely wiped off.

Five Phases of Brahman

Bhṛgu, son of the celebrated teacher Varuṇa, aspired to know the Brahman and approached his father for understanding the same. The latter did not give him a ready-made answer and put his son on guided self-exploration.[37] He was asked to practise penance and learn the truth for himself. The father told him that even the food, breath, eye, ear and mind could be defined as Brahman provided they or any one of them satisfied the below noted basic qualifications of that Supreme Reality :

> "From which beings are born, whereby being born they live, to which they go hence and enter again."

The son was directed to perform penance in pursuit of the above-quoted Basic Truth. Accordingly, he concentrated himself in thought and by the askesis (concentration of thought) of his brooding, he successively arrived at the conclusion that food (matter), vital air, mind and knowledge, and individually severally constituted the ultimate reality because each of them in their own respective way fulfilled the above qualifications. However, the father was not satisfied. This was evidently, because of the very partial and imperfect representation which each out of matter, life-breath, mind and intellect could give to Brahman. Accordingly, the son was directed to make further exploration by doing more penance. He did so and ultimately the truth dawned on him that Bliss or the beatific consciousness can be regarded as the source of all things whatsoever. It has further been said that this piece of knowledge shall be for ever mysteriously known as the *Bhārgavī Vāruṇī Vidyā* and that this is "exalted in the highest heaven." He who knows this, becomes established. He becomes the master of food and its eater, great in progeny, cattle, splendour of holiness and fame (S. 28). It obviously means that this wisdom is even honoured among the gods.

Supremacy of Single Gadhead

The first eighteen verses of the last Book[38] of the Taittirīya Āraṇyaka do, rather with single minded devotion, bring out the supremacy of the single Godhead in diverse ways. He has been stated to be omnipresent throughout the universe right from the depth of deep oceans upto the seat of the highest heaven. This Prajāpati is greater than the great, is set in the heart of each creature and is the seed of all creation (S. 29). The entire universe takes origin from Him and ultimately resolves in Him. All the gods, past and future are sustained by that Imperishable One who resides in the highest heaven. He is all enveloper, all permeating and the sole creator of all the inanimate and animate creation including the crude Nature (Prakṛti). Despite all this, He is the subtlest and the greatest of all, imperceptible, ancient, unlimited and far beyond the ambit of ignorance (S. 30). He alone is righteousness and truth. He is the venerable Brahman contemplated by the wise. Acts of worship and social utility are also that Reality. As navel of the universe, that Brahman is the source and sustainer of all creation. That very Prajāpati is, diversely speaking, the gross elements, the Sun, the moon etc., immortality and Brahman himself (S. 31). He is the sole origin of all units of time right from a moment to a year, seasons etc. and He also gave birth to the firmament and the heaven. None can possibly intellectually comprehend the higher, the lower and the lateral limits of that Godhead (on account of his undisputed omnipresence). None can also have control over Him which, ipso-facto, justified the epithet of being gifted with 'Great Glory' for Him. His form cannot be beheld nor can he be seen with the physical eye by any body. Those who know Him as set in their heart and meditate on Him with undistracted mind become immortal (S. 32). That sole Godhead is the only primeval source of all creation, the Great Person beyond the periphery of ignorance, of golden hue, bestower of brilliance on the gods, their controller and priest, prime controller of the entire universe by His very greatness, giver of physical and mental powers, sustainer of diverse planes of the universe. By knowing Him one transcends death and there is no other path leading to the attainment of liberation

(S. 33). He has unlimited physical, mental and intellectual capacities and is the Sole Creator. He exists as the warp and woof in all the created beings and is set in their hearts. He who knows that All-pervasive. One becomes worthy of receiving the honour due to a father even from his own natural father (S. 34). Supreme qualities of the Supreme-Being have further been reiterated in the next three verses which may very pertinently be quoted in original at the end of this chapter (S. 35-37).

A large portion of the tenth Book consists of extracts from various Saṁhitās. In fact, credit does seem to go to the compiler of this Book as a very large number of the best stanzas found in the various recensions of the Vedas and some other Upanishads in the praise of Brahman have been collected here. Inevitably repetition of the some superlative qualities of the single Godhead could not possibly be avoided. Thus, incoherence and lack of unity in the treatment of the subject-matter is permeating all through the eighteen verses analysed above. However, they seem to have been placed in the very beginning of this Book with a view to sublimate the supreme qualities of Prajāpati.

Brahman—Sole Origin of Microcosm and Macrocosm

The third verse[39] of X. 10 says that "from Him arise all the seas and the mountains. From Him, flow rivers of all kinds and from Him, all herbs and essences come forth. It is through Him that the Inner Soul dwells in beings" (S. 38). Further affirmation also flows from verse No. 6 that the entire universe is non-different from the Supreme-Brahman. This verse lays down that the Ātman has dwelling in the purity. He is the Vasu in the inter-regions, the Sacrificer at the altar; the guest in the dwelling home. He dwells in men (as consciousness), in gods (the most excellent), in the right and in the sky. He is (all that is) born of water, sprung from the earth, born of right and born of mountains. He is the Truth and Mighty one[40] (S. 39). The succeeding stanza[41] says that "the beings born from Brahman (identified here with Prajāpati) are not separate from Him. Before their birth, nothing whatsoever existed other than Him, who entered all the creatures of the world. Prajāpati has identified Himself with the creatures. He imparts lustre to the three luminaries—fire, sun and the moon. He is endowed with sixteen parts" (S. 40). Stanza[42] X.10.19 once again clearly states that the Brahman (identified here with Rudra) is that "Highest Reality."

Rudra, the great seer is the first born among gods and is superior to all. Behold the Golden-germ being born. May that Lord endow us with clear remembrance." (S. 41). The all-enveloping character of the Supreme Godhead has further been reiterated in this section through another verse[43] which lays down that "Other than whom, there is nothing higher; nothing minuter; nothing greater; That Person who stands still like a tree established in heaven, fills whole of the universe" (S. 42).

Brahman as Mere Spectator in the Cosmogonic Process

Whereas the third verse in X.10 clearly states that the Godhead is the sole origin of the entire macrocosm and is also all-permeating, and the next following fourth stanza[44] specifically mentions certain classes as special abodes or symbols of that Supreme-Being, the fifth verse rather in full contradistinction and also in an antithetical way, unequivocally mentions the latter to be a mere silent spectator in the entire process of cosmogony. Assertion of this stanza does not at all fit in the context of the subject enunciated in the earlier and the immediately supervening verses. However, in a rather truly deistic spirit, God is described in this verse[45] as only the spectator of actions, as being absolutely free from the influence of qualities and as thus, living apart from contamination with Nature (S. 43). This stanza makes the Nature and the Individual Soul as instrumental to entire creation with practically no role being played by the Supreme-being.

Immense Qualities of Nārāyaṇa

Cataloguing the supreme and innumerable qualities of Nārāyaṇa, it has been said[46] that He is multi-headed, multi-eyed, producer of all prosperity, imperishable and supreme controlling Divine Person. He is all dominating, eternal, omniform, remover of sins, all-pervasive puruṣa and the entire world subsists in dependence on him. Nārāyaṇa is the Lord of the universe, ruler of individual souls, auspicious, permanent, supremely worthy of being known, soul of the universe, the last resort, the Supreme Reality known as Brahman, the highest of all, the Supreme Light and the Infinite Self (S. 44). Whatever is visible and heard throughout the length and breadth of the universe, that is fully pervaded by Nārāyaṇa from inside as well as outside. He is limitless, changeless, omniscient, giver of prosperity and dwelling in the sea of one's heart which is like the inverted bud of a lotus. As individual soul, the Nārāyaṇa resides in a narrow space in the hearts of all the creatures.

Aham Brahma'smi

Section I.27 ends with a highly mystical stanza. It opens with the prayer that may God be the fulfiller of all my desires/aspirations followed by the unequivocal assertion that 'I am myself that Eternal being'. It is supervened by the prayer, "Oh God! May I attain the highest heaven, be listener of discourses and be blessed with wealth/prosperity and off-springs while I am arranging the watery bricks here in the construction of the fire-alter" (S. 45).

Though the 67th prose passage of section X.1 of the Taittirīya Āraṇyaka has been set amidst a ritualistic context; yet it is highly philosophical and spiritualistic. It unequivocally states that "That Supreme Light which shines as the substratum of the liquid element—I am that. I am that supreme light of Brahman. Whatever I am, I am Brahma. I am veritably Brahma. I am nothing else but Brahma" (S. 46).

Identity Between the Self and the Absolute and Doctrine of Self-Realisation

Very often a question has been raised as to what is the relation between the Self and the Absolute. It has been maintained that the Absolute is the only reality; but what can be said about the reality which is empirically called the Self. From the phenomenal point of view, it may be said that it exists as a separate entity; but transcendentally, it is identical with the Absolute. Evidently, he who realises in himself this truth that his own self and the self of the universe are one, the greater truth that it is the same eternal spirit which is embodied in himself as well as in the universe, is not extinguished, the moment he dies. Withdrawing from the world of physical matter to the subtle and still more subtle levels of existence, in an ordered manner, he finally arrives at the inmost self that is of bliss. This is fully supported from the following passage[47] :

> "The spirit who is here in a man and the spirit who is there in the Sun, it is one and there is no other. He who knows this, on departing from this world, proceeds on to that self which consists of food, proceeds on to that self which consists of

breath, proceeds on to that Self which consists of mind, proceeds on to that Self which consists of understanding, proceeds on to that Self which consists of bliss." (S. 47).

The above rather unmistakably proves that within the self, there are various selves; but the true knower must advance to the highest self. By implication, it is also clear that the man without knowledge fails to reach this consummation.

Seat of the Soul in Human Body and the Nature of Brahman

In the Vedic literature as a whole, the heart is regarded as the seat of the soul. However, in a passage[48] of the Taittirīya Āraṇyaka, in a very cryptic style and with a good deal of prohetic insight, the seer of the text gives his reflections as to the way in which the soul in the heart moves by a passage through the bones of the palate right upto the skull and on the way greets the Brahman who is his Lord and master. While the soul in the heart is characterised as the manomaya puruṣa, the Brahman that resides in the brain is called manasaspati; the soul's overlord. "What we feel as the space inside the heart, therein is this immortal golden being, namely mind (or soul). What we know as hanging like a nipple between the bones of the palate, through it, is the entrance to the Lord[49] on the passage right upto the skull where the hairs are made to part. Bhūḥ......Bhuvaḥ......Suvaḥ......Mahaḥ. When these (mystic) words are uttered, the soul moves right up-to Brahman. The soul gains autonomy, joins the Ruler of mind (or soul), becomes the lord of speech, sight, hearing and knowledge, becomes (in short) the Brahman, whose body is space, whose soul is the real, whose delight is life, whose mind is bliss, who abounds in tranquility and is immortal."

The above passage rather makes an audacious effort to pinpoint the seat of the soul in the human body and its ultimate identity with Brahman who has been stated to be all permeating in the macrocosm and embodiment of bliss, tranquility and immortality. Physically speaking, the place of the soul has been depicted to be confined only between the heart and skull; but no final word has been said about its exact location in the human frame. In case, it is admitted that the Ātman resides in the portion between the heart and skull only; then the remaining organs of the body have, ipso-facto, to be at least presumed, if not admitted, to be without the raison d'etre called the soul and thus should be non-functionary or practically paralysed. However, we do not experience so. In fact, every limb of the human body, right from the toe upto the end of the hair of the head, functions perfectly well and in unison with each other. This is a very potent indicator to the fact that the sole and supreme sustainer of the human body functions unfailingly, uniformly and effectively even in the minutest human organ. Accordingly, it is rather difficult to agree with the author of this Hermit-text that the soul is physically confined to any particular region of the human body. In contrast to this assertion, the seer of the Aitarey Āraṇyaka[50] has shown deeper mystic insight and exactitude when he unequivocally asserts that the soul prevails wholly in all the limbs upto hair and nails.

As regards the macrocosmic Supreme Soul called Brahman, there are hardly any two opinions that He is all-permeating and has all the above-said essential ingredients of tranquility, immortality etc. In fact, His all-pervasiveness has also been rather immaculately stated in the afore-mentioned section of the Aitareya Āraṇyaka when it lays down that all beings down to insignificant creatures like ants are born, thus pervaded.

Nature of the Soul and Faculty of God-Realisation

Despite the heterogeneous nature of the verses collected in this section,[51] the first and twenty-third verses do dilate on the nature of the soul and as to how the realisation of God is to be attained. The first verse, inter alia, says that "the soul of the living being is subtler than the subtle and yet greater than the great, and is placed in the cavity of the heart. The unstriving person beholds Him and becomes freed from sorrow—when through the grace of the Creator, he sees His greatness"[52] (S. 48).

The second verse referred to above lays down that "in the citadel of the body, there is the small sinless and pure lotus of the heart which is residence of the Supreme. Further in the interior of this small area, there is the sorrowless Ether. That is to be meditated upon continually." (S. 49). Thus, both of these stanzas do reveal that the soul is extremely minute as well as great. Obviously, the nemesis of the theory which attributes a spatial extension to the soul lies just in these contradictions. The only way out of this difficulty lies on the supposition that the soul transcends all spatial limitations.

Coming over to the faculty of God-realization as embodied in both of these verses, it may be stated that the closing part of the second stanza emphasizes on meditation on the Self and the first stanza does pre-suppose grace of God for self-realization even after the entire mental and intellectual fabric of the man is fully purified and he becomes free from all sorrow. Thus, this verse clearly envisages bestowal of the grace of God as a condition precedent to revelation of the Self.

Instrumentality of Renunciation in Liberation

In addition to afore-mentioned purification of one's practical life, two verses (X.10.21-22), inter alia lay added emphasis on the principle of renunciation for attainment of liberation. The first verse[53] says that "immortality cannot be attained by work, progeny, or wealth. One can reach life eternal only by renunciation. That (Brahman) which the hermits attain is beyond the heaven; yet it shines brilliantly in the cave of the heart." (S. 50). The succeeding verse[54] further reiterates that only those of the ascetics, who have well understood the meaning through the Vedanta knowledge and have purified their nature through practice of renunciation, are liberated into the region of the Brahman at the time of dissolution of their bodies (S. 51). Thus, evidently, renunciation has a great role to play in the attainment of salvation.

Nature of the Individual Soul

Elucidating the immense and supreme qualities of Nārāyaṇa, it has been said[55] that he is beset in a very narrow space in the human heart. This soul is of the nature of a great fire, self-effulgent, facing all sides, consumer and assimilator of food, undecaying and intelligent. It warms up the entire body right from the sole of the foot to head. The soul, which is like a flame of fire, is located in the centre of the body in a very small and exalted place. Giving further details of the soul, it has been said that it is dazzling like the flash of lightning in a blue cloud, slender like the awn of a paddy, of golden hue, brilliant and extremely subtle (S. 52). Right in the centre of that flame dwells God. He is veritably Brahmā, Śiva, Indra, the Imperishable One and the highest king of heaven (S. 53). Thus, this stanza unequivocally establishes the identity between the individual and universal souls—'Ayam Ātmā Brahma.'

The above elucidated philosophy is further corroborated by

two stanzas given in subsequent sections.[56] The first verse says that "the Supreme Being moves inside the heart of created beings possessing manifold forms. O Supreme! you are the sacrifice, Viṣṇu, the expression vaṣaṭ, Rudra, Brahmā and Prajāpati" (S. 54). The second verse declares that, "the Supreme Lord who is the master of the entire world and enjoyer of all things be gratified. As a person dwelling in the body, He is of the size of thumb and is present even in the toe." (S. 55). Eulogisation of Nārāyaṇa as the Supreme Godhead is definitely a development much later to the Saṁhitās and Brāhmaṇas. This lavish extolment of Nārāyaṇa should, very naturally, be a potent reason to give this Tenth Book the title of Nārāyaṇopanishad.

Renunciation, the Best Means for Attainment of God and Importance of Syllable OM

Sections X.62-63 primarily delineate the various modes of penance, their comparative merits and limitations. Truthfulness, abstention from food, control of the sense organs, tranquility of mind, charity, virtue, procreation, Vedic fires, agnihotra, sacrifice, contemplation on the Supreme and renunciation have, one after the other, been catalogued as various penances because these qualities are ordinarily very difficult to be adopted in life. Just as Brahman is Supreme in the universe, likewise nyāsa or renunciation is the best of all penances. It has been said to be the very embodiment of Brahman who verily is the Universal Spirit, Blissful, Self-born, Prajāpati and Controller of Time. Brahman is supreme and the inner-most self of all the creatures. He is pervasive throughout the entire universe. He is all that is perceptible at present, was in the past and will be in the future. Brahman can be comprehended only by the desire to know Him, perfect purity of actions, faith and truthfulness. He is storehouse of riches, splendid and beyond the ambit of ignorance. Having realised Him through the mind and heart, the person so enlightened does not fall prey to death or in other words, he is saved of the repeated cycles of birth and death. Hence, of all the penances, nyāsa (renunciation) has been said to be the best (S. 56). The sole Godhead is the supreme bestower of wealth, omniform, life sustainer, creator, ordainer of the entire macrocosm and hence the need for paying obeisances to Him for attainment of His glory. Such obeisances can be made by making oneself contemplate on syllable OM. This verily is the mysterious and most secret doctrine of the gods. Knower of this attains the greatness of the Almighty. This also, ipso-facto, very emphatically brings out the efficacy of contemplation on syllable Om as a means of God-realisation.

Raptures of Mystic Ecstasy

The Taittirīya Āraṇyaka[57] contains a mystic monologue which contains the essence of the raptures of spiritual experience. This experience is almost identical with that of Sage Vāmadeva in Aitareya Āraṇyaka. The utterances of Triśaṅku in this section are remarkable for the grandeur of the ideas involved in them. After Triśaṅku had attained Self-realisation, he tells us, he felt as if he was the "Mover of the Tree." What is the Tree to which Triśaṅku is referring? It may be the Tree of the Body, or it may even be the Tree of the world. It is not uncustomary for the sages and seers of Hermit-texts and subsequent writers to speak of the body or the World as verily a Tree. In fact, Triśaṅku tells us that, like the true soul that he was, he could move the Tree of the bodily or worldly coil. He tells us, further more, that his glory was "like the peak of a mountain," which is as much as to say that when he had come to realise the self, he felt that everything else looked so mean and insignificant to him from the high pedestal of Ātmanic experience that he felt as if he was on the top of all things whatsoever. Triśaṅku tells us furthermore that "the source from which he had come was purity itself. This obviously, seems to refer to the Purity of the Divine Life from which all existence springs. Then, again Triśaṅku tells us that he was as it were "the immortal being in the Sun." Furthermore, Triśaṅku says that he regarded himself as "a treasure of unsurpassable value" referring probably to the infinite wealth of Ātmanic experience that he had obtained. Finally, he tells us that he was verily, "the intelligent, the immortal and the Imperishable One," thus identifying himself with absolute Spirit (S. 57).

Again there is another post-ecstatic monologue[58] in this very Āraṇyaka which tells us in a passage of unsurpassed grandeur throughout both the Āraṇyaka as well as post-Āraṇyaka literature that when a man transcends the limitations of his earthly, etheric, mental, intellective and beatific-sheaths, he sat in the utter silence of solipsistic solitude, singing the song of universal unity. "How wonderful, how wonderful, how wonderful; I am the food, I am the food, I am the food; I am the food-eater, I am the food-eater, I am the food-eater; I am the maker of their unity, I am the maker of their unity, I am the maker of their unity." Metaphysically speaking, these utterances only mean that the mystic concerned was himself all matter and all spirit as well as the connecting link between them both, and epistemologically, that he was himself the subject-world and the object-world and also the entire subject-object relation—a stage of spiritual experience which can well be characterised in modern idealistic way as a stage where the difference between the field, the fighter, and the strife vanishes altogether—the culmination of the unitive song; namely; "I am the first born of the Law;[59] I am older than the gods; I am the navel of Immortality; he that gives me, keeps me; him, who eats all food, I eat as food; I envelop the whole universe with splendour as of the Sun." (S. 58).

NOTES AND REFERENCES

1. Vasukra is mentioned as a sage in Ṛgveda as the son of Indra, RV. X. 27; 28, 3-5, 9, 11; X. 29. As one belonging to the family of Vasiṣṭha, he is referred to in RV. IX. 97.28-30.
2. AA., II.1.4.
3. AA., II.1.5.
4. AA., I.3.8.
5. AA., II.1.3.
6. AA., II.3.3.
7. Commentary (Page 153) as given in Aitareya Āraṇyaka as published by Ānandāśrama Sanskrit series No. 38.
8. Page 217 of AA. edited by A.B. Keith, 1909.
9. AA., II.1.2.
10. AA., III.2.3.
11. AA., II.3.8.
12. Śvet. U., V.10.
13. AA., II.3.8.
14. AA., II.3.8.
15. AA., II.1.3.
16. AA., II.3.8.
17. Bṛh. U., IV.4.12.
18. AA., II.6.1.
19. AA., I.3.8.
20. AA., II.6.1.
21. AA., III.2.4.
22. AA., II. 3.7.
23. AA., II. 3.2.
24. AA., I.2.3.

25. AA., I.2.4.
26. AA., II.4.3.
27. AA., V.3.3.
28. Many more examples of such pseudo-mysticism can be quoted from sections I.1.3; I.2.1-2; I.3.8; II.1.3,5,8; II.3.4-5 and III.1.3-5 of Aitareya Araṇyaka.
29. TA., I.8.
30. TA., III. 11.
31. Its first part is also found in Vājasaneyi Saṁhitā, XXXI. 18.
32. TA., III.14.
33. TA., VIII.1.
34. TA., IX.10.2-4.
35. TA., VIII.6.
36. TA., VIII.7.
37. TA., IX.1-6.
38. TA., X.1.
39. This verse is also found in Muṇḍaka Upanishad with minor variations.
40. TA., X.10.6. This is known as Haṁsa-mantra describing the Supreme Reality. Its original place is in the ṚV., IV.40.5. It is found in VS., X.24 and XII.14; TS., III.2.10.1 and Śat. Br., 7.3.11.
41. TA., X.10.7.
42. This verse is also found in Śvet. U., IV.12 and with a little variation in III. 4, *ibid.*
43. TA., X.10.20. Also found in Śvet. U., III.9.
44. Quoted from TS., III.4.11.
45. This verse is also found in Śvet. U., IV. 5.
46. TA., X.11.
47. TA., VIII.8.
48. TA., VII.6.
49. Indra, paraphrased as Indandra, breaking through skull in Aitereya Āraṇyaka, II.4.3.
50. AA., I.3.8.
51. TA., X.10.
52. This stanza is also found in KU (1.1.20) with minor variation and an exact duplicate in Śvet. U., III.20.
53. This verse is also found in Kaiv. U. 2, 3 with minor variation.
54. This verse is also found in Muṇḍ U., III.2.6 with minor variation.
55. TA., X.11.11, 12.
56. TA., X.31,38.
57. TA., VII. 10.
58. TA., IX. 10.5,6.
59. This finds mention with a little difference in the Ṛgveda (X 61.19) and also in the Taittirīya Brāhmaṇa (2.8.8.1).

SOURCES III

ऐतरेयारण्यकम्

१. एतं ह्येव बह्वृचा महत्युक्थे मीमांसन्त एतमग्नावध्वर्यव
एवं महाव्रते छन्दोगा एतमग्यामेतं दिव्येतं वायावेतमाकाश
एतमप्स्वेतमोषधीष्वेतं वनस्पतिष्वेतं चन्द्रमस्येतं
नक्षत्रेष्वेतं सर्वेषु भूतेष्वेतमेव ब्रह्मेत्याचक्षते ॥ (३.२.३)

२. तद् वियूया कवयो अन्वविन्दन्
नामायत्ता समतृप्यन् श्रुतेऽधि ॥ (२.३.८)

३. तदिदं कर्म कृतमयं पुरुषो ब्रह्मणो लोकः । (२.१.३)

४. यदक्षरं पंचविधं समेति युजो युक्ता अभियत्संवहन्ति ।
सत्यस्य सत्यमनु यत्र युज्यते तत्र देवाः सर्व एकं
भवन्ति ॥ (२.३.८)

५. अथ नामधेयं सत्यस्य सत्यमिति ।
प्राणो वै सत्यं तेषामेष सत्यम् ॥ (बृ.आ.उ.२.३.६)

६. आत्मेत्येवोपासीतात्र ह्येते सर्व एकं भवन्ति । (बृ.आ.उ.१.४.७)

७. यदक्षरादक्षरमेति युक्तम् ॥ (२.३.८)

८. एष ब्रह्मैष इन्द्र एष प्रजापतिरेते सर्वे देवा इमानि च
पंच महाभूतानि पृथिवी वायुराकाश आपो ज्योतींषीत्येतानीमानि
च क्षुद्रमिश्राणीव बीजानीतराणि चेतराणि
चाण्डजानि च जारुजानि च स्वेदजानी चोद्भिजानि
चाश्वा गावः पुरुषा हस्तिनो यत् किंचेदं प्राणि जङ्गमं
च पतत्रि च यच्च स्थावरं सर्वं तत्प्रज्ञानेत्रम् ।
प्रज्ञाने प्रतिष्ठितं प्रज्ञानेत्रो लोकः प्रज्ञा प्रतिष्ठा ।

प्रज्ञानं ब्रह्म ।

स एतेन प्रज्ञेनाऽऽत्मनाऽस्माल्लोकादुत्क्रम्यामुष्मिन् स्वर्गे
लोके सर्वान् कामानाप्त्वाऽमृतः समभवत्समभवत् ॥ (२.६.१)

९. अथाधिदैवतं चक्षुः श्रोत्रं मनो वाक्प्राणस्ता एताः पंच
देवता इमं विष्टाः पुरुषं पंचो हैवैता देवता अयं विष्टः
पुरुषः । सोऽत्राऽऽलोमभ्य आ नखेभ्यः सर्वः साङ्ग आप्यते
तस्मात्सर्वाणि भूतान्यापिपीलिकाभ्य आप्तान्येव जायन्ते ।
तदुक्तमृषिणा । सहस्त्रधा पंचदशान्युक्थेति पंच हि
दशतो भवन्ति । यावद् द्यावापृथिवी तावदित्तदिति

ऐतरेयारण्यकम्

याबती वै द्यावापृथिवी तावानात्मा ॥ (१.३.८)

१०. कोऽयमात्मेति वयमुपास्महे कतरः स आत्मा ।
येन वा पश्यति येन वा शृणोति येन वा गन्धानाजिघ्रति
येन वा वाचं व्याकरोति येन वा स्वादु चास्वादु
च विजानाति यदेतद्धृदयं मनश्चैतत्संज्ञानमाज्ञानं विज्ञानं
प्रज्ञानं मेधा दृष्टिर् धृतिर्मतिर्मनीषा
जूतिः स्मृतिः संकल्पः क्रतुरसुः कामो वश इति ।
सर्वाण्येवैतानि प्रज्ञानस्य नामधेयानि भवन्ति ॥ (२.६.१)

११. स योऽतोऽश्रुतोऽगतोऽमतोऽनतोऽदृष्टोऽविज्ञातोऽनादिष्टः
श्रोता मन्ता द्रष्टाऽऽदेष्टा घोष्टा विज्ञाता प्रज्ञाता सर्वेषां
भूतानामन्तरपुरुषः स म आत्मेति विद्यात् ॥ (३.२.४)

१२. तद्वा इदं बृहतीसहस्रं संपन्नं तद्यशः संपन्नं तद्यशः स
इन्द्रः स भूतानामधिपतिः स य एवमेतमिन्द्रं भूतानामधिपतिं
वेद विस्रसा हैवास्माल्लोकात्प्रैतीति ह स्मा ह
महिदास ऐतरेयः प्रेत्येन्द्रो भूत्वैषु लोकेषु राजति ॥ (२.३.७)

१३. पुरुषे त्वेवाऽऽविस्तरामात्मा स हि प्रज्ञानेन संपन्नतमो
विज्ञातं वदति विज्ञातं पश्यति वेद श्वस्तनं वेद लोकालोकौ
मर्त्येनामृतमीप्सत्येवं संपन्नः ॥ (२.३.२)

१४ इदमदर्शमिती३ तस्मादिदन्द्रो नामेदन्द्रो ह वै नाम
तमिदन्द्रं सन्तमिन्द्र इत्याचक्षते परोक्षेण परोक्षप्रिया इव
हि देवाः परोक्षप्रिया इव हि देवाः ॥ (२.४.३)

तैत्तिरीयारण्यकम्

१५. सुवर्णं धर्मं परिवेद वेनम् । इन्द्रस्याऽऽत्मानं दशधा
चरन्तम् । अन्त समुद्रे मनसा चरन्तम् । ब्रह्माऽन्वविन्दद्
दशहोतारमर्णे । अन्तः प्रविष्टः शास्ता
जनानाम् । एकः सन्बहुधा विचारः । शतँ शुक्राणि
यत्रैकं भवन्ति । सर्वे वेदा यत्रैकं भवन्ति । सर्वे
होतारो यत्रैकं भवन्ति । स मानसीन आत्मा जनानाम् ।
अन्तः प्रविष्टः शास्ता जनानाँ सर्वात्मा ।
सर्वाः प्रजा यत्रैकं भवन्ति । चतुर्होतारो यत्र संपदं
गच्छन्ति देवैः । स मानसीन आत्मा जनानाम ॥ (३.११)

तैत्तिरीयारण्यकम्

१६. य आण्डकोशे भुवनं विभर्ति । अनिर्भिण्णः सन्नथ
लोकान् विचष्टे । यस्याऽऽण्डकोशं शुष्ममाहुः
प्राणमुल्बम् । तेनक्लृप्तोऽमृतेनाहमस्मि ॥ (३.११)

१७. अन्तः प्रविष्टं कर्तारमेतम् । अन्तश्चन्द्रमसि मनसा
चरन्तम् । सहैव सन्तं न विजानन्ति देवाः ।। (३.११)

१८. इडायै सृप्त घृतवच् चराचरम् । देवा अन्वविन्दन्
गुहाहितम् ॥ (३.११)

१९. वेदाहमेतं पुरुषं महान्तम् । आदित्यवर्णं तमसस्तु
पारे । सर्वाणि रूपाणि विचित्य धीरः । नामानि
कृत्वाऽभिवदन् यदास्ते ॥ (३.१२)

२०. तमेवं विद्वानमृत इह भवति । नान्यः पन्था
विद्यतेऽयनाय ।। (३.१२)

२१. यो देवेभ्यो आतपति । यो देवानां पुरोहितः । पूर्वो
यो देवेभ्यो जातः । नमो रुचाय ब्राह्मये ॥ (३.१३)

२२. तमेव मृत्युममृतं तमाहुः । तं भर्तारं तमु गोप्तारमाहुः ।
स भृतो भ्रियमाणो बिभर्ति । य एनं वेदसत्येन
भर्तुम् ॥ (३.१४)

२३. असज् जजान सत आबभूव । यं यं जजान स उ गोपो
अस्य । यदा भारं तन्द्रयते स भर्तुम् । परास्य भारं
पुनरस्तमेति ॥ (३.१४)

२४. ॐ ब्रह्मविदाप्नोति परम् । तदेषाऽभ्युक्ता । सत्यं
ज्ञानमनन्तं ब्रह्म । यो वेद निहितं गुहायां परमे
व्योमन् । सोऽश्नुते सर्वान् कामान्त्सह । ब्रह्मणा
विपश्चितेति ॥ (८.१)

२५. असन्नेव स भवति । असद् ब्रह्मेति वेद चेत् । अस्ति
ब्रह्मेति चेद्वेद । सन्तमेनं ततो विदुरिति ।। (८.६)

२६. तत्प्रतिष्ठेत्युपासीत । प्रतिष्ठावान् भवति । तन्मह
इत्युपासीत । महान्भवति । तन्मन इत्युपासीत ।
मानवान्भवति । तन्नम इत्युपासीत । नम्यन्तेऽस्मै
कामाः । तद्ब्रह्मेत्युपासीत । ब्रह्मवान्भवति । तद्

तैत्तिरीयारण्यकम्

ब्रह्मणः परिमर इत्युपासीत । पर्येणं म्रियन्ते द्विषन्तः
सपत्नाः । परि येऽप्रिया भ्रातृव्याः ।। (६·१०)

२७. असद्वा इदमग्र आसीत् । ततो वै सदजायत ।
तदात्मानँ ३ स्वयमकुरुत । तस्मात् तत्सुकृतमुच्यत
इति । यद्वै तत्सुकृतम् । रसो वै सः । रसँ ह्येवायं
लब्ध्वाऽऽनन्दी भवति । को ह्येवान्यात्कः प्राण्यात् !
यदेष आकाश आनन्दो न स्यात् । एष ह्येवाऽऽनन्दयाति ।
यदा ह्येवैष एतस्मिन्नदृश्येऽनात्म्येऽनिरुक्ते-
ऽनिलयनेऽभयं प्रतिष्ठां विन्दते । अथ सोऽभयं
गतो भवति ।। (८·७)

२८. भृगुर्वै वारुणिः । वरुणं पितरमुपससार । अधीहि
भगवो ब्रह्मेति । तस्मा एतत्प्रोवाच । अन्नं प्राणं
चक्षुः श्रोत्रं मनो वाचमिति । तँ होवाच । यतो वा
इमानि भूतानि जायन्ते । येन जातानि जीवन्ति ।
यत्प्रयन्त्यभिसंविशन्ति । तद्विजिज्ञासस्व । तद् ब्रह्मेति ।
स तपोऽतप्यत । स तपस्तप्त्वा ।

अन्नं । ब्रह्मेति व्यजानात् । अन्नाद्ध्येव खल्विमानि
भूतानि जायन्ते । अन्नेन जातानि जीवन्ति । अन्नं
प्रयन्त्यभिसंविशन्तीति । तद्विज्ञाय । पुनरेव वरुणं
पितरमुपससार । अधीहि भगवो ब्रह्मेति । तँ होवाच ।
तपसा ब्रह्म विजिज्ञासस्व । तपो ब्रह्मेति स तपोऽतप्यत ।
स तपस्तप्त्वा ।।

प्राणो ब्रह्मेति । व्यजानात् । प्राणाद्ध्येव खल्विमानि
भूतानि जायन्ते । प्राणेन जातानि जीवन्ति ।
प्राण प्रयन्त्यभिसंविशन्तीति ।
तद्विज्ञाय । पुनरेव वरुणं पितरमुपससार । अधीहि
भगवो । ब्रह्मेति तँ होवाच । तपसा ब्रह्म विजिज्ञासस्व ।
तपो ब्रह्मेति । स तपोऽतप्यत । स
तपस्तप्त्वा ।
मनो ब्रह्मेति व्यजानात् । मनसो ह्येव खल्विमानि
भूतानि जायन्ते । मनसा जातानि जीवन्ति । मन
प्रयन्त्यभिसंविशन्तीति ।

तैत्तिरीयारण्यकम्

तद्विज्ञाय। पुनरेव वरुणं पितरमुपससार। अधोहि
भगवो ब्रह्मेति। त ँ३ होवाच। तपसा ब्रह्म विजिज्ञासस्व।
तपो ब्रह्मेति। स तपोऽतप्यत। स
तपस्तप्त्वा॥
विज्ञानं ब्रह्मेति व्यजानात्। विज्ञानाद्ध्येव जायन्ते
खल्विमानि भूतानि जायन्ते। विज्ञानेन जातानि
जीवन्ति। विज्ञानं प्रयन्त्यभिस बिशन्तीति।
तद्विज्ञाय पुनरेव वरुणं पितरमुपससार। अधीहि भगवो
ब्रह्मेति। त ँ३ होवाच। तपसा ब्रह्म विजिज्ञासस्व।
तयो ब्रह्मेति। स तपोऽतप्यत। स तपस्तप्त्वा।

आनन्दो ब्रह्मेति व्यजानात्। आनन्दाद्ध्येव
खल्विमानि भूतानि जायन्ते। आनन्देन जातानि
जीवन्ति। आनन्द प्रयन्त्यभिसंविशन्तीति।
सैषा भार्गवी वारुणी विद्या। परमे व्योमन्
प्रतिष्ठिता। स य एवं वेद प्रतितिष्ठति। अन्नवानन्नादो
भवति। महान् भवति। प्रजया पशुभिर्ब्रह्मवर्चसेन।
महान्कीर्त्या॥ (९.१.६)

२९. अम्भस्य पारे भुवनस्य मध्ये नाकस्य पृष्ठे महतोमहीयान्।
शुक्रेण ज्योतीँषि समनुप्रविष्टः प्रजापतिश्चरति गर्भे अन्तः॥
(१० १)

३०. अतः परं नान्यदणीयसँ हि परात्परं यन्महतो महान्तम्।
यदेकमव्यक्तमनन्तरुपं विश्वं पुराणंतपसः परस्तात्॥ (१०.१)

३१. (क)
तदेवर्तं तदु सत्यमाहुस्तदेव ब्रह्म परमं कवीनाम्।
इष्टापूर्तं बहुधा जातं जायमानं विश्वं बिभर्ति भुवनस्यनाभिः॥
(ख)
तदेवाग्निस् तद्वायुस् तत्सूर्यंस् तदु चन्द्रमाः।
तदेव शुक्रममृतं तद् ब्रह्म तदापः स प्रजापतिः॥ (१०.१)

३२. न संदृशे तिष्ठति रूपमस्य न चक्षुषा पश्यति कश्चनैनम्।
हृदा मनीषा मनसाऽभिक्लृप्तौ य एनं विदुरमृतास्ते भवन्ति॥
(१०.१)

तैत्तिरीयारण्यकम्

३३. वेदाहमेतं पुरुषं महान्तम् । आदित्यवर्णं तमसः परस्तात् ।
तमेवं विद्वानमृत इह भवति, नान्यः पन्था विद्यतेऽयनाय ॥ (३.१२)

३४. प्र तद्वोचे अमृतं नु विद्वान् गन्धर्वो नाम निहितं गुहासु ।
त्रीणि पदा निहिता गुहासु यस्तद् वेद सवितुः पिता सत् ॥ (१०.१)

३५. स नो बन्धुर्जनिता स विधाता धामानि वेद भुवनानि विश्वा ।
यत्र देवा अमृतमानशानास् तृतीये धामान्यध्यैरयन्त ॥ (१०.१)

३६. परि द्यावापृथिवी यन्ति सद्यः परि लोकान् परि दिशः परि सुवः ।
ऋतस्य तन्तुं विततं विचृत्य तदपश्यत्तदभवत्प्रजासु ॥ (१०.१)

३७. परीत्य लोकान् परीत्य भूतानि परीत्य सर्वाः प्रदिशो दिशश्च ।
प्रजापतिः प्रथमजा ऋतस्याऽऽत्मनाऽऽत्मानमभिसंबभूव ॥ (१०.१)

३८. अतः समुद्रा गिरयश्च सर्वेऽस्मात्स्यन्दन्ते सिन्धवः सर्वरूपाः ।
अतश्च विश्वा ओषधयो रसाश्च येनैष भूतस्तिष्ठत्यन्तरात्मा ॥
(१०.१०)

३९. हँसः शुचिषद् वसुरन्तरिक्षसद्धोता वेदिषदतिथिर्दुरोणसत् ।
नृषद् वरसदृतसद् व्योमसदब्जा गोजा ऋतजा अद्रिजा ऋतं बृहत् ॥
(१०.१०)

४०. यस्माज् जाता न परा नैव किंचनाऽऽस य आविवेश भुवनानि
विश्वा ।
प्रजापतिः प्रजया संविदानस्त्रीणि ज्योतींषि सचते स षोडशी ॥
(१० १०)

४१. यो देवानां प्रथमं पुरस्ताद् विश्वाधिको रुद्रो महर्षिः ।
हिरण्यगर्भं पश्यत जायमानं स नो देवः शुभया स्मृत्या संयुनक्तु ॥
(१०.१०)

४२. यस्मात्परं नापरमस्ति किंचिद्यस्मान्नाणीयो न ज्यायोऽस्ति
कश्चित् ।
वृक्ष इव स्तब्धो दिवि तिष्ठत्येकस्तेनेदं पूर्णं पुरुषेण सर्वम् ॥
(१०.१०)

तैत्तिरीयारण्यकम्

४३. अजामेकां लोहितशुक्लकृष्णां बह्वीं प्रजां जनयन्तीं सरूपाम् ।
अजो ह्येको जुषमाणोऽनुशेते जहात्येनां भुक्तभोगामजोऽन्यः ॥
४४. [क] (१०.१०)
पतिं विश्वस्याऽऽत्मेश्वरं शाश्वत शिवमच्युतम्
नारायणं महाज्ञेयं विश्वात्मानं परायणम् ॥
(ख)
नारायणः परं ब्रह्म तत्त्वं नारायणः परः ।
नारायणः परो ज्योतिरात्मा नारायणः परः ॥ (१०.११)
४५. कामप्रयवणं मे अस्तु । स ह्येवास्मि सनातनः ।
इति नाको ब्रह्मिश्रवो रायो धनम् । पुत्रानायो देवीरिहाऽऽहिता ॥
(१.२७)
४६. आर्द्रं ज्वलति ज्योतिरहमस्मि । ज्योतिर्ज्वलति ब्रह्माहमस्मि ।
योऽहमस्मि ब्रह्माहमस्मि । अहमस्मि ब्रह्माहमस्मि ।
अहमेवाहं मां जुहोमि स्वाहा ॥ (१०.१)
४७ स यश्चायं पुरुषे । यश्चासावादित्ये । स एकः ।
स य एवंवित् । अस्माल्लोकात् प्रेत्य । एतमन्नमयमात्मानम्
उपसंक्रामति । एतं प्राणमयमात्मानमुपसंक्रामति । एतं
मनोमयमात्मानमुपसंक्रामति । एतं विज्ञानमयमात्मानमुपसंक्रामति ।
एतमानन्दमयमात्मानमुपसंक्रामति ॥ (८.८)
४८ अणोरणीयान् महतो महीयानात्मा गुहायां निहितोऽस्य जन्तोः ।
तमक्रतुं पश्यति वीतशोको धातुःप्रसादान् महिमानमीशम् ॥
(१०.१०)
४९. दह्रं विपापं वरवेश्मभूतं यत्पुण्डरीकं पुरमध्यसंस्थम् ।
तत्रापि दह्रे गगनं विशोकं तस्मिन् यदन्तस् तदुपासितव्यम् ॥
(१०.१०)
५०. न कर्मणा न प्रजया धनेन त्यागेनैके अमृतत्वमानशुः ।
परेण नाकं निहितं गुहायां विभ्राजते यद्यतयो विशन्ति ॥
(१०.१०)
५१. वेदान्तविज्ञानसुनिश्चितार्थाः संन्यासयोगाद्यतयः शुद्धसत्त्वाः ।
ते ब्रह्मलोके तु परान्तकाले परामृतात् परिमुच्यन्ति सर्वे (१०.१०)
५२. नीलतोयदमध्यस्था विद्युल्लेखेव भास्वरा ।
नीबारशूकवत्तन्वी पीता भास्वत्यणूपमा ॥ (१०.११)

तैत्तिरीयारण्यकम्

५३. तस्याः शिखाया मध्ये परमात्मा व्यवस्थितः ।
स ब्रह्मा स शिवः सेन्द्रः सोऽक्षरः परमः स्वराट् ॥ (१०.११)

५४. ओमन्तश्चरति भूतेषु गुहायां विश्वमूर्तिषु ।
त्वं यज्ञस् त्व विष्णुस् त्वं वषट्कारस् त्वं
रुद्रस् त्वं ब्रह्मा त्वं प्रजापतिः ॥ (१०.३१)

५५. अङ्गुष्ठमात्रः पुरुषोऽङ्गुष्ठं च समाश्रितः ।
ईशः सर्वस्य जगतः प्रभु प्रीणातु विश्वभुक् ॥ (१०.३८)

५६. स वा एष पुरुषः पंचधा पंचात्मा येन सर्वमिदं प्रोतं
पृथिवी चान्तरिक्षं च द्यौश्च दिशश्चावान्तरदिशश्च स वै
सर्वमिदं जगत् स भूतं स भव्यं जिज्ञासक्लृप्त ऋतजा
रयिष्ठाः श्रद्धा सत्यो महस्वान्तमसोपरिष्टात्
ज्ञात्वा तमेवं मनसा हृदा च भूयो
न मृत्युमुपयाहि विद्वान्
तस्मान्नयासमेषां तपसामतिरिक्तमाहुः ॥ (१०.६३)

५७. अहं वृक्षस्य रेरिवा । कीर्तिः पृष्ठं गिरेरिव । ऊर्ध्वपवित्रो
बाजिनीव स्वमृतमस्मि । द्रविणं सवर्चसम् । सुमेधा अमृतोक्षितः ।
इति त्रिशङ्कोर् वेदानुवचनम् ॥ (७.१०)

५८. स य एवंवित् । अस्माल्लोकात्प्रेत्य । एतमन्नमयमात्मानमुपसंक्रम्य ।
एतं प्राणमयमात्मानमुपसंक्रम्य ।
एतं मनोमयमात्मानमुपसंक्रम्य । एतं विज्ञानमयमात्मा-
नमुपसंक्रम्य । एतमानन्दमयमात्मानमुप संक्रम्य । इमांल्
लोकान्कामान्नीकामरुप्यनुसंचरन् । एतत्साम गायन्नास्ते ।
हा३वु हा३वु हा३वु । अहमन्नम् अहमन्नम् अहमन्नम् ।
अहमन्नादो३हमन्नादो३हमन्नादो । अहंश्लोककृदहं
श्लोककृद् अहंश्लोककृत् । अहमस्मि प्रथमजा ऋत३स्य ।
पूर्वं देवेभ्यो अमृतस्य ना३भायि । यो मा ददाति स इदेव
मा३ऽऽवाः । अहमन्नम् अन्नमदन्तमा३द्मि । अहं
विश्वं भुवनम् अभ्यभवा३म् सुवर्न ज्योतीः ॥ (९.१०)

CHAPTER
FOUR

Symbolism, Its Nature, Origin, Application in the Sacrificial Cult and Details thereof in the Aitareya and Taittirīya Āraṇyakas

Symbolism

God or the 'Ultimate Truth' is taken to be unknowable and indefinable. Consequently, a definite approach to the reality is made by suggestive type or symbol—an approach that can perhaps never find its goal; but can only draw nearer and nearer to the symbol or likeness which most fully and faithfully reflects the true and embodies the largest part of a reality, which in its entirety, is inconceivable by human mind and inexpressible in the language of man. The symbol is the necessary and helpful intermediary between the inadequate capacity of the mind of the worshipper and the incommunicable nature and the fulness of the unknown whom he adores.

All the great gods had their resemblances, animal or material forms, in which they presented themselves embodied to human-sight, which served to recall to the worshipper the deity, whose mind and character, they more or less inadequately reflected. Other more rare and refined symbols were presentative of qualities or attributes, as the lotus, the emblem of spotless purity. All idols, totems, fetishes are symbols. The wise man does not worship the symbol, the shape in clay or wood or stone; but is thereby reminded of the invisible substance or reality which they each represent.

Use and purpose of symbols

The use and purpose of the symbols is two-fold :

1. To set forth in visible or audible likeness what cannot be really or fully expressed to the physical eye or ear or even clearly conceived by the limited faculties of the human mind. All language is in the last resort symbolic, and religious language is in an especial degree, for it endeavours to present a mystery or a reality too deep for words;

2. The image or symbol serves the purpose also of providing in material and suitable form, a convenient object of reverence, to meet the religious needs of those whose minds through darkness or ignorance, are unable to grasp the conception of an unseen formless deity. Such men, if left without a physical object to which their reverence and fear may attach themselves, will wonder in amaze of doubt, disquiet and unbelief. It is better that they should worship erroneously, worship a thing than that they should not worship at all. In Hinduism, the pūjā of the multitude (Janatā Janārdana) to the image of the god is reverent and sincere. In some respects also and within definite limits, the Indian contention has justified itself that the symbol has proved a sign-post and a guide to better, higher thoughts and to a truer worship of Him whom no form can express or language describe.

Nature of Symbolism

The most symbolic names or titles of Brahman are Hiraṇyagarbha, (the golden germ), Svayaṁbhū, Viśvakarman, the mystical syllable OM, Sat Chit Ānanda etc. The vehicles of the gods are practically symbols of their presence and power—the goose of Brahman, the garuḍa or the monstrous eagle of Vishnu, the bull (Nandī) of Śiva, the fabulous sea monster (Makara) of Varuṇa, the monkey of Hanumāna, the elephant Airāvata of Indra, the buffalo and dogs of Yama, the lotus of Saraswati wife of Brahmā and also of Lakshmi, wife of Vishnu. The sacred Tulsi plant in the court-yard of the dwelling is the mark of the deity's presence. The Sāligrāma, the sacred-ammonite stone, is another mystical and well-known symbol, Liṅga or phallus is an important symbol of lord Śiva. Images or symbol of Grāmadevatās, the village divinities under sacred trees are supposed to watch over the interests of inhabitants of the village. The piṇḍa or balls of cooked rice are used at the commemorative services for the deceased relatives. The most important and widely recognised symbol of this character is probably the sacred foot-print, which typifies both the presence and the authority of the god. Planets like Mercury, Venus, Mars, Jupiter and Saturn have the signs of bow, square, triangle, lotus, an iron sword respectively. The Sun and Moon have symbols of disk and crescent respectively.

Hindu coins and seals also bore symbols, which were very numerous and diversified. Besides, figures of gods and goddesses, the commonest emblems were the trident denoting empire, the elephant or bull, power; the umbrella, a royal dignity and right; the crescent, a lunar dynasty; a thunderbolt, spear, armed might.

Origin of Symbolism

It has already been stated above that the image or symbol serves the purpose of providing in material and suitable form a convenient object of reverence, to meet the religious needs of those whose minds through darkness or ignorance, are unable to grasp the conception of an unseen formless deity. The so-called spiritually gifted persons have always constituted a microscopic minority throughout the length and breadth of this vast universe. The natural phenomenon like daily and regulated rising and setting of the sun, storm, rain, hail-storm, disease, death etc. always left the earliest human-beings dumb-founded and helpless victims to the actions and vagaries of nature and the supernatural forces. Naturally, all this contributed to the sensations or feelings of appreciation, awe etc. in their minds. So, even the earliest human-beings in their inherent simplicity, came to develop a deep-seated faith in the existence of some super-natural power, controlling the various cosmic actions and phenomena. Ipso-facto, symbolical worship of that "Supreme Controller" of the universe must have started through the medium of worship of Sun, wind, rain-god thunder-bolt etc. So, the origin of symbolical worship appears to be concomitant with the origin of the atheist human-being on this earth. However, with regard to the development of Aryan culture and religion, it can safely be said that the development or beginning of idol or symbolical worship is of much later origin. The Yajurveda unequivocally asserts[1] that the Godhead has no form. With the penetration of the Aryans into southern India, greater and more intimate contacts developed with the aborigines thereof. The latter had entirely a different culture. Hence, as a result of such inter-mixture of ideologically different sects, progressive development of ritualistic cult, tantric and puranic literature etc., the symbolical or image-worship seems to have made its debut among the Aryans. As Phallic emblems and other icons have been discovered in Mohenjo-Daro ruins, it is reasonable to think that worship of idols was prevalent among people who represented that civilisation, and they were most probably the non-Aryan Dravidians. The practice of image worship was adopted, it seems, at first by the lower masses and then in course of time, it gradually became a common mode of religious worship among Hindus. We find references to it in some of the Dharma Sūtras, in Manu and later Smṛtis. It can, therefore, be said that temples and the worship of images had already come into existence by the 4th or 5th century B.C. (Manu, 2.176). By that time Deva pūjā had taken the place of Deva yajña which was the religious practice among the ancient Aryans. For some time, Deva Yajña and Deva Pūjā went on side by side till ultimately the latter practically supplanted the former. Image-worship is generally found in polytheistic religions. Among orthodox Hindus, we find people socially disunited and even antagonistic to one another on account of their having different gods as objects of worship. The worshippers of Śiva remained, for centuries, in bitter opposition to the worshippers of Vishnu. This was an important cause of disunity. Symbolical worship even now continues among large sections of the Hindus who identify themselves as Sanātanists, Śaivites, Vaishnavas, Śakti-worshippers etc.

Application of Symbolism in Sacrificial Cult

Neither the performance of rituals nor symbolical worship was ever the subject-matter of the Hermit Texts. In fact, idol or symbolical worship in the present day sense was unkown at the time of the Āraṇyakas. During the Brāhmaṇical period, performance of the ritual in the rigidly prescribed manner was believed to result in the inevitable bestowal of the besought boons by the gods. Thus, this ritualistic cult had made the gods subservient to the proper performance of the ritual and the gods of the Saṁhitā period had lost their independence and inherent benevolence. The Āraṇyakas basically sought to re-establish the supremacy of the Godhead as the Sole Creator and Controller of the entire universe. They also reiterated the identity between the Ātman and Brahman. However, the elaborately evolved ritualism had taken deep roots in the minds of the Aryans at that time. Hence, the Āraṇyakas could not, very prudently, openly denounce the ritualism and the values held high by it. Ipso-facto, the seers of the Hermit-Texts had not only hard times to face; but had also to use very cautious language so as not to offend the protagonists of the ritualistic cult and also to successfully propagate and re-crown the supremacy of the single Godhead. Hence they, at times, harnessed into service symbolical language which did have its mystic significance also. Thus, symbolism has sparingly been imported into the Aitareya and Taittirīya Āraṇyakas; but that too is confined to the use of symbolical language only which is, however, deeply surcharged with mysticism. Some of the examples thereof are given below :

A. SYMBOLISM AS FOUND IN THE AITAREYA ĀRAṆYAKA

Mahāvrata

The opening sentence of the Aitareya Āraṇyaka says that Indra having slain Vṛtra became great. When he became great, then there came into being the Mahāvrata. Therefore, the Mahāvrata ceremony bears the name of Mahāvrata (S. 1). Truly speaking, there should be no affinity or proximity of time between the actual occurrence of the mythological episode of killing of Vṛtra by Indra and subsequent evolution of the ritual known as Mahāvrata at some stage of the incessant revolution of the wheel of time. However, ignoring altogether this obviously immense intervening time-gap, the ceremony of Mahāvrata has been given a symbolic identification with the greatness that dawned on Indra after vanquishing his mighty foe Vṛtra and the tremendous worldly gains in the form of material prosperity, social uplift etc. that accrue to the sacrificer after performance of the ceremony of Mahāvrata.

Uktha

According to the usual connotation in rituals, the word 'uktha' means a stotra, a hymn or a set of hymns. No doubt, an uktha is always looked upon with a sense of reverence and a medium of worship of God; but in the Aitareya Āraṇyaka,[2] the word has been greatly mystified and used as a symbol of great reverence both in respect of the gods and the Self. Certain key-notes have been evolved so as to pin-point the three worlds and the most important celestial functionary in each of these worlds which has been connoted by using the word 'Arka'. Keith has translated 'Arka' as praise; but Sāyaṇa holds it to mean 'a reverential god'. However, it remains a fact that the functionary holds pivotal position/importance in the world of which it is the 'Arka' and the same cannot be denied and much less under-rated in any way. Complete identity has rather been laboriously worked out in the three worlds and certain important limbs of the human body on the one hand and the aforesaid celestial functionaries and certain important organs of the human body on the other. A deep note of mysticism has been struck when it has been stated that the man is great and prajāpati. The eighty hymns are the common food or the stotra to be recited in each of the godly and human 'Ukthas'. By food, all functionaries/creatures exist and are maintained. The following chart shall clearly bring out each of the Ukthas, so elucidated in respect of the gods as well as the human-frame :

Uktha of the gods	*Arka*	*Uktha of man*	*Arka*
(*i*) The Earth	Agni	Mouth	Speech
(*ii*) The Sky	Air	Nostrils	Breath
(*iii*) Younder Heaven	Sun	Forehead	Eye

The symbolical description of Uktha of the human body becomes all the more subtler in a succeeding section [3] It has already been stated in an earlier section[4] that in each of the five sense organs of the human body, there is latent a deity, who in fact, is the real functionary in the diverse functions of our sense-organs. It was further stated therein that it is the puruṣa or the 'Self' in all these organs who is the sole cause of their actual functioning. The Man or Puruṣaḥ pervades wholly and completely throughout all the limbs right upto hair and nails. Such clear and unequivocal description of Ātman in this section of the first Āraṇyaka seems to have assumed the symbolical name of 'Uktha' in section II.1.4, even though the description has not become so subtle as the all-permeating character of Ātman in the former section. All the same, it has definitely become subtler as compared to mere physical description of the human uktha in section 2, ibid. The parable of leaving the human body and re-entry into it one by one in turn by speech, eye, ear, mind and finally the breath is a mere illustration to prove the fact that the body cannot exist without the vital air. It has become the mainstay of the human frame and thus acquired the definition or conception of being the 'Uktha' as compared to speech, eye, ear and mind. It has also been proved in this section that all other limbs of the human body can function only if the breaths continue to perform the functions assigned to them. The section also specifically clarifies that the deities controlling the functioning of other sense organs admitted the breath to be their leader and themselves as mere subsidiaries to him.

Uktha as Creator of day and night : Section II.1.5 ibid, opens with the statement that the gods carried the Uktha forward. Being carried forward, he was stretched out. (Because men say) he has been carried forward, the morning came into being. (Because men say) he has gone to rest, the evening came into being. Day is breathing forth (Prāṇa), night is breathing down (Apāna).

Uktha has been identified with the vital airs in the preceding section of the second Āraṇyaka. However, it has earlier been stated that Prajāpati is the solitary seed or origin of everything in this universe. Ipso-facto, the so-called Uktha or the Prāṇa also derives the source of its existence from Prajāpati. Hence, God, the Prajāpati and not merely the Uktha is creator of days and nights. The day has symbolically been stated to represent the Prāṇa (expiration) and the night as the apāna (inspiration) of prajāpati. All this symbolical description, in fact, signifies the mystic truth that God alone is the regulator of time in this universe.

Controlling and all pervasive powers of Uktha : The Aitareya Āraṇyaka[5] also details out the supreme controlling authority of the Uktha viz., Prāṇa. A stotra usually comprises of a number of hymns that are composed in various metres. On this very analogy, the various parts of the hypothetical physical frame of the centripetal concept of the powerful 'Uktha' or Prāṇa have been described. In this elucidation of the diverse powers of the Uktha as a saviour, guide, controller etc. the basic identity of the Uktha with the Prajāpati should never be lost sight of.

Speech has been stated as rope and the diverse names of all the objects as the knots of this rope. So, by speech and giving of names to everything in this world, all this is bound or controlled. Thus, speech and the process of nomenclature have a very basic role to play in organising the affairs of this world and they both take their origin from the 'Uktha'. A person who knows this basic philosophy, becomes an object of worship.

Next, the various metres of an Uktha or a stotra have been stated to be various parts of hypothetical body of the universally powerful Uktha and this knowledge has been stated to be gifted with the power of securing the knower thereof against the ill-effects of his sinful actions at all places (S.2).

Then, have been quoted two Vedic verses (RV, I.164.3 and I.55.8) to assign to the Uktha the powers that are enjoyed by God himself as per details in these verses. The uktha or Prāṇa has been stated to be guardian, 'Never tiring' 'continuously pulsating', 'illuminator' 'omnipresent' and 'enveloper of all'. Then follows the unequivocal assertion that everything in the world is covered by breath. Just as in a set of hymns, the bṛhatī metre is the biggest, similarly the Prāṇa has a dominating role to play in the universe. It not only supports the ether; but all the creatures right upto ants are also covered or pervaded by it (S. 3). All this is symptomatic description of the omnipotence and omnipresence of the Prajāpati —the real Uktha.

Creative powers of Puruṣa

In II.1.2, a metaphysical pronouncement has been made in unequivocal terms that the Uktha (hymn) is Puruṣa. He is great and is Prajāpati. Thus, the ultimate identity of Puruṣa and Prajāpati has been established. In section 7 ibid , the creative powers of the puruṣa have been detailed out. The creative agents are the various psychic faculties of the Puruṣa as per details given below :

Agent of creation	*Elements or god created*
(*i*) Speech	Earth and fire
(*ii*) Breath	Sky and air
(*iii*) Eye	Heaven and sun

(*iv*) Ear — Quarters and moon

(*v*) Mind — Waters and varuṇa

It has also been repeatedly clarified that the field of jurisdiction of the above five sense organs is co-extensive with the physical dimensions or effectiveness of the five gross elements, Sun, moon, heaven and god Varuṇa as created by each of them separately. The creative organs of the Puruṣa and the diverse elements created by them are also co-existent with each other. The former do not decay till the latter decay. All this description of the powers of the Man is a symbolical description of the creative powers of God—the Prajāpati. This section delineates the Puruṣa as the efficient cause of the creation. Bringing into existence of Varuṇa in the very beginning of all creation is a special feature of this Āraṇyaka Ipso-facto, the seers of the Āraṇyaka had firm faith that the off-springs should lead virtuous lives and hence, the necessity of creation of Varuṇa, the dispenser of virtue, at the very initial stage (S. 4).

It has already been elucidated in the preceding section that Puruṣa is the efficient cause of creation of the five basic gross elements, Sun, moon, heaven and the god Varuṇa. This section[6] carries the process of creation still further as per details given below :

(*i*) Like the first stanza of the creation Hymn of the Ṛgveda (X. 129), this section also opens with the question if these were waters as the root (cause of creation) and the animate/inanimate creatures as the off-shoot (S. 5). Thus, water was the material cause of creation. Sāyaṇa considered waters as an expression of the five elements; but Keith took it as an unnecessary idea.

(*ii*) A seer, known by the name of Mahidāsa Aitareya said, "I know my origin to be right from the gods and from me upto gods, I know the process of creation." Sāyaṇa explains it as '*devaiḥ sahitaṁ tad abhinnam mat svarūpaṁ.*' Dr. Mangala Deva Śāstri[7] explains it that 'my greatness envelopes the deities and that of the deities' envelopes me. From philosophic point of view, there is complete identity between man and the gods'. Mahidāsa further fortified his above observation by asserting that gods are gifted from this world and they are also likewise supported

(S. 6). Thus, the inherent nature of man and gods is identical with that of the Brahman and the latter is both the efficient as well as the material cause of all creation.

Importance of Prāṇa

After detailing out the material and efficient causes of creation of the world, this section[8] brings out the importance of Prāṇa (vital-airs) in life in the following terms :

(*a*) It is called giri (hiding place). It is also called hiding place of Brahman (Brahma-giri). It is a well known fact that during sound sleep all the senses enter into Prāṇa. It, therefore, ipso-facto, forms the basis of the senses. The argument of Sāyaṇa that the Prāṇa is swallowed up and hidden by other senses is apparently unintelligible and also unacceptable. The plain reading of the terminology of the Āraṇyaka does not at all signify anything of this type. It only states, "This is the hiding-place, eye, ear, mind, speech and breath. They call it the hinding place of brahman." It only means that the sense organs are more important in the functioning of the body and Prāṇa has the most vital role to play. with its exit, even the immortal element would leave the body. That is why, it has been given the epithet of 'Brahma-giri.'

(*b*) He is the life, breath, being and 'not being'. Sāyaṇa felt that the Jivātman constitutes the base of life and induces all actions. The Soul also remains in the body so long as the Prāṇa pulsates therein. Hence, the above epithet of 'Bhuti' and as soon as the vital airs leave the body, the stage of 'abhūti' is reached. Ipso-facto, the basic importance of Prāṇa is unmistakably established.

(*c*) He is death and immortality. Sāyaṇa explains it that death occurs when the Prāṇa leaves the body and remaining of the breath within the body is its immortality. Ānandatīrtha renders that 'at death, they see the bodies deserted by 'Vāyu'.

Obviously, the above assertion of the Āraṇyaka is not correct and is opposed to the basic philosophy contained in the Yajurveda[9] which clearly states that at the time of death, the breath joins the wind. Thus, the so-called Prāṇa just enters the atmospheric air and is not something immortal. That is something else and is known by the name of Ātman which is immortal as per aforesaid verse of the Yajurveda. However, it may constantly be borne in mind that in the present section, the entire description is symbolical and the Prāṇa or Puruṣa or the Uktha actually represents the immortal Self in us. This interpretation is further fortified from the fact that with a view to corroborate the above statement viz. Prāṇa is death and immortality, a Vedic verse (RV. I. 164. 8) has been quoted by the seer of the Āraṇyaka. Briefly speaking, this verse, *inter alia* states that propelled by his own power, down and up he goes. Besides, the immortal and the mortal live together; the deity is immortal; the immortal and mortal go in different directions; they (the people) know only the one and not the other and finally who knows this becomes immortal in yonder world and is seen as immortal by all the beings (S. 7).

All this description is of the metaphysical level and unmistakably pertains to the immortal Ātman and not the mortal body. Prāṇa as such, is a part of the mortal physical frame and cannot by itself assumed the status and characteristics of the Ātman in the creatures. Evidently the entire description about basic importance of Prāṇa in this section is merely a creation of the ingenuity of the minds of the commentators; otherwise, the text does no where call the Prāṇa as giri, asu, bhūti etc. In fact, it has clearly been said that this is life, this is Prāṇa. This clearly signifies that which is life, is symbolically speaking, also Prāṇa. This does not, by any stretch of imagination equate and identify Prāṇa and Ātman. In fact, the real immortal element in the body is the latter.

B. SYMBOLISM AS FOUND IN TAITTIRĪYA ĀRAṆYAKA

Allegorical or symbolical worship makes its debut for the first time in section II. 17 of the Taittirīya Āraṇyaka. The process of atonements by a priest who performs any sacrifice for some ignoble sacrificer has been described here, under the guise of another suggestively similar. The process of any worship does, ordinarily, presuppose presence of a few articles of material equipment like laddles, offerings etc. However, no such material equipment is needed for performance of an atonement as referred to above. What is required is retirement to a Jungle, seating onself on some neat and clean place in healthy environments and doing of self-study. Mere observance of fast by the atoner shall constitute the sacrificial fee, the very place shall be the upa sada, the seat, the Soma-pressing; his speech, the curved wooden laddle; his mind, the upa-bhṛt; his resolution or will, the dhruvā; his Prāṇa, the oblation; the Sāma-verses, the Adhvaryu; the atoner himself, the sacrifice; breathing last by him, the gift or donation. Thus, the narrative description of a sacrifice has been disguised under a process which is entirely mental, intellectual and at the best supramental. This is nothing but allegorical presentation of the subject of sacrifice. This process has been carried much farther in sections 1 to 7 of Book III—when the author of the Āraṇyaka does not deal with any superficial ritualism; but gives the ritual an altogether metaphysical interpretation. In these sections, the diverse items of the material equipment have been represented as per some of the following details :

Serial No.	*Material Equipment*		*Represented by*	
1.	Sruk		Reflecting capacity	(III. 1)
2.	Ghee		Mind	(-do-)
3.	Fire-altar		Speech	(-do-)
4.	Barhi grass		Recitation	(-do-)
5.	Hotā	(*i*)	Vāk-pati	(-do-)
		(*ii*)	Earth	(III.2)
		(*iii*)	Agni	(III 3)
		(*iv*)	Mahā-havis	(III.5)
		(*v*)	Vāk	(III 6)
6.	Haviṣ	(*i*)	Breath	(III.1)
		(*ii*)	Mind	(III.6)
7.	Adhvaryu	(*i*)	Sāma verses	(III.1)
		(*ii*)	Heaven	(III.2)
		(*iii*)	Aśvins	(III.3)
		(*iv*)	Satya-havi seerṣ	(III.5)
		(*v*)	Vāta	(III 6)
8.	Agnīt	(*i*)	Rudra	(III.2)
		(*ii*)	Tvaṣṭā	(III.3)
		(*iii*)	Acyutapājā seers	(III.5)
9.	Upa-vaktā	(*i*)	Mind	(III.1)
		(*ii*)	Bṛhaspati	(III.2)
		(*iii*)	Mitra	(III.3)
		(*iv*)	Acyutamanā seers	(III.5)
10.	Consecration		Wife of the sacrificer	(III.6)

The allegorical or symbolical description of the sacrifice has not ended here. The Sun, the air, the heaven, the intermediary spatial regions, the sacrifice and the earth constitute respectively the eye, breath, back-side, Ātmā, limbs and other parts of the body of the sacrificer. Brāhmaṇa, Agni, Earth, Air, Moon, Prajāpati etc. have also been named as ten hotās[10] who play diverse roles of Bhartā, Pratiṣṭhā etc. in the sacrifice. This allegorisation finds further elaboration in section III. 9 when so-called spouses of a large number of deities have been catalogued.

NOTES AND REFERENCES

1. VS., XXXII. 3.
2. AA., II. 1.2.
3. AA., II. 1.4.
4. *Ibid.*, 1.3.8.
5. AA., II. 1.6
6. AA., II. 1.8.
7. AA., Paryālocanam, p. 34.
8. AA., II. 1.8.
9. VS., XL. 17.
10. T.A., III. 7.

SOURCES IV

ऐतरेयारण्यकम्

१ इन्द्रो वै वृत्रं हत्वा महानभवद्यन्महाव्रतम् अभवत् (१.१.१)
तन्महाव्रतस्य महाव्रतत्वम् ।

२. छादयन्ति ह वा एनं छन्दांसि पापात्कमणो यस्यां
कस्यांचिद् दिशि कामयते य एवमेतच्छन्दसां
छन्दस्त्वं वेद । (२.१.६)

३. सर्वं हीदं प्राणेनाऽऽवृतम् ।
सोऽयमाकाशः प्राणेन वृहत्या विष्टब्धस्तद्यथाऽयमाकाशः
प्राणेन बहत्या विष्टब्ध एव सर्वाणि भूतान्यापिपी-
लिकाभ्यः प्राणेन वृहत्या विष्टब्धानीत्येवं विद्यात् । (२.१.६)

४. बरुणोऽस्य प्रजां धर्मेण दाधार । (२.१ ७)

५. आपा३इत्याप इति तदिदमाप एवेदं वै मूलमदस्तूलमयं
पितैते पुत्राः । (२.१.८)

६. एतद्ध स्म वै तद्विद्वानाह महिदास ऐतरेय आऽहं मां
देवेभ्यो वेद ओ मद् देवान् वेदेतः प्रदाना
ह्येत इतः संभृता इति । (२.१.८)

७. अपाङ्प्राङेति स्वधया गृभीत इत्यपानेन
ह्ययं यतः प्राणो न पराङ् भवति ।
अमर्त्यो मर्त्येना सयोनिरित्येतेन हीदं सर्वं सयोनि
मर्त्यानि हीमानि शरीराणी३ अमृतैषा देवता ।
ता शश्वन्ता विषूचीना वियन्ता न्य१न्यं
चिक्युर्न निचिक्युरन्यमिति निचिन्वन्ति हैवेमानि
शरीराणी ३ अमृतैवैषा देवता । (२.१.८)

CHAPTER
FIVE

Metaphysics, its Subject Matter and Details of Metaphysical Contents of Aitareya and Taittirīya Āraṇyakas

Metaphysics

It is not easy to give a quite satisfactory definition of metaphysics. It will be convenient to divide the treatment of it into three parts :

1. the general nature of knowledge;
2. the conception of reality and its chief applications; and
3. the bearings of metaphysics on other subjects, especially ethics and religion.

Knowledge

The term is ambiguous. It is employed in a very wide sense; but it is very commonly understood in a narrower sense. Thus, knowledge is frequently distinguished from those modes of apprehension which are called sensation, perception and imagination. It is thus confined to those modes of apprehension which involve definite thought or conception. It is now customary to use the term 'cognition' for all these modes of apprehension. There are, however, some differences in our ways of knowing which is very necessary to bear in mind. The most fundamental are :

(*a*) simple apprehension and judgment;

(*b*) immediacy and mediacy;

(*c*) acquaintance and description;

(*d*) enjoyment and contemplation; and

(*e*) experiencing and experienced.

Experiencing and Experienced

Whenever there is knowledge of any kind, there is some one who knows and something that is known. Knowledge does not exist in vacuo, but at some particular centre; and that centre is not primarily aware of itself; but of some particular object. Whenever any one reflects upon his knowledge, he at once becomes aware of this double aspect : he realizes not only that something is apprehended; but he apprehends it. Now, when any one reflects further upon his knowledge and especially when by intercourse with his fellowmen, he is able to compare his own knowledge with that of others, he very soon comes to realize that some of the things that he apprehends are more closely connected with his particular way of apprehending them than others are. Some of the things that we have or enjoy do not specially belong to ourselves; but simply as objects that we contemplate and others as being more peculiarly as our own or bound up with our attitude as experiencing. Thus, we may be led to rather recognise a subjective and an objective aspect in all modes of apprehension. This is an important distinction.

Conception of Reality

The study of the theory of knowledge leads to the recognition that, in one sense at least, there is no meaning in the antithesis between the real and the unreal. Sometimes our apprehension of things is very incomplete; and, when we gain a fuller apprehension of them, we may be said to know them more truly.

The earliest attempts at a constructive theory of the cosmos and certainly one of the most interesting and remarkable is that which is set forth in the Āraṇyakas. The difficulties of the subject, especially at so early a stage of human thought, prevent it from being dealt with in a perfectly lucid way; but the doctrine that the cosmos is to be conceived as an unchanging spiritual unity, manifesting itself, especially in human life, in a process of slow development, appears to be definitely indicated. This view showing itself most clearly in the conception of a long series of successive embodiments, gained a firm hold on Eastern thought. It is a view to which western thought also has recurred from time to time; but in general, Western thought starts rather from the multiplicity of existing things, and makes only very tentative efforts to apprehend the central unity.

Bearing of Metaphysics

It would be a great mistake to suppose that the value of metaphysical speculation is to be measured exclusively by its success in providing us with a coherent doctrine of the cosmos. Any one who thinks seriously about the ultimate problems of knowledge and reality is almost bound to make some attempt to think about the universe as a whole. A chief element in the higher forms of religion consists in a certain intensification of the moral consciousness by its more definite concentration on the conception of intrinsic value—as in such saying as 'What shall it profit a man, if he shall gain the whole world, and lose his own soul?' This intensification is generally combined with the conviction that the object of ultimate valuation is real and attainable. A conviction of this kind is sometimes based on a definite metaphysical doctrine. At other times, it is based rather on some form of intuition or of revelation or on the authority of some great teacher or simply on the intrinsic force of the moral principle itself. The founders of religions and their most influential prophets have generally connected their teaching with some doctrines of a more or less explicitly metaphysical character. Buddhism, which is perhaps the most purely ethical form of religion that has ever had an extensive influence, seems to be rather intimately connected with those Indian forms of metaphysical construction that had their origin in the Āraṇyakas. It conceives of what has ultimate value as the realization of the higher self to be achieved by the control of the lower, and especially by the suppression of the lower forms of desire.

The gospel of love is the most inspiring, because it implies, when its meaning is fully developed, that everything has value. It is sometimes urged that metaphysical and religious views of the cosmos, by representing the attainment of moral ideal as involved in the nature of things, have certain tendency to weaken the moral motive, by making it appear that individual effort is unnecessary. It is not so. On the whole, none of the deeper forms either of metaphysical construction or of religious insight has represented the ideal as attainable in any other way than through the individual choice of what is best.

In common parlance, metaphysics may be stated to be the practical form of mysticism. In its earliest experiences, the humanity considered natural phenomena/forces like rain, fire, thunder-strike, sun etc. as superior to itself which could make it happy or unhappy. It, therefore, thought it expedient to please them and devised ways and means to do so. The means so developed gradually evolved themselves into a practical cult that can be discussed under what is known as metaphysics. The original concept of supernaturalism and its relationship with the humanity, however, continued to be the subject matter of what is termed as mysticism. Thus, besides the evolution of the cosmos, leading of morally upright life full of universal love for its fellow-beings seems to be the raison d'etre or the core subject of metaphysics. Unity of a single Godhead and its all-peremeating character are also very important ingredients of the subject-matter of metaphysics. In the context of this background, a brief resume of the metaphysical contents of the Aitareya and Taittirīya Āraṇyakas is given in the supervening paragraphs :

A. METAPHYSICAL CONTENTS OF AITAREYA ĀRAṆYAKA

Importance of speech in life

Certain sections of the first two Āraṇyakas of the Aitareya Āraṇyaka do bring out a rather penetrating and sifting analysis about the immense importance of speech in human life. It has rather been conspicuously stated[1] that speech is denoted by 'rich in prayer' (S. 1). Sāyaṇa explains it that it is through the intellect that every thing is realised or understood. Bringing out the close relationship between human mind and speech, it has specifically been stated[2] as follows :

"All desires rest on the mind, for with the mind man conceives all desires. Speech yields all desires, for by speech man expresses all desires." (S. 2).

The above does depict a basic process of the functioning of the human faculties, primarily the mind. The Bhagawad Gītā also says, "*Dhyāyato viṣayān puruṣaḥ Saṅgas teṣūpajāyte*[3]......"

The second part that speech yields all desires seems to be only a partial truth. It is true that the speech is conducive to realisation of some of the desires as it is only through its medium that a human being expresses his desires ; but it is equally true that by mere expression itself, our desires are not fulfilled. As a matter of common observance, it can confidently be asserted that majority of us have to toil hard in life to produce wealth. This basic truth of life has, therefore, rightly been, in a way codified as "*udyamena hi siddhyanti kāryāṇi na manorthaiḥ.*"

A simple Sanskrit word called 'tat' has not only been stated[4] to be the first utterance of a growing child; but also of Prajāpati himself. This brings out the basic factum that by speech names are made. There are numerous creatures in this universe and equally diverse are other types of botanical and zoological growths and had there been no conception of speech in the world, identification, differentiation, specification, nomenclature etc. of the multitude of creatures and vegetational growth would have become impossible. This, ipso facto, would have put a permanent embargo on all development of thought, philosophy, science, languages and what not ? Hence, this basic fact that all nomenclature is based on speech has not only very significantly but rather mystically been brought out in this one of the oldest texts regarding development of human thought and philosophy.

All-pervasive Nature of Speech

Reiterating the all-pervasive nature of speech, it has been stated[5] that Brahman and speech are co-extensive and inseparable. Like the Brahman, the speech is also all-pervasive. (S. 3). This part of the Āraṇyaka is, therefore, remniscient of the all-permeating character of speech as brought forth in hymn X. 125 of the Ṛgveda.

While asserting that God is the sole seed or creator of the universe, it has very cryptically been stated[6] that all actions originate from speech (*Vāco retaḥ karma*). This statement is self-explanatory and hardly needs further elaboration about the basic importance of speech.

Dominant Role of Speech in Life

The Āraṇyaka[7] lays down that the entire out-growth (zoological, botanical or otherwise) in this universe is cognised through a specific name. These names are like various knots in the continuous rope of speech. It is through the process of giving names that all things are identified. The nomenclature and further description of the qualities, properties etc. of the entire animate and inanimate world has to be done through the medium of speech (S. 4). Without the agency of speech, the entire world would just have been dumb.

Speech and Truth

The great litany (Mahad Uktham) has been stated[8] to be the highest development of speech. The speech has further been classified as five-fold, measured, unmeasured, music, truth and falsehood. Examples of each of these classes have been quoted. It is significant to note that 'OM' has been quoted as example of truth and 'no' as that of falsehood. Sāyaṇa explains 'no' as "*Sarvaprapañ casya Niṣedhakaḥ*." This interpretation also appears to be significantly correct because in the ultimate analysis of things, brahman alone is truth and everything else is untruth: Taittīriya Āraṇyaka[9] also declares Brahman to be Real, Knowledge and Infinite. Thus, truth is one of the prime characteristics of Brahman which is the ultimate Reality.

It has further been stated[10] that the flower and fruit of speech is what is true. One who speaks the truth becomes famous and of splendid renown. The untrue is the root of speech, and, as a tree with roots exposed dries up and perishes, so a man who speaks untruth, exposes his roots, dries up and perishes. The Āraṇyaka, therefore, advises that a man should not speak untruth; but should rather guard himself against it. This very view was subsequently reiterated in question VI of the Praśna Upanishad wherein it is said that, "verily to his roots, he withers, who speaks untruth."

Relationship between Speech and Prāṇa

A seer called Kauṇṭharavya says,[11] "Speech is united with breath,

breath with the blowing air, the air with the All-gods, the All-gods with the world of heaven, the world of heaven with Brahman. This is the union of the former with the latter." (S.5). According to another sage called Pañcālcaṇḍa, "The union is speech. By speech are the Vedas composed, by speech the metres. By speech friends are united, by speech all beings, therefore, speech is all this. When one reads or speaks, breath is in speech, speech then swallows breath, breath then swallows speech. They swallow each other. Speech indeed is the mother, breath the son." (S. 6). This intimate and rather indispensable relationship between speech and Prāṇa has been further fortified by quoting a Ṛgvedic Verse (X, 119.4).

In whole of the above discussion, greater and more fundamental importance has been attached to speech rather than to Prāṇa. This is rather in contradiction of the immense importance of Prāṇa as brought out in detail with great perseverence in the second Āraṇyaka. Besides, basically speaking, the Prāṇa and not speech has the inherent significance. Prāṇa has already been stated in this Āraṇyaka to be the 'Uktha' and with its exit from the body, all functionaries like eyes, tongue, ears etc., ipso facto, stop functioning. How can a subservient organ like speech be the mother of Prāṇa as made out above. Apparently, this is both inconsistent as well as unsustainable.

Prāṇa as Creator

In the first two sections of this Chapter,[12] Prāṇa has been portrayed as the creator of the principal vedic seers (viz. Śatarcins, Mādhymas etc.), Kṣudrasūktas and Mahāsūktas, a hymn, verses, half/quarter verses, syllables, and even the sounds. All sorts of aberrations-etymological, rational or irrational have been harnessed to at least superficially bring home the fact that the Prāṇa is really the creator of all of them. The closing sentence of the second section unequivocally declares that all vedas, all sounds and all the verses are Prāṇa. These two sections of this Āraṇyaka do go a long way to clearly establish the universal belief among the followers of ancient Indian tradition that all vedas, hymns and Ṛks are divine creation. The modern educated Hindus take them as the out-pourings of the divine inspiration of the seers. The arguments given in these two sections to prove the basic hypothesis are hardly rational ; but they do forcefully bring out the fact that the seer of the Āraṇyaka had a firm and rather implicit faith that the prāṇa or Uktha or Prajāpati was the sole creator of all the vedic seers and their inspired writings.

All-pervasive Character of Prāṇa

A colloquy[13] between the vedic seer Viśwāmitra and god Indra has been invoked to assert the all-pervasive character of Prāṇa. It has been asserted that all the creatures are prāṇa and he that shines is also prāṇa. He pervades all the quarters. He is the food and support of all creaturest (S. 7).

It has been asserted[14] that recitation of one thousand bṛhtīs purifies the reciter so much that he becomes full of knowledge, devatāmayaḥ, Brahmamayaḥ, Amṛtamayaḥ and attains the gods. This is followed by an intensely metaphysical note that "what I am, He is; what He is, I am." (S. 8). Such a practical conviction develops after complete purification of the mind and at that stage, the man starts realising complete identity between individual and the supreme self. The foregoing assertion of this Āraṇyaka is the precursor of the following two subsequent upanishadic dictums :

(i) *Ayam Ātmā Brahma*, and

(ii) "*Yo Sāv asau puruṣaḥ so' ham asmi.*"

The truth and validity of the above assertion has been further fortified by quoting a quarter of the ṛk or verse from the Ṛgveda (I. 115.1) wherein through the symbol of the sun, the all-permeating God has unequivocally been stated to be the ātmā or life-line of all animate and inanimate creatures. Thus, this section not only puts forth the basic principle that there is complete identity between individual and the Supreme self, but also that the latter is the summum bonum of all kinds of existence.

Creative Powers of God

'Puruṣa evoktham ayam eva mahān Prajāpatiḥ', says the Aitareya Āraṇyaka.[15] Thus, there is perfect identity between the self in the man and the lord of the universe or Prajāpati. They have both been termed as 'uktha' in this Hermit-text. This section[16] carries forward the aforesaid fundamental assertion and brings out the creative powers of the 'Ātmokthan Pañcavidham' or the self, the five-fold hymn. The five basic gross elements, viz., earth, air, ether, water and light originate from the Self, the five-fold hymn. From the 'Self' every thing arises and ultimately resolves into him (S. 9).

This section proceeds further to elucidate the distinctive functions of the afore said five basic elements. The earth and water have been termed as food because of them are foods compunded. Light and air are the feeder, for by them he eats food. Sāyaṇa interprets that the entire vegetation grows from the earth with the aid of water. So, both have rightly been termed as food. Through the vital airs, the digestive heat is generated and hence the air and light do perform the basic functions of a feeder. The fifth element of creation, viz., ether has been termed as the bowl (Āvapanam) because in the ether, all is ultimately poured or in other words, it may be stated that the prāṇa, when it leaves the physical frame of the creatures, merges with the ether.

Further distinction has been made in this section between the vegetational world and the animals. The trees and plants are food and animals, the feeder because they eat trees and plants.

Like the man, the animals who are gifted with teeth in both the upper and lower jaws have been categorised by this section as the feeders while other animals have been termed as the food. The former overcome the latter type of animals. This assertion proves that the seers of the Āraṇyaka had an acute discerning eye and the above proposition is based on an accurate power of observance that in general, the animals that are gifted with teeth in both the jaws do have dominance in the animal world – as for example, the lion in the jungle and man elsewhere because of the latter's superiority in discrimination, discernment and intellect.

Synthesis of Ethical life and knowledge of the Absolute

In contrast to the plethora of ritualistic details in the first Āraṇyaka, the succeeding Book of the Aitareya Āraṇyaka opens with a very philosophic statement that may very pertinently be quoted below :

> "This is the path;[17] this is the sacrifice; this is brahman; this is truth. Therefore, let no man diverge from it; let no man transgress it. For they did not transgress it; of old, those that did transgress it, were overcome" (S. 10).

The above statement has, if actually followed in life, immense practical importance as well as wisdom. The aim of human existence is happiness in this life and attainment of liberation after death. The statement in question contains a formula for attainment of both. The truth does remain that we should lead an upright and ethical life. This would, ipso facto, if coupled with hard work, devotion to duty etc., lead to happiness. This part of this opening stanza of the Āraṇyaka is consistent with the Ṛgvedic prayer that we may never give up the path of good in our life (RV, X. 57.1). Alongwith morally upright life, the man should also strive attainment of knowledge of the Absolute Self or the Brahman, who, in the ultimate analysis, is the sole origin and repository of whatever exists in this universe. This is obviously the supreme objective worth achievement though leading of a morally upright life is the essential grounding therefore. The Āraṇyaka says with full authority and faith that this alone is the path or mode of life worth being led. This very principle seems to have been a little more developed and stated more clearly subsequently in the Īśa Upanishad as follows :

Vidyāṁ cāvidyāṁ Ca, yas tad Vedobhayam Saha
Avidyayā Mṛtyuṁ tīrtvā, vidyayāmṛtam aśnnute.

Practical Code of Conduct and Importance of Charity in life

In verses 11 and 14 of Chapter XL of the White Yajurveda, simultaneous knowledge of Avidyā and Vidyā, asambhūti and sambhūti has been spelt out as an elixir for success in this life and that hereafter. It has been clearly stated therein that through avidyā and vināśa overcome death and through vidyā or sambhūti, attain immortality. Almost similarly unfailing formula seems to have been put forth in the Aitareya Āraṇyaka[18] though under different nomenclatures, viz., OM and no. Before dilating further on the matter, it appears quite pertinent to reproduce below the translation of the relevant portion of this section as done by Keith :

'The word OM is empty and goes forward. So if a man says OM, then that is taken from him; if he should say OM to everything, he would empty himself and be unable to have delights. The syllable 'no' is full for one's self. If a man should say 'no' to everything, his fame would be evil and he would destroy himself. Therefore, should one give at the proper time, and at the proper time he should refrain from giving. So does he unite the true and the untrue. From their union, he grows and becomes greater (S. 11).

From the above, it appears that the word 'OM' has two meanings. The first is metaphysical and the second 'affirmative yes'. In the above quoted first sentence, it has been stated that the word 'OM' is empty and goes forward. This is mere literal translation by Keith and virtually conveys no sense. Sāyaṇa explains this as 'Brahman who is free from worldly attachments' (S. 12). This appears to be a very plausible and rational interpretation.

Then starts the second meaning of the word 'OM'. The very first sentence says that when a man says 'OM' or yes to any demand from others, then he has to comparatively empty himself or surrender something. If he says 'yes' or agrees to accede to every demand, then he would naturally empty himself in full or in other words, lose stock of his wordly possessions and shall not be able to satisfy his own needs. Sāyaṇa also agrees with this view.

The next portion of this very section[19] deals with the so-called misers. The sentence opens with the assertion that a person who has a patent 'no' to all prayers for charity from him, his estate mounts up and his homestead is full of wordly wherewithal. However, this assertion is not universally true because accumulation of wealth does not primarily depend upon the capacity or willingness to spare ; but so many other more important factors like size of income from various sources, extent and vastness or otherwise of those sources, pattern of expenditure, abstinence from wasteful expenditure, leading of a restrained life etc. However, the Āraṇyaka rightly goes on to assert that one who does not practice any munificence at all, he would have ill-fame and would be just like a living dead person. These observations of the ancient seers are very candid and have universal validity even today. Finally puts forth the Āraṇyaka, a sane code of conduct in between the above elucidated two extremes of charity without restraint and utter lack of it. It says that give charity at the proper time and at the proper time, do refrain from giving. In this way, there shall be a proper union of 'yes' and 'no' to various demands for charity in life. From their union in life, the man would grow and become greater. The advice is really significant and of practical adoption in life.

Practical Ethics in Aitareya Āraṇyaka

A major part of the Aitareya Āraṇyaka deals with the ceremony of Mahāvrata. The upanishadic part, no doubt, primarily deals with the creation of the universe, identity of the Ātman and brahman etc. ; but all the same, certain passage are there in this part which dilate on practical ethics in life. In II. 5, some of the duties of the father towards the mother of his child and the child himself have been briefly, but very significantly delineated. 'After impregnation, the women rears the embryo and subsequently nourishes the same when it develops into a child. The embryo is, according to the Āraṇyaka, the very self of the man that is communicated to the wife through sexual union. As a nourisher, the woman is to be dutifully nourished (by her husband). The woman bears the germ. The man supports the child before and after the birth of the child. In fact, when he supports the child before its birth and thereafter, he supports in truth himself for the continuation of these worlds.' (S. 13). Thus, the father cannot arrogate to himself that when he supports the wife and the child, he is their supporter; but the seers of the Āraṇyaka enjoin upon him the moral duty to support and nourish them. This, he is required to do because the childern are a mere projection and continuation of his very self through the medium of procreation.

Likewise, it has been envisaged that the son too is required to perform certain specific and praiseworthy deeds in life. The Āraṇyaka clearly lays down that the son is appointed for performance of holy deeds (S. 14). Thus, the wise seers of the Āraṇyaka do enjoin upon the off-springs not only to be religious; but also to do good deeds so that the world may obviously be a place worthliving.

God as inducer of good deeds

Inter alia, it has significantly been laid down that God alone is the inducer of good deeds. The relevant passage[20] (S. 15) clearly reveals that it is through the inducement of the Imperishable One that a man undertakes the performance of a laudable ritual like the Mahāvrata and it is through the performance of such one-day ritual that the man attains the Undying One. Thus, it is evident that God induces the man to do good deeds. It is also made out that through the performance of the rites, the Eternal One is attained.

Creation of the Universe

A very philosophical Ṛgvedic verse,[21] *inter alia*, lays down that in the beginning there was no air. That One alone was there and He breathed by dint of his own strength. Exactly similar is the sole creator of the universe in the Aitareya Āraṇyaka[22] as well when in the very opening sentence, it says that in the beginning, Ātmā alone was there and there was nothing else blinking. He though of creating the worlds. He created these worlds, water, lights, mortal and waters. This water is above the heaven, and heaven supports it. The lights are the sky. The mortal is earth, those underneath are the waters (S. 16). A number of commentators like Bothlingk, Deussen, Sitārāma etc. feel that heaven must come in somewhere and it is sufficient if it comes in as a support. Ānandatīrtha explains ambhas as mahas and the other worlds beyond the heaven where waters were originally placed. Rajārāma takes it as 'the blue firmament'.

Creation of guardians of the worlds

In furtherance of the process of creation, the Sole Original Existence, namely the Ātman thought that the worlds have already been created by him; let him now create the guardians of the world. He formed the person, taking him out from the waters (S. 17). Thus, came into being, the Cosmic Puruṣa or the so-called virāj of later vedanta. This entity is also now known as 'iśvara' in contradistinction to the concept of Brahman and he is taken to be *de facto* controller or administrator of the universe.

Creation of Cosmic Puruṣa

The Ātman brooded over the Cosmic Man and when the latter was brooded over, a mouth burst forth as an egg does. From the mouth came speech, from speech fire. Nostrils burst forth. From the nostrils came forth prāṇa, from prāṇa wind. Eyes burst forth. From the eyes came forth sight, from sight the Sun. Ears burst forth. From the ears came forth hearing, from hearing the quarters. Skin burst forth. From the skin came forth hairs, from hairs plants and trees. The heart burst forth. From the heart came forth mind, from mind the moon. The navel burst forth. From the navel came forth down-breath (apāna), from down-breathing, death. The generative organ burst-forth. From the organ, came forth seed (retaṣ), from seed water.

Creation of man with all faculties

Thus far, the Cosmic Man, the deities and cosmic senses and forces have been created by the Sole Creator who has here been designated as Ātman or in other words, in the process of cosmology, the cosmic puruṣa and the cosmos have been evolved from the Absolute Existence. In the next section, [23] the process of evolution moves on to create the microcosm. This section opens with the sentence that the deities so-created fell into this great ocean and they were troubled by hunger and thirst. They, therefore, requested the Ātman to grant them a place where they could rest and eat food. He first led a cow and then a horse to them; but they were not satisfied. Ultimately he led a man to them and the latter said, "Well done! Man is indeed well done." The Ātman said to the deities, "Enter according to your places." Then fire, having become prāṇa, entered the nostrils. The Sun, having become sight, entered the eyes. The quarters, having become hearing, entered the ears. The plants and trees, having become hairs, entered the skin. The moon, having become mind, entered the heart. Death, having become down-breathing, entered the navel. The waters, having become seed entered the generative organ. Last of all, hunger and thirst also prayed to the Ātman for a place. The latter assigned both of them to the cosmic deities and made them sharers with the deities. Hence, to whatever deity an oblation is offered, hunger and thirst are partners in it.

Keith feels that this section reverses the former section.[24] There Ātman produced the worlds, the puruṣa and the deities. The deities now enter into puruṣa. In the Brāhamaṇas, the Brahman creates the world and then enters it; but here the deities have no creative power, and the section only seems to show the reciprocal dependence of the deities and the senses, of the great cosmic forces and the microcosm.

The view taken by Keith that there is a reversal of the order of creation is not correct. It seems to be based on lack of proper appreciation of the order of creation delineated in these two sections which correctly describe the creation of the cosmic forces from the Sole Subject; viz. Ātman and decends to the creation there from of the individual creatures who are inevitably subject to the dual sensations of hunger and thirst. Thus, the order of creation described in these two sections is perfectly intelligible and it rightly evolves from the Macrocosm to the microcosm.

Creation of food

After having created the worlds and their guardians, the Ātman or the Absolute thought that He may create food[25] for them. He brooded over the waters. From the waters so brooded over, form (Mūrti) was born. This form was indeed food. The food when created sought to go away. He was fain to seize it. He sought to grasp it by various organs—speech, prāṇa, eye, ear, skin, mind and the generative organ; but failed. Ultimately, he succeeded to grasp food by down-breathing or apāna. Thus, it is vāyu who lays hold of food and vāyu is he who lives by food or in other words, the life breath remains in the body through the essence of food (*Annarasena hi prāṇa dehe badhyate*). That is why, Sāyaṇa quotes Bṛhadāraṇyka Upanishad (II,2,1); "annam dāma."

Entry of the soul into the body

The Sole Creator of the universe thought, "how can this be without me ? By which way, shall I enter ?" He thought, if speech distinguishes, if prāṇa palpitates, if eye sees, if the ear hears, if the skin feels, if the mind thinks, if down-breathing digests, if the organ sends forth, what then am I ? Saṅkara illustrates by the metaphor, "Unless the lord keeps the city, the watchers watch in vain." There must be soul in the body. Sāyaṇa compares Bṛhadāraṇyaka Upanishad,[26] which, *inter alia* says that which performs the functions of all the five types of breaths is the Soul and is present in all things. He also quotes Ṛgveda, VI, 47.18 :

"*Rūpam rūpam pratirūpo babhūva,*

tadasya rūpam praticakṣṇāya."

Having split open the top of the skull, the soul entered by that door. That door is called vidṛti, the place of happiness. There are three dwelling places of him and three dreams.

The three dwelling places have been variously interpreted. Saṅkara gives two explanations. The first is that of right eye, inner mind and ether in the heart. Ānandatīratha explains the mind as in the throat and identifies the heart with the ether. He thus gets the triad, right eye, throat and heart. Sāyaṇa follows him and cites the Brahma Upanishad, III; "*netre jāgaritam vidyāt, kaṇṭhe svapnam samādiset, suṣuptaṁ hṛdayasthaṁ tu.*" Saṅkara and others explain the states as a waking, dreaming and deep sleep, for all are sleep as compared with true knowledge of brahman. The other explanation is that referring to another birth, viz., one's own body and those of one's mother and father. Keith feels that it is no doubt quite wrong; but Sāyaṇa reconciles the two by assigning two kinds of Saṁsāra, dinavyavahāra and janmāntara-svīkāra, to which the theories correspond.

Man as replica of God

As soon as the soul (or the God in man) entered the body, he looked through all beings, to see whether any one wished to proclaim another self. He saw this person only as the most widely extended brahman (S. 18). Ipso facto, it is established that the Brahman is all permeating so much so that each creature, howsoever, insignificant it might be, has His subtle representative within itself which is now-a-days given the name of 'ātman' or the individual soul.

Doctrine of Transmigration of Soul

"The earth is both the food and the feeder because all that exists springs from it. Whatever goes forth, (heaven) consumes it all. Whatever goes thence, the (earth) consumes it all." (II. 1. 2).

The above statement clearly proves that after death, when the creatures go to the yonder world, the latter consumes them or in other words, they do go to another world and when, on re-birth, they come from there, this (earth) consumes them (S. 19). This clearly proves the doctrine known by the name of transmigration of soul. Sāyaṇa has also confirmed the same; but Keith differs.[27] He feels that the earth consumes what the heaven sends; e.g. rain, not persons who are born again, or as Sayaṇa says sacrificers who having enjoyed heaven after death return again to earth. It is not proved that such an idea is known to this Āraṇyaka.

This view of Keith is obviously against the plain language of the Āraṇyaka and is obviously not acceptable.

Section II.1.3 ibid. further corroborates the above-said principle of transmigration of soul when it says that the man is moulded by his deeds (*Tad idam karma kṛtam ayaṁ puruṣaḥ*).

Sāyaṇa explains kṛtam as done in a former birth; but Keith feels this an unnecessary introduction of transmigration theory. He simply feels that the passage only means that action is the man; the man is what he does.

The view taken by Keith is not supported by the original text which is self-explanatory and clearly supports the interpretation given by Sāyaṇa.

It has been said[28] that a man has three births. This seems to be elucidation of the idea put forth in the preceding section[29] that the individual soul has three dwelling places. Rājārāma Rāmkrishan Bhāgavata[30] describes these three births as follows :

(*a*) the seminal soul when it is transferred has its first birth;

(*b*) the second, birth as a human-being; and

(*c*) death and rest in the indestructible heaven.

The third sleep is the sleep of death beginning in this, and ending in the heavenly world.

The views of Rājārāma find almost full corroboration from the original text of the Aitareya Āraṇyaka[31] when it states :—"In man, he is from the first as a germ. That seed is strength gathered from all the limbs and he thus bears a self in his self. When he connects the seed to the woman, then he causes it to be born. That is his first birth (S. 20). When the son is born, it is the second birth of man. The self in the father having done its duty and attained old age departs, and departing hence is born again. This is his third birth (S. 21). This is clear and unequivocal proof of the elucidation of the doctrine of transmigration in this Āraṇyaka. The concept has been further fortified by quoting a relevant stanza from the Ṛgveda (IV. 27.1) and the vedic parable of the seer Vāmadeva[32] who while lying in the womb declared : 'Within the womb, I learnt all the births of these gods. A hundred brazen forts restrained me; but like a hawk, I escaped swiftly downwards. Knowing this, he stopped forth after the destruction of the body, and having enjoyed all delights in the world of heaven, he become immortal.' (S. 22).

Parallelism in Macrocosm and Microcosm

There is a well known philosophical saying in Sanskrit namely; "Yathā piṇḍe tathā brahmāṇḍe." Exactly in the reverse order has been drawn a parallelism between the Macrocosm and Microcosm in the first two sections of this Book.[33] This portion of the Āraṇyaka deals with the philosophy underneath the basic union in the cosmic and microcosmic forces in the world. The opening few sentences detail out a broad spectrum of the universal forces or the deities. It has been laid down therein that the earth and heaven are the first and second halves respectively. The air or ether is the uniting force or medium between the two. In the microcosm or the individual, speech and mind are respectively the two halves and breath is the union between them. Another class of seers[34] felt that out of speech and mind, the latter is the first half or in a way, more important because by mind, a person first resolves and then utters speech. The compact of mind, speech and breath is like a chariot with three horses.

The seer Śākalya felt that the earth and sky are the two halves and rain is their union. Prajanya is the uniter. Thus, when it rains heavily and continuously for day and night, then people say, "Earth and heaven have united." On this analogy of the cosmos, in the microcosm, it has been said[35] that every man is egg-like which has two halves. One is that of earth and the other of heaven, and between them is ether, just as there is the ether between earth and heaven. In this ether, the breath is fixed, as is the air in that ether. Sayaṇa explains that there are two distinct parts of the human body. From feet up to the lower lip represents the earth and the upper portion represents the ether. Apparently, there is hardly any rationale in this sort of interpretation.

As there is sun in the heaven, lightning in the sky and fire in the earth, accordingly the human body is also gifted with three lights, namely; eye in the head, heart in the body and seed in the member (S. 23).

B. METAPHYSICS IN TAITTIRĪYA ĀRAṆYAKA

Transmigration and concept of Heaven and Hell

The Taittiriya Āraṇyaka[36] lays down that there are four types of deaths. These have been named as 'param', 'Avamam', 'Madhyamam' and the fourth. The Sun, air, fire and moon have been given out as respective causes of the above-said four categories of deaths. The sinners are afflicted by death categorised above as 'param' and also suffer from perennial scarcities. They also go through an unending circle of births and deaths. On the contrary, the righteous people are gifted with all the worldly where-withal and attain heaven after death. Though not clearly stated, yet this appears to be the type of death called 'Avamam'. Those who have both good and bad deeds to their credit; they meet with the middling type of death. The fourth type of death has not been defined in the original text. However, it has clearly been stated that moon is the cause of this kind of death. In his commentary, Sāyaṇa has stated that the moon is the lord and an effective creator of all vegetation. Hence, those who die on account of paucity of necessary eatables or food meet with this kind of death. This has also been termed by Sāyaṇa a low type of death.

On account of the sins committed by them, the sinners are afflicted with diverse ordeals in hellish worlds located somewhere between the earth and heaven. They are re-born in this world either with incomplete or disabled limbs or become creatures that are not born from the womb. By the force of their (low) deeds; they meet with death after death. Just as insignificant insects are killed by us instantaneously; such sinners too are likewise put an end to by the gods. One who knows this and hears religious discourses for a long time, he overcomes sudden or accidental death and becomes the honourable guest of God after death. He also attains salvation. Obviously with a view to stress the importance of good deeds in human life, the last verse of the Yajurveda has been quoted, wherein it is prayed—"O Agni, lead us by the good path to prosperity. Oh God; you know all our deeds. Destroy our sins of deceit. (In return) we shall adore thee by repeated salutations." Thus, this ethical instruction also lays stress on leading of morally upright life.

Transmigration

After explaining that an immortal Self of the nature of light and a store-house of golden hue entered the human body, the Āraṇyaka[37] proceeds to state that a person who has realised the inherent nature of his Self is blessed with longevity, freedom disease and accidental or sudden death. He is blessed both by good and evil forces in both the worlds (S. 24). Reiterating the doctrine of transmigration of soul, another verse says that the human beings are (rather helplessly) carried by their deeds to assume various embodiments or incarnations from this world to the yonder and vice versa just as particles of sand are flow off by a current of strong wind (S. 25). Then follows a prayer to the Lord of Death that all his old and new emissaries who hover around, (the sacrificer) may get off and Yama may appoint a beautiful place as dwelling for the sacrificer at any time—may be by day, by night or even while laying the watery bricks on the fire altar (S. 26).

Transmigration, Concepts of Heaven, Hell and Re-birth

Verses contained in Book VI of the Taittirīya Āraṇyaka abound in clear references to concepts of transmigration, heaven, hell and re-birth. A number of verses clearly implore the gods that the departed soul may go to the world of the good and pious persons or may be re-born on the earth according to its deeds. Another verse takes the soul as a source of light and implores for its merger with the supreme source of light which has been termed as the third light (S. 27). This is an obvious reference to salvation. The world to which go the valient warriors, the seers and the good-hearted persons have also been sought for the departing soul. Another vedic verse quoted here[38] (RV, I.50.10) puts forth the prayer that the parting soul may emerge from intense darkness or ignorance, ascend to the highest heaven and attain the best of the gods (viz. Sūrya) which is the sublimest source of light. It has further been specifically implored that the departing soul may go ahead to the ancestors or to the highest heaven or even come back to this world for re-birth according to its deeds (S. 28). In the alternative, it may make a home for itself in the highest heaven, get a spouse and live together happily (S. 29). The envoys of yama do exercise due discrimination while taking off from this world, the truthful and untruthful persons (S. 30), the devotees of God and benevolent persons (S. 31).

Concept of Heaven and Hell

The Taittirīya Āraṇyaka[39] lays great stress on leading of a morally upright life. The virtues so stressed have been separately dealt with in this work. As a necessary corollary thereof, the Āraṇyaka rightfully puts forth prayers to varuṇa, the deity who maintains moral order in the universe, to grant to the doers of meritorious deeds the worlds which they deserve and to the sinful, the world of death called 'Hiraṇmaya'. He is also requested to be kind and bestow heaven on us (of course after death) (S. 32).

Creation of the Universe

While delineating the process of initial creation of the universe ;[40] it has been said that in the beginning, it was all water and nothing else. Prajāpati made appearance on a lotus-leaf and thought of creation. He found that the unmanifest could be instrumental in the creation of the manifest. He brooded over himself and shook his body. Certain categories of seers called Āruṇas, Ketus etc. arose from the flesh of Prajāpati. From his nails and hair, another class of seers came into being. The constituent fluids of his body were a part and parcel of the waters. From out of the waters, a tortoise[41] came out. He told Prajāpati that he existed there already. It was, in fact, the Primeval Puruṣaḥ. He acquired to Himself numerous heads, numerous eyes, numerous feet. The Primordial Man took water in his both hands and placed it towards the eastern side of the altar of Āruṇaketuka fire by reciting the mantra—"Evā hy eveti." There arose the Sun. The direction of its origin came to be known as the east. Placing of subsequent handfuls of water on different sides of the fire-altar resulted in creation of fire, air, indra, pūṣan, gods, human beings, ancestors, Gandharvas and fairies. With the placing of each handful of water, the aforesaid verse was also recited by the Primordial Man. Alongwith the above gods, men etc. were created all the remaining directions and intermediate regions. Whatever drops of water fell outside the fire-altar, from them the demons and the like were created. It is on account of falling of such drops that they came to be so low. Thus, the Brahman appearing in the guise of a tortoise created the entire world and is his Own Creator. Since the entire creation was from waters, so, ipso facto, everything was in loose form and not steady. So, Prajāpati bestowed steadiness or firmness on everything by, entering therein himself (of course as soul as understood today in common parlance). This is supported by a verse which lays down that having created all the Gross Elements, creatures, all the directions/intermediate regions, the Prajāpati himself entered in all of them. He is, therefore, indubitably the "First-born of all creation."

The above account of creation of the universe makes it clear that it was Prajāpati and not the absolute Brahman in whose mind arose the desire that he may undertake creation. He brooded over and shook his body. As explained above, the Absolute Brahman (who existed even earlier than Prajāpati) made appearance as a tortoise and Prajāpati entered the bodies of the creatures as soul. Thus, this narrative makes the modern vedantic 'Kārya-Brahma' instrumental for creation rather than the 'Kāraṇa-Brahma.' Secondly, it is not understood how the Āruṇaketuka fire was in existence in the fire-altar around which water was poured in handful before fire, wind etc. were formally created. Besides, the concept of tortoise being responsible for the entire creation seems to be the preceding ideology of subsequent incarnations known by the names of Matsya and Varāha etc. Thus, the new ideology that took birth at the time Taittirīya Āraṇyaka seems to have acquired greater dimensions and clearer concept during the rise of subsequent Puranic literature. Thirdly, it is quite significant to repeat that it is Prajāpati and not the Absolute Brahma that entered the diverse creation as soul. All this is inconsistent with the detailed process of creation illustrated in II.4.1-3 of the Aitareya Āraṇyaka. In this Āraṇyaka and the Ṛgvedic hymn X.129, it is the Absolute Unmanifest and not the Prajāpati, who thought of procreation. It is once again the multi-headed, multi-eyed and multi-footed puruṣa who is responsible for the entire creation in the Ṛgvedic hymn called Puruṣa-Sukta (X. 90). No doubt, certain traits of this Ṛgvedic Puruṣa have been imported into the creative tortoise of the Taittirīya Āraṇyaka ; but all the same, this so-called eternal tortoise became active only when Prajāpati brooded over him. Thus, but for the initial activity on the part of Prajāpati, the Absolute Unmanifest would not have taken any initiative in creation of the universe and would have preferred to lie dormant. It is also not known as to how Prajāpati himself came into existence of his own. Thus, the account of creation given in the Taittirīya Āraṇyaka not only suffers from certain basic infirmities as detailed out above ; but is also very pithy as compared to the corresponding accounts in the Ṛgveda and the Aitareya Āraṇyaka.

Supplementing the above account of the creation of the universe, the present section[42] contains all the 16 verses of Puruṣa hymn (X. 90) of the Ṛgveda. In fact, two more verses have been embodied in this section. Elucidating the process of creation of the universe, it has been said that in the beginning there was Puruṣa alone who was multi-headed, multi-eyed and multi-footed. It not only permeated the entire universe; but was beyond that also. All the past and future animate and inanimate creatures are nothing but Puruṣa only. He is lord of immortality. Whatever living existence is there in the world; that waxes greater by food. His greatness is really lofty; but Puruṣa is still greater. All creatures are one-fourth of Him and three-fourth of his Eternal Self is in heaven. The entire universe is created and recreated by the remaining one-fourth thereof. He permeates the entire animate and inanimate creation. From Him, virāj was born. From that virāṭ, another (third) Puruṣa was born. This third Puruṣa spread Himself eastward and westward over the earth. When gods prepared the sacrifice with Puruṣa as their offering; the spring, summer and winter seasons become ghee, wood and oblations respectively. They sprinkled the earliest born Puruṣa with water who was offered as oblation in this sacrifice. With Him, the deities and all Sādhyās and Rishis sacrificed. From that sacrifice, in which Primordial Puruṣa was completely offered as sacrifice, ghee was created. He formed the creatures of the air, domestic as well as wild animals. From that great sacrifice, Ṛgvedic verses, Sāma-hymns, metres, yajus, horses, cattle with two rows of teeth, kine, goats and sheep were generated. From His mouth, arms, thighs and feet Brahmins, Rājanayas, Vaiśyas and Śūdras were produced. Similarly moon, Sun, Indra, fire, air, atmosphere sky, earth, regions were generated from mind, eyes, mouth, breath, navel, head, feet and ears respectively.

The Course of Evolution from the Primal Ātman

A very elaborate explanation of the generation of all the objects in the universe is offered in the Upanishadic portion of the Aitareya Āraṇyaka.[43] It can safely be regarded the fullest account of the process of evolution of the universe in the forest texts and the supervening upanishads. We are told there, that in the beginning the Ātman alone existed, and there was no other blinking thing whatsoever. The Ātman thought to himself; let me create the worlds; whereupon he created the four worlds, namely those of the super-celestial region of waters, the heavens with their celestial lights, the mortal earth and the subterranean region of waters. After these worlds were created, the Ātman proceeded to create first a World Person (Puruṣa)—an intermediate entity between the Ātman and the subsequently created universe. Continuing the process of creation, the Ātman created the individual soul last of all. It was the Ātman Himself which entered the bodies of the creatures—thereby a complete metaphysical identity between the individual soul and the supreme soul was established.

Likewise, the Taittirīya Āraṇyaka[44] also lays down : "From this Soul (Ātman) verily space arose; from space, wind; from wind fire; from fire, water; from water, the earth; from the earth, herbs; from herbs, food; from` food, semen; from semen, the person (S. 33). This is a complete enumeration of the five different elements which are described as having proceeded one after another from the primeval Ātman; who, to all intents and purposes, is described in the passage as not playing any very active part in creation. It is significant to note that the expression that is used in the passage to designate the fact of emanation is saṁbhutaḥ. Obviously, it entails not a process of any positive creation; but that of gradual evolution from the Supreme Source called Ātman. Thus, the process of coming into existence of universe as delineated in the Taittrīya Āraṇyaka (which portion now constitutes the Taittirīya Upanishad) does depict the Supreme Brahman to be Sole Originator of this universe.

Emanation of the Universe

Before describing the process of emanation of the universe, this section[45] puts forth two questions whether the wise and the ignorant are equal in death and both are overtaken by the same fate. Does the man, who has not the knowledge, go to the world of the Brahman when he dies or does he fail to do so ? Does the man of knowledge, when he sheds the body, go on to taste and share the riches of the Brahman ? The Āraṇyaka does not explicitly reply to both of these questions. However, with a view to prove that the Brahman is the Supreme Source of all the worlds and that the entire creation is one connected and seried manifestation of the one Brahman, the seer of the Hermit text immediately proceeds to explain the emanation of the universe out of Brahman. The Creator desired that He may become many and may Himself procreate. He practised penance or concentrated on Himself in thought and by the force of His brooding, created, all things that exist. Having created them entered into them, become Himself both the manifest and the unmanifest, the defined and the undefined, the based and the unbased, the conscious and the unconscious, the true and the false. He became all truth, even whatsoever here exists. Therefore, they say of Him that He is truth (S. 34).

Continuing the process of elaboration of the emanation of this universe from God, it has been said[46] that "at the beginning of all things, what existed was Non-Existent and Unmanifest. From this, manifest Existence was born. Manifest (or Being) shaped itself of its own accord. It is thus that it is called well-made or self-made." (S. 35). Obviously, in this agnostic conception of a primal non-existent, this forest text is anticipated by that famous Nāsadīya Sūkta, which tells us that at the beginning of all things, there was neither Being nor Not-Being; but what existed was only an ocean of Night (RV X.129.3). By Not-Being, we must understand not absolute Not-Being; but only relative Not-Being, the primal semblance of existence as contrasted with later concrete existence.

Evolution of the Macrocosm

Despite the heterogeneous nature of the verses collected in section X. 1 and the ritualistic pattern they have been set in, there are three verses quoted from Ṛgveda (X. 190.1-3) which very precisely delineate the process of evolution of the macrocosm from the Supreme Being. It has been said that from the self-illuminating Supreme, truth (of thought) and truthfulness[47] (of speech) were born, thence was night generated, thence also the watery ocean.[48]

From the watery ocean, the year was subsequently produced. Then, the ruler of the sentient and insentient beings ordained days and nights.

In the beginning, the Creator created the Sun, the moon, the sky, the earth, the firmament and heaven (S. 36).

Concept of Atman

The Taittrīya Āraṇyaka[49] rather very beautifully states that the soul is neither male or female, nor is it of an intermediate sex : What body it takes in that body does he lie ensconced. The same Ātman permeates in all the animate and inanimate beings. All the creatures worship the same God who pervades in all animals as well as the gross elements. This very God is omnipresent and after having entered the various bodies (as Ātman), feels bound to them. In some bodies, it is known as female while in others as male. Though gifted with eyes, the people do behave like blind persons on account of lack of discrimination in discerning the intrinsic nature of various manifestations. There takes place a complete identification of the Ātman with the body in which it resides. Due to this erroneous identification, the self-conscious Ātman feels bound to wordly lurements and possessions. It has no visible or discernible physical frame; but all the same, it feels attracted towards costly things like jewels, gold, etc. of the world and wants to wear and praise them (S. 37). All this is attributable to the lack of proper appreciation by human beings of the real nature of their Self.

Unlike other trees, the wordly tree has its roots above and branches below. Hence, a person who is aware of this basic philosophy refuses to believe that the Ātman is subject to death and the diverse phases of life (accompanied by pleasures and pains) leave him unaffected. He takes them affecting only the body and not the soul residing therein (S. 38). Inherently speaking, the Ātman has His abode and sustenance only in the Sole Supreme-Being of the world. It is neither subject to death nor is in any actually grieved in any situation.

Three noteworthy verses of the Taittirīya Āraṇyaka[50] give certain significant facts about the features of the human body and real nature of the Self. It has been stated that the human body has eight wheels (like skin, flesh, bones etc.), nine gates (like eyes, ears, nostrils, mouth etc.) and it is the invincible abode of gods. In this body, there is a golden sheath or store which is the abode of happiness and is beset with a light. One who knows this body (which is beset with an immortal existence) as abode of Brahman, on him both Brahma and Brahmā bestow long life, eminence and offsprings. Brahmā entered this lustrous and golden (human) fortress which is remover of sins, beset with fame and is also invincible (S. 39).

The Epistemology of Self-consciousness

The five Kośas or the sheaths of the soul have been elucidated in sections 1 to 5 of Book VIII of Taittirīya Āraṇyaka. After explaining the first three sheaths, namely, the physical, the astral and the mental; the seer of the Āraṇyaka rather makes a very cryptic observation regarding the essentially unknowable nature of the self. "From the ultimate reality, words together with the mind turn back because of their inability to comprehend its fullness. One who knows the bliss of Brahman does not at all fear at any time[51] (S. 40). This observation, studded almost midway in the elucidation of the various bodies or sheaths of the soul, has indeed great significance. The seer of the Āraṇyaka seems to have well realised the limitations and imperfections of the human mind to know the Self which is the eternal knower of objects. No doubt God and the Self are unknowable; but the sage of the Āraṇyaka seems to disbelieve that they are objects of faith only. On the contrary, he felt that God and the Self are both objects of mystical realisation. It is impelled by this conviction that sage of the Āraṇyaka invokes into service greater and more powerful faculties like knowledge and the Self of Bliss itself to unravel the real nature of the secret of the Manifestation or the Ultimate Reality. Thus, it has been proved that even though the Self is generally "Unknowable" ; yet all the same, there is no bar for the Supreme Knower to know itself. The Self can be realised through self-contemplation in which the Self is most mysteriously both the subject and object of knowledge.

Significance of OM and its identification with Brahman

While detailing out as to how the Brahman-Yajña is to be performed,[52] it has been said that when all the preliminaries have been completed; then first of all; 'OM' should be recited. This 'OM' is representative of the three vedas. In it entire speech is contained and it is the Supreme Imperishable One (S. 41). OM has three more AUM which it might easily be seen to contain. Sāyaṇa quotes from Atharva Veda, Chhāndogya, Aitareya and Kaṭha Upanishads to elucidate all the three ingredients of the above statement. Furthermore, this Āraṇyaka unequivocally declares that all the ṛks and all gods find their supreme abode in the symbol OM and a person who does not know this significance, he will gain no benefit from the study of Ṛgveda (S. 42). This obviously brings out the supreme significance of this syllable.

The Tartirīya Āraṇyaka[53] unequivocally declares that OM is Brahman. It further declares that all this is Brahman. With OM, the Sāmans are chanted. Śastras to be recited by the hotṛ priest in certain sacrifices begin with OM and Śom. It is with OM that the Adhvaryu and Brahmā priests utter the response and the introductory eulogy respectively. It is with prior recitation of OM that one assents to the offering to fire. With OM, a Brahmin begins to recite that he may attain Brahman and verily does he so (S. 43). All this hardly needs any comments. It is also to be noticed that OM is described as not merely the supreme means of meditation; but the goal to be reached by the meditation itself. The OM occupies in Indian philosophy the same position which the logos occupies in Christology.

Ethics

The Taititrīya Āraṇyaka [54] attaches great importance to the adoption of high ethical values in life. It has been laid down that a human being owes a debt to the deities and he may de discharged of the same by doing good deeds. Just as a child after delivery is freed of the confinement of the womb; so, "Oh God! release us of all our misdeeds and bestow happiness on us." Open up routes of the sacred worlds. We may also practise charity so as to attain heaven. Then, comes the advice to a married couple to continue to perform yajña in life; be amiable to each other and also do righteous deeds. The earth and Aditi are our mother; the atmosphere brother and the sin is our enemy. The heaven is like our father. They promote our well-being. We may not attain to those low worlds to which go the persons who die issueless (S. 44). Heaven is attained by good hearted, straight forward and righteous persons after being relieved of all the diseases. From there, we can joyfully see our ancestors as well as successors (S. 45). Whatever food, gold and other possessions have wrongfully been acquired and thereafter consumed by the reciter or offered to the deities, he may be relieved of the sin so committed mentally or through word of the mouth. The desire to be sinless permeates section II.7. Performance of the Kūsmāṇḍa yajña cleanses a person of all his sins and is essential for self-purification. Sinners like thieves of gold, killers of a learned Brahmin, embryo and a sodomite have no right to perform the above-said sacrifice. During the period of consecration, personal morals are also to be strictly kept high. Meat eating, sexual intercourse, sleeping on a cot and telling of lies is strictly prohibited. In fact, the consecrated person has been advised to depend only on milk, rice-gruel or a mixture of boiled and coagulated milk. At the most, he can take rice, roasted barely or powder thereof.

The Book VI of the Taittirīya Āraṇyaka[55] is also studded with certain verses which unequivocally advocate and uphold leading of morally upright life. Most of these verses are contained in the Ṛgveda and one or two in the Yajur and Atharvedas. The prayer[56] goes forth to God to wash off our sins and also purify our means of livelihood. We may successfully escape the clutches of death and live a long life. We may be rich in children and possessions, cleansed, purified and regular performers of yajña (S. 46). Verses are also there which say, "Oh God! you are birthless. Take off all our sins and hatred or enmities. You are yavaḥ (a particular astron). So, likewise free us from our sins and repugnances."

The first eight verses contained in section 11 are contained in Ṛgveda (I. 97) and also in Atharvaveda (IV. 33). The closing part of all the eight verses unfailingly puts forth the prayer that God may take off all our sins. The first verse also solicits for purification of our earnings. Third verse also contains the prayer that even those who are revile from among us, they too, like the good ones, be devotees of God. It has further been prayed that as water automatically flows down from the slopes and also from higher level to lower levels; similarly sins may flow off from our lives. Both of these verses (No. 9 and 10) are not found in any of the vedas. All the above quoted verses are very emphatic protogonists of honest earnings, freedom from sins in our lives, performance of yajña and leading of a pure and above-board life.

The invocation (S. 47) contained in the very opening stanza of this section[57] speaks of the firm determination of the speaker that he shall speak of the right and of what is true. This vow has special significance and much more so in the modern times—particularly when materialism and obsession of reaping immediate gains has taken pre-eminently predominating sway over the thoughts, words and deeds of the human-beings. In the present days, there is oft-repeated advocacy of being tactful and diplomatic in our conversation and diverse other deliberations in our daily mundane life. Such a behaviour pre-supposes action according to the exigencies of the occasion irrespective of the moral and ethical considerations involved. In case the above-quoted vow of sticking to Ṛtam and Satyam is to be practically adhered to in life; then there is hardly any scope for in-play of tactfulness and diplomacy in our lives. The latter do pre-suppose that falsehood can be invoked into service if that serves our material ends. As soon as this is done, the above vow loses all practical significance. There is no midway if spiritual exaltation and revelation of the Self is to be attained in this life. If this objective is to be made a practical feasibility; then so-called tactfulness and diplomacy shall have to be carefully and vigilantly warded off in our lives. Sticking to the right and truth in life does not in any way entail that we are to be dry, curt, unhelpful and discourteous in our speech and actions. On the contrary, it does cut short the need of much of the verbosity and avoidable reasoning. A truthful person is simply required to be sweet; but firm in his various deliberations. No adumbration or presentation of ostensible show of sincerity and friendship is required to be put up. Things become self-evident and a truthful and right thinking person soon comes to be assessed in his true perspective without any extra effort or appeasement on his part. In case the pledge to epeak the truth and the right is adhered to in life; the path to self-realisation is also progressively enlightened so much so that fundamentally sound preposition of Mahābhārata that "happiness lies in good conduct" lands in the life of the practiser of truth and he becomes a veritable abode of happiness in this very life.

The repetition of Śānti, śānti at the end of this invocation has a message to convey. No doubt, Saṅkara has interpreted it to represent the ādhidaivika, ādhyātmika and ādhibhautika aspects of peace in life; but this repetition of peace, peace does firmly and emphatically stress on the raciter that he is to carry on the various deliberations of his life with full equanimity, even-mindedness and peace inside as well as outside himself. He is not to be carried away by momentary reactions; but is invariably to be guided and led by basic human and moral considerations so that he may be a wise person in the real sense. An upanishadic verse does reiterate that wise persons who know the significance of immortality, do not seek anything stable in this world wherein everything is unstable (Kathopanishad, II.1.2).

The Taittirīya Āraṇyaka[58] catalogues the most important of all the observances that are essential fer leading a happy life. A human being desirous of the same must have in life perfect purity of heart or righteousness, truthfulness, austerity, self-control, tranquility and humanism. He must perform daily oblations to the fire. He must respect and entertain the guests. He must procreate, produce children and thus propagate the race. He must also regularly carry on self-study and teaching of the Veda and other books of true knowledge. We are also told the opinions of three different moralists, each of whom insisted upon a special virtue. The sage Satyavachas Rāthītara taught the virtue of Truth. The sage Taponitya Pauruśiṣṭi insisted upon the virtue of penance. Finally, the sage Nāko Maudgalya said that there was no virtue higher than the study and teaching of the Sacred Books, for that, he said constituted penance (S. 48). This section attaches greatest significance to and unmitigated emphasis on self-study and teaching for achievement of the objective of happiness in life.

Section VII.11 is most hortative. It adopts a deliberately didactic tone and impresses a number of virtues to be adopted. It contains a direct moral advice imparted by the teacher to the outgoing pupil. When the pupil has finished the course of his studies at his master's house or hermitage, the master by way of parting advice, tells him to speak the truth, to respect the law or Dharma; and not to swerve from the study of the Vedas; after having offered to the preceptor the kind of wealth he would choose, he should go into the world to marry and to produce children so that the family lineage may not be broken. The pupil is further advised not to desist from the duties that are due to gods and the fathers; to regard the parents, the preceptor and the guest as his gods. In general, the pupil is advised only to perform those actions which might be regarded as faultless by the society. Those, says the Spiritual Teacher, who are higher than ourselves in Brahminhood, should be respected by "giving a seat"— an expression which is otherwise interpreted as implying also that in the presence of such, not a word should be breathed by the disciple." The teacher also tells the disciple to practise charity with faith and not with unfaith, with magnanimity, modesty, awe and sympathy (S. 49).

Coming over to the rules for moral conduct, this section tells the disciple that he should follow only the good actions of the Spiritual Teacher; that he might even more profitably follow the good actions of those who are still better situated than the Spiritual Teacher. If ever, he should seek to find out the intimate nature of duty or conduct, then he should always be guided by this one principle only, namely, how the Brahmins, who are sound in judgement, devoted to good deeds, not led by others and lovers of virtue, conduct themselves in that particular case (S. 50). This quotation evidently implies the maxim that we should always mould our conduct on the pattern of conduct of those who are better than ourselves and are in a position to give us rules of conduct by their example. There is an Oligarchy in Morality, as there is an Oligarchy in the Society or the State. It is the voice of the Moral Oligarchy which, according to this section, ought to prevail in supplying us with the pattern of conduct.

Need for being hospitable towards guests has once again been reiterated rather in greater detail in this Āraṇyaka.[59] It has been commanded that residence be not denied to anybody at your dwelling as that is the rule. Therefore, in any way whatsoever one should acquire much food. The stranger in the dwelling should, therefore, be addressed to arise (and partake of food) as the same is ready. Serving of food without delay; with some delay and finally with lot of delay has identical repercussions as to how the host shall himself be treated whenever he happens to be a guest with somebody else (S. 51).

The first eighteen verses of this section[60] rather constitute a collection of such verses from the various extant and inextant saṁhitās which are characteristically henotheistic in their approach in delineating the supreme qualities of Prajāpati. Thereafter have been given a plethora of verses that contain prayers to diverse gods and goddesses like Mahādeva, Rudra, Durgā, Kātyāyana, Durgi, Nārāyaṇa, Vāsudeva, Vishnu, earth, Varuṇa, Agni, Indra, Jātavedas, waters; personified birds/grass like Garuḍa, Dūrvā etc.

The multiplicity of these verses given rather in quick succession repeatedly brings out the prayers for our riddance from sins, evil deeds and various fears. Varuṇa has been entreated to grant his saving grace to the devotee for having enjoyed what belonged to bad people and also having accepted gifts from sinners. Whatever sins have been committed by the reciter and his people in thought, word and deed, the same may completely be destroyed by Indra, Varuṇa, Bṛhaspati and Savitṛ (S. 52). Whatever injurious, impure and troublesome is there in the waters may be destroyed. A significant prayer puts forth that whatever sins have been committed by the reciter by unlawful eating, unlawful drinking and accepting gifts from a sinful person; the same may be effaced by the hand of King Varuṇa Being thus sinless, stainless and unbound by evil and bondage; the supplicant may ascend to the blissful heaven and enjoy living in the close company of Brahman Himself (S. 53). Doing of wrong actions, breaking of the vow of chastity, committing of theft, killing of an embryo and outrage of a preceptor's honour have been catalogued as great sins and prayers go forth for being absolved of the same (S. 54) followed by repeated prayers to the seers, Vasus etc. for purification of our lives. Prayers are also there in plenty to the various deities to bestow on us a span of 100 years of healthy life, prosperity, removal of all troubles, full protection to ourselves, our children and cattle, enhancement of happiness in our lives and grant of good fortune. All this analysis lays added emphasis on leading of a morally exalted life with full faith in God who was taken as the Supreme helper, guide and repository in life.

Moral Uprightness—A means to mystical perfection

It is for the second time that book VIII of the Taittirīya Āraṇyaka quotes (with a minor verbal change) the stanza[61] which means that the words and mind both fail to attain the Brahman. One who knows the bliss of the Brahman does not at all feel afraid of anything (S. 40). This repetition has a significance in so much so that the Ultimate Reality is unseizable in terms of thought and speech. Earlier this stanza was inserted midway in the elaboration of the five kośas and here in the later section,[62] it has immediately succeeded the narration regarding gradual rise of the Self from those of food, prāṇa etc. to that of bliss. This obviously means that the Brahman is only an object of mystical realisation rather than anything attainable by the human organs and speech. Ipso facto, the entire life has to be faultlessly attuned to a higher moral standard so as to culminate in mystical realisation. If such morality is ensured in life, then there is no feeling of repentance for the man. He never thinks as to why he did not do good deeds or why he did only evil actions. He has come to learn of the nature of Reality and has thus gone beyond the reach of these duals (S. 55). Thus, according to the seers of the Āraṇyakas, leading of a morally exalted life has a positive correlation with ultimate realisation of the Self.

Significance of good deeds in life

The Taittirīya Āraṇyaka[63] precisely and very aptly brings out the importance of good deeds and abhorrence of falsehood in human life. The relevant verse says that "just as the fragrance of a tree in full blossom is wafted by the wind from a distant place, similarly the fragrance of meritorious deeds spreads to a distant place. Again if a sword is laid across a pit with its sharp edge upwards and a man intends to walk on it with his bare feet, he shall, ipso facto, be perturbed by the very thought of either injuring his feet if he walks on the sword or of falling into the pit. Similarly a man must guard himself nay hate telling of lies or committing sins" (S. 56). The path of virtue alone is the royal road for the seekers of liberation. This view is further fortified from a Ṛgvedic verse (V. 82.5) quoted in the next section[64] which unequivocally puts forth the prayer that "Oh Divine Being ! take off all sins from our lives and fill all the virtues in us" (S. 57). The seer of the Āraṇyaka does not seem to feel satisfied with leading of a virtuous life when we are awake or up and doing. He goes further and quotes another Ṛgvedic prayer (V. 82.4) which, *inter alia*, contains the prayer to the Almighty that evil thoughts may be wiped off even from our dreams. All this supports the inevitable surmise that vedic seers looked upon the faculty of God realisation not from psychological, but from moral point of view.

Universal brotherhood among men

The present day world is seriously ravaged by strifes, mutual rivalries and such like animosities among the nationals of various countries. Despite so many political, racial, and economic causes such animosities are basically attributable to the fact that each nation or class or group of persons even in a single country feel themselves as distinct and specifically distinguishable from other such class or classes of men and women. This is based on sheer ignorance about their identical origin and growth from the same Mother Earth. Existence of this knowledge—nay belief and its adoption in life can play wonders in bringing about harmony, sweetness, coherence, brotherhood, co-operation, give and take, magnanimity etc. among all the human brethsens of the world. This can emerge not only among various nations; but even among the diverse members of a single nation or country. This is one of the greatest and indubitably rare lessons that the vedic literature bestows on the present day strife-torn humanity. The vedas have declared that all men are sons of the same Immortal Father.[65] This has, in a way, been reiterated in the Taittirīya Āraṇyaka,[66] when it unequivocally declares that "Aditi is the selfsame Mother of gods, celestial ministrels, men, manes, demons and all other creatures and is gifted with rare qualities like fertility, extensiveness, greatness, deified motherliness, praiseworthiness, virtue etc." (S. 58). Ṛgveda also, *inter alia*, declares[67] that "Aditi is mother, father and son; Aditi is all the goods; Aditi is the five classes of men." Hence, from this common origin, all human-beings have a big lesson to learn of living in peace with each other.

Purification of entire fabric of life

The verses contained in these sections[68] lay great stress on self-control and purification of all our physical limbs, mind, intellect, intentions, aims and all the five bodies or sheaths of the soul, freedom from sinful life and subduing of diverse passions so that the entire fabric of life may first of all rise to a higher moral pedestal before the man can possibly conceive of attaining self-realisation. Thus, the vedic literature repeatedly looks upon the faculty of self-realisation not from the psychological, but from moral point of view in life.

Five Sheaths of the Soul

First five sections of Book VIII detail out what are known as sheaths or bodies of the soul. These are Five Persons—the Annamaya, the Prāṇamaya, the Manomaya, the Vijñānamaya and the Ānandamaya. Each of them envelopes or ensouls the previous one and governs its respective fields of Matter, Life, Mind, Knowledge and Bliss :

(*i*) *The Physical Sheath* (*Annamaya Kośa*) : While explaining the emanatory theory of cosmogony, it has been said that from the primeval Ātman, the five gross elements were evolved. From the earth, emanated herbs and plants; from the latter food and from food, man was born. Thus, even man, the highest evolved creature that walks on the earth, is a product of the physical substance of matter called food. He is, therefore, inherently speaking, essence of food (S. 33).

Man comes into being with the birth of his body which is constituted of the essence and the modifications of Matter and he dies with the disintegration of that body of matter. Whatever the other principles active in him like mind, life etc., they depend for their existence and functioning on the physical body and are, normally, wholly conditioned by it. Whichever way one looks at this human being in creation, horizontally or vertically, he is an evolute of Matter-Food.

"Poised in the principle of Matter, it (Spirit or Self) becomes the physical self of a physical universe in the region of a physical Nature : Spirit is then absorbed in its experience of Matter; it is dominated by the ignorance and inertia of the tāmasic Power proper to physical existence. In the individual, it becomes a materialised soul, annamaya puruṣa, whose life and mind have developed out of the ignorance and inertia of the material principle and are subject to their fundamental limitations. For life in Matter works in dependence on the body; mind in Matter works in dependence on the body and on the nervous being; spirit itself in Matter is limited and divided in its self-relation and its power by the limitations and divisions of the matter-governed and life-driven mind. This materialised soul lives bound to the physical body and its narrow superficial external consciousness, and it takes normally the experiences of its physical organs, its senses, its matter-bound life and mind, with at most some limited spiritual glimpses as the whole truth of existence (Śri Aurobindo).[69]

(*ii*) *The Astral Sheath* (*Prāṇamaya Kośa*) : Physical substance (Matter) provides indeed the base, the hard rock of existence. But it needs something else to vivify it, to enliven it. That is done by Prāṇa, the Life force. Without this life-element in it, Matter is dead matter. Enlivening the physical form of all entities in the universe, there flows a life-energy. That is, why, the Āraṇyaka proceeds on to say that there is a second and inner self which is other than that of the substance of food. It is made of the vital stuff called Prāṇa. The Self of vital air fills the Self of food and it is like the shape of man... This Self of vital air is the soul in the body of the former one which was of food.

Of this Prāṇamaya Puruṣa,[70] the in-breath is the head; the diffused breath that distributes and the Apāna (the breath of death which gives away the vital force out of the body) are the twin sides; earth (physical matter) is its base and foundation; and ether is the very soul of its being.

The gods, men and beasts live and breathe under the dominion of prāṇa; for it is the life of created things and is called the Life-Stuff of All.[71]

The spirit can be poised in the principle of life, not in matter. The Spirit so founded becomes the vital self of a vital world, the Life-soul of a Life-energy in the reign of a dynamic Nature. In the individual, this spirit becomes a vital soul, prāṇamaya puruṣa. This vital soul lives in a vital body composed of a substance much subtler than physical matter. It is a substance surcharged with conscious energy, capable of much more powerful perceptions, capacities, and sense-activities than the gross atomic elements of earth-matter can offer. Prāṇa is, therefore, to be experienced and realised as Brahman itself, as a manifestation of Brahman as Power for its fullest potency to be dynamised in oneself. It has, therefore, rightly been said in the Āraṇyaka that those who worship the Eternal (Brahman) as vital air, reach Life to the uttermost.

(*iii*) *The Mental Sheath* (*Manomaya Kośa*) : The vital air which vitalises the physical body does not, however, operate all by itself. It is not a blind, mechanically active force. It is informed, guided and led by the operation of a principle of consciousness. Wherever there is life, there is behind it an operating consciousness which in its awakened form is termed Mind. The self of this Mind-plane of existence is called the monomaya puruṣa.

More internal than that which is made up of vital air is another self which is made of Mind. The Self of Mind fills the Self of vital air ... And this Self of Mind is the soul in the body to the former one which was of vital air.[72]

Above matter and life stands the principle of mind, nearer to the secret of origin of things. The spirit poised in mind becomes the mental self of a mental world and dwells there in the reign of its own pure and luminous mental nature. In the individual, the spirit so poised becomes a mental soul, mano-maya puruṣa. The mind in its own plane is not limited by life and obstructed by matter. This mental soul lives in a mental or subtle body which enjoys capacities of knowledge, perception, a free delicate and extensive mentalised sense-faculty not limited by the grosser conditions of the life-nature or the physical nature.

(*iv*) *Intuitional Sheath* (*the Supramental Person*) : The above elucidated Mental sheath is not the last word. In the very nature of things, mind is imperfect, incomplete and patently too limited in its field and power to be the ultimate puruṣa of the manifestation, individual or universal. Mind is dependent. It cannot know or act by itself. It depends upon the senses and other faculties for its functioning. By its own constitution, the human mind proceeds by a separative, analytic process of thought and can hence arrive at only partial truth of things. It is only a greater faculty with a larger sweep of Vision and Power that can possess the Knowledge and the Secret of the Manifestation. Such an active Principle is Knowledge and the Supreme Being expressed and governing it is the Vijñānamaya puruṣa. The Āraṇyaka, therefore, says that there in an inner self which is other than that which is of Mind and it is made of Knowledge. The Self of Knowledge fills the Self of Mind... And this Self of Knowledge is the soul in the body to the former which was of Mind.[73]

The word vijñāna is not synonymous with buddhi or intellect. It is the term for a higher principle in the cosmic manifestation. This is what is called Mahas or the supermind. It is a knowledge proper to a higher grade of the Spirit's Being. It is at once Knowledge and Power. Of this Supramental Person, it has been said that Faith is its head, Truth and Ṛta are its two sides and the Mahas (the vast light) is its base and yoga (union) is the ātman of its being. Such a Knowledge Power directs the sacrifice and all deeds. All the gods offer adoration to him as to Brahman and Elder of the Universe. If a person worships Brahman as the Knowledge and neither swerves from it nor falters, then he casts off all of his sins and attains all desires.

The transition from the mind-self to the knowledge-self is the great and the decisive transition in the yoga. It is the shaking off of the last hold on us of the cosmic ignorance and our firm foundation in the Truth of things.

(*v*) *The Beatific Sheath* (*The Self of Bliss*) : Even the self of Knowledge-Power is not the inner-most self. There is behind it another Self which constitutes the soul of the Vijñānamaya puruṣa, in fact the ultimate core of all other Puruṣas, of all the tiers of manifestation. The Hermit text goes on to say that "there is yet a second and inner self which is other than this which is of knowledge and it is fashioned out of Bliss (ānanda-maya). The Self of Bliss fills the Self of Knowledge. The Bliss Self is made in the image of a man according as is the human image of the other. This Self of Bliss is the soul in the body to the former one which was of knowledge."[74]

It is this Ānandamaya Puruṣa who makes possible the

existence of all the Puruṣas. Bliss is the very nature of Brahman. It is from the fountain spring of Ānanda in its supreme ebullience that all creation issues forth, is motivated and maintained. The Self of Bliss is not supported by any other Self like the previous selves; but it is based, indeed arises directly out of Brahman of which it is the very nature.

Of this Self, a spontaneous Joy (moda) and Happiness (pramoda) are the twin sides; love is its head. Brahman itself is its direct base and Ānanda (the Supreme Bliss) is the core (ātman).

Beatificism

In our mundane life, material prosperity as well as spiritual exaltation are both essential for leading a happy life. However, the Taittirīya Āraṇyaka[75] makes an interesting analysis of the conception of bliss. Physical good has itself been taken as an aspect of 'bliss' as spiritual good constitutes the acme of 'bliss.' A scale of values has been detailed out connecting the so-called physical bliss on the one hand with the highest spiritual bliss on the other. It has been stated that the unit of measurement may be taken to be "the happiness of a young man of noble birth and of good learning, who is very swift, firm and strong and to whom is granted the possession of the whole earth full of wealth. Of a hundred such blisses is made the bliss of the human genii; of a hundred blisses of these genii is made the bliss of the divine genii; of a hundred of these latter blisses of the manes is made the bliss of the gods who are born gods; of a hundred of these is made the bliss of the gods who have become gods by their actions; of a hundred blisses of these gods is made the bliss of highest gods; of a hundred blisses of these gods is made the bliss of Indra; a hundred blisses of Indra constitute the bliss of Bṛhaspati; of a hundred such blisses is made the bliss of Prajāpati; and a hundred blisses of Prajāpati make the bliss of Brahman; and each time, it has been told that all the blisses, severally and progressively, belong to the man who is well versed in the Vedas and is free from all desires" (S.59).

Obviously the above quoted repeated affirmations reveal that a seeker, while he is still in flesh and blood, can realise in himself each of the states of beatitude in the higher grades of being provided he strives and equips himself that wise. This possibility which is ever-present before a human-being is not open to other orders in creation. Ipso facto, it is to this Bliss of Brahman that the man who knows arrives. Here is the clear answer to the questions posed in an earlier section[76] as to what is the state in which the man of knowledge finds himself after death and what of him who has not the knowledge.

Psychology of Fear and Functioning of Cosmos

Looking to the archaic past in which the seers of the Āraṇyakas lived in India, it is really surprising to find that they could have developed so much psychological reflection to their credit. They were not only foremost in their age in philosophical reflection in general; but were so in psychological reflection in particular. Analysing the psychology of fear, it has been said that a man finds himself firmly established in fearlessness so long as he realises the invisible, bodiless, undefinable and supportless Brahman as his real self. As soon as this basic conception becomes weak or feeble and distinctive notion of individuality envelops him; he is at once greatly engrossed by the psychology of fear, "It is only when a feeling of otherness gains lodgment in us that we come to entertain the emotion of fear.[77] That indeed is the fear of one who thinks of himself[78] as knower. Through the fear of Him (*i. e.* Brahman) the wind blows, the Sun rises, fire, Indra and death Speed along." Thus, it is this basic sense of fear or otherness which is the basic cause of unhappiness, misery, strife, despise etc. However, this basic notion or emotion permeating among all has a constructive off-shoot also. The Āraṇyaka itself unequivocally puts forth that it is under the fear of the Supreme that even all cosmic activity like blowing of the wind, rising/setting of the Sun etc., takes place. The regularity and perfection with which all the cosmic forces function do presuppose the existence of an intelligent guide. This is a clear proof of God in the laws of the universe.

Definition of Austerity

The Taittirīya Āraṇyaka[79] lays down that righteousness, truthfulness, hearing of Vedas, control of sense organs, charity, and Yajña constitute austerity. The Brahman has manifested Himself as the three vyāhṛtis. Meditate upon Him. This is austerity par excellence (S. 60). All the six items separately emphasised here as 'austerity' practically include all that is required for a complete moral and spiritual discipline.

NOTES AND REFERENCES

1. AA., I. 1.4.
2. AA., I. 3.2.
3. Bhagavad Gītā., II. 62.
4. AA., I. 3.3.
5. AA., I. 3.8.
6. AA., II. 1.3.
7. AA., II. 1.6.
8. AA., II. 3.6.
9. TA., VIII. 1.
10. A.A., II. 3.6.
11. AA., III. 1.6.
12. AA., II. 2.
13. AA., II. 2.3.
14. *Ibid.*, II. 2.4.
15. AA., II. 1.2.
16. *Ibid.*, II. 3.1.
17. AA., II. 1.1.
18. AA., II. 3.6.
19. AA., II. 3.6.
20. AA., II. 3.8.
21. RV., X. 129.2.
22. AA., II. 4.1.
23. AA., II. 4.2.
24. A.A., II. 4.1.
25. *Ibid.*, II. 4.3.
26. Bṛh. Up. III. 4.1.
27. AA. Keith, A.B., p. 202 (note 9).
28. AA., II. 5.1.
29. *Ibid.*, II. 4.3.
30. As given by Keith in AA. P. 234 (note 9). Original not consulted.
31. *Ibid.*, II. 5.1.

32. He is a Ṛgvedic sage and the fourth Book of Ṛgveda is ascribed to him and his descendants. Mysticism attributed to him in the Ṛgveda is not relevant here.
33. AA., III. 1. 1-2.
34. Śūravīrao Māṇḍūkeyaḥ (AA., III. 1.1).
35. A., III. 1.2.
36. TA., I. 8.
37. TA., I. 27.
38. TA., VI. 3.
39. *Ibid.*, X. 1.
40. TA., I. 23.
41. It has been maintained by some scholars like Dr. S.A. Dange (Pastoral Symbolism From The Ṛgveda, published by the University of Poona, July, 1970) that the vedic symbolism should be explained from the point of view of anthropological studies such as folk-philosophy or proto-philosophy. However, this is not a universally accepted view.
42. TA., III. 12.
43. AA., II. 4.
44. TA., VIII. 1.
45. TA., VIII. 6.
46. TA., VIII. 7.
47. According to Bhaṭṭabhaskara, commentator of this Āraṇyaka, ṛtam implies the totality of sentient beings and satyam, the individual souls.
48. Sāyaṇa observes that samudra means both firmament and ocean; the epithet arṇava is added to distinguish the latter.
49. T.A., I. 11.
50. TA., I. 27.
51. *Ibid.*, VIII, 4.
52. TA., II. 11.
53. TA., VII. 8.
54. TA., II. 6.8.
55. TA., VI. 10-11.
56. RV., X. 18.2.
57. TA., VII. 1.
58. TA., VII. 9.
59. TA., IX. 10.1. Earlier, it has been laid down in TA., VII. 11 that, *inter-alia*, a guest be served as a god.
60. TA., X. 1.

61. TA., VIII. 4, 9.
62. *Ibid.*, VIII. 9.
63. TA., X. 9.
64. TA., X. 10.10.
65. Śṛṇvantu viśve amṛtasya putrāḥ.
66. TA., X. 21.
67. RV., I. 89.10.
68. TA., X. 51-57, 60.
69. On Yoga, p. 531. Not consulted in original. cf. Pandit, M.P., The Upanishads, p. 137.
70. TA., VIII. 2.
71. TA., VIII. 3.
72. TA., VIII. 3.4.
73. TA., VIII. 4-5.
74. TA., VIII. 5-6.
75. TA., VIII. 8.
76. TA., VIII. 6.
77. TA., VIII. 7-8.
78. Hume and Sri Aurobindo have translated it by taking the reading as manvānasya [of a thinker (who is of course conceited)]. As the euphonic combination of viduṣo manvānasya and viduṣo' manvānasya is virtually the same; Sāyaṇa Saṅkara etc. have translated it as amanvānasya.
79. TA., X. 8.

SOURCES V

ऐतरेयारण्यकम्

१. वाग्वै धियावसुः । (१.१.४)

२. मनसि वै सर्वे कामाः श्रिता मनसा हि सर्वान्कामान्
ध्यायति । सर्वे हास्मिन् कामाः श्रयन्ते य एवं वेद ।
वाग्वै सर्वान् कामान् दुहे वाचा हि सर्वान् कामान् वदति ॥ (१.३.२)

३. यावद् ब्रह्म विष्ठितं तावती वागिति यत्र ह क्व च ब्रह्म
तद् वाग्यत्र वा वाक् तद् वा ब्रह्म त्येतत् तदुक्तं भवति ॥ (१.३.८)

४. तस्य वाक्तन्तिर् नामानि दामानि तदस्येदं वाचा तन्त्या
नामभिर् दामभिः सर्वं सितं सर्वं होदं नामनी ३ँ सर्वं
वाचाऽभिवदति ॥ (२.१.६)

५. वाक्प्राणेन संहितेति कौण्ठरव्यः प्राणः पवमानेन पवमानो
विश्वैर् देवैर् विश्वे देवाः स्वर्गेण लोकेन स्वर्गो लोको
ब्रह्मणा सैषाऽवरपरा संहिता ।। (३.१.६)

६. वाक्संहितेति पंचालचण्डः ।
वाचावै वेदाः संधीयन्ते वाचा छन्दांसि वाचा मित्राणि
संदधति वाचा सर्वाणि भूतान्यथो वागेवेदं सर्वमिति ।
तद्यत्रैतदधीते वा भाषते वा वाचि तदा प्राणो भवति वाक्तदा
प्राणं रेंहृढयथ यत्र तूष्णीं वा भवति स्वपिति वा प्राणे तदा
वाग्भवति प्राणस्तदा वाचं रेहृढि तावन्योन्यं
रीहढो वाग्वै माता प्राणः पुत्रः ॥ (३.१.६)

७. तमिन्द्र उवाच प्राणो वा अहमस्म्यृषे प्राणस्त्वं प्राणः
सर्वाणि भूतानि प्राणो ह्येष य एष तपति स एतेन रूपेण सर्वा
दिशो विष्टोऽस्मि तस्य मेऽन्नं मित्रं दक्षिणं तद् वैश्वामित्रमेष
तपन्नेवास्मि ॥ (२.२.४)

८. तद्योऽहं सौ सौ योऽसौ सोऽहम् ॥ (२.२.४)

ऐतरेयारण्यकम्

९. आत्मोक्थ पंचविधमेतस्माद्धीदं सर्वमुत्तिष्ठत्येतमेवाप्येति ॥ (२.३.१)

१०. एष पन्था एतत् कर्मैतद् ब्रह्मैतत् सत्यम् ।
तस्मान्न प्रमाद्येत् तन्नातीयात् ।
न ह्यत्यायन् पूर्वे येऽत्यायंस्ते परा बभूवुः ॥ (२.१.१)

११. पराग्वा एतद्रिक्तमक्षरं यदेतदो३मिति तद्यत्किंचोमित्याहात्रैवास्मै
तद्रिच्यते स यत्सर्वमों कुर्याद् रिंचादात्मानं स
कामेभ्यो नालं स्यात् ।
अथैतत्पूर्णमभ्यात्मं यन्नेति स यत्सर्वं नेति ब्रूयात्
पापिकाऽस्य कीर्तिर्जायेत सैनं तत्रैव हन्यात् ।
तस्मात् काल एव दद्यात् काले न दद्यात् तत् सत्यानृते मिथुनी
करोति तयोर् मिथुनात् प्रजायते भूयान् भवति ॥ (२.३.६)

१२. परमुत्कृष्टं जगत्कारणमखण्डैकरसं ब्रह्मतत्त्वमंचति गच्छति
प्रतिपादयतीति पराक् । अत एव संसाराद् बहिर् भूतं
सद् रिक्तं संसारभोगशून्यम् ॥
[पृष्ठ १६९—मन्त्र २.३.६. के नीचे सायण की टिप्पणो]

१३. साऽस्यैतमात्मानमत्र गतं भावयति सा भावयित्री भावयितव्या
भवति । तं स्त्री गर्भं बिभर्ति सोऽग्र एव कुमारं जन्मनोऽग्रेऽधि
भावयति । स यत् कुमारं जन्मोऽग्रेऽधिभावयत्यात्मानमेव
तद् भावयति । एषा लोकानां संतत्या ॥ (२.५.१)

१४. सोऽस्यायमात्मा पुण्येभ्यः कर्मभ्यः प्रतिधीयते ॥ (२.५.१)

१५. जीवाक्षरेणैव जीवाहराप्नोति जीवाह्वा जीवाक्षरमिति ॥ (२.३.८)

१६. आत्मा वा इदमेक एवाग्र आसीन्नान्यत्किंचन मिषत ।
स ईक्षत लोकान्नु सृजा इति । स इमाँल्लोकानसृजत ।
अम्भो मरीचीर्मरमापः ॥
अदोऽम्भः परेण दिवं द्यौः प्रतिष्ठाऽन्तरिक्षं मरीचयः
पृथिवी मरो या अधस्तात्ता आपः ॥ (२.४.१)

१७. स ईक्षतेमे लोका लोकपालान्नु सृजा ।
सोऽद्भ्य एव पुरुषं समुद्धृत्यामूर्छयत् ॥ (२.४.१)

ऐतरेयारण्यकम्

१८. स जातो भूतान्यभिव्यैख्यत्किमिहान्यं वावदिषदिति
स एतमेव पुरुषं ब्रह्मततममपश्यत् ॥ (२.४.३)

१९. यद्ध किंचेदं प्रेर्ता३इ तदसौ सर्वमत्ति यदु किंचातः
प्रैती ँ३ तादेयं सर्वमत्ति सेयमित्याद्याऽत्त्री ॥ (२.१.३)

२०. पुरुषे ह वा अयमादितो गर्भो भवति यदेतद्रेतः।
तदेतत् सर्वेभ्योऽङ्गेभ्यस्तेजः संभूतमात्मन्येवाऽऽत्मानं
बिभर्ति तद्यदा स्त्रियां सिंचत्यथैनज्जनयति तदस्य
प्रथमं जन्म ॥ (२.५.१)

२१. अथास्यायमितर आत्मा कृतकृत्यो वयोगतः प्रैति।
स इतः प्रयन्नेव पुनर्जायते तदस्य तृतीयं जन्म ॥ (२.५.१)

२२. गर्भे नु सन्नन्वेषामवेदमहं देवानां जनिमानि विश्वा।
शतं मा पुर आयसीररक्षन्नधः श्येनो जवसा निरदीयमिति।
गर्भ एवैतच्छयानो वामदेव एवमुवाच स एवं
विद्वानस्माच्छरीरभेदादूर्ध्वं उत्क्रम्यामुष्मिन्स्वर्गे लोके
सर्वान्कामानाप्त्वाऽमृतः समभवत् ॥ (२.५.१)

२३. यथा सौ दिव्यादित्य एवमिदं शिरसि चक्षुर्यथाऽसावन्तरिक्षे
विद्युदेवमिदमात्मनि हृदयं यथाऽयमग्निः पृथ्व्यामेवमिदमुपस्थे
रेतः ॥ (३.१.२)

तैत्तिरीयारण्यकम्

२४. पराङ्ंत्यज्यामयी। पराङ्ंत्यनाशकी। इह
चामुत्र चान्वेति। विद्वान्देवासुरानुभयान् ॥ (१.२७)

२५. सिकता इव संयन्ति। रश्मिभिः समुदीरिताः।
अस्माल् लोकादमुष्माच्च। ऋषिभिरदात् पृश्निभिः ॥ (१.२७)

२६. अपेत वीत वि च सर्पतातः येऽत्रस्थ पुराणा ये च नूतनाः।
अहोभिर् अद्भिरक्तुभिर्व्यक्तम्। यमो ददात्ववसानमस्मै ॥ (१.२७)

२७. इदं त एकं पर ऊ त एकं तृतीयेन ज्योतिषा संविशस्व।
संवेशनस्तनुवै चारुरेधि प्रियो देवानां परमे सधस्थे ॥ (६.३)

तैत्तिरीयारण्यकम्

२८. संगच्छस्व पितृभिः स ँ् स्वधाभिः समिष्टापूर्तेन परमे व्योमन् ।
यत्र भूम्यै वृणसे तत्र गच्छ तत्र त्वा देवः सविता दधातु ।। (६.४)

२९. उत्तिष्ठ प्रे हि प्रद्रवौकः कृणुष्व परमे व्योमन् ।
यमेन त्वं यम्या संविदानोत्तम नाकमधिरोहेमम् ।। (६.४)

३०. वैवस्वते विविच्यन्ते यमे राजनि ते जनाः ।
ये चेह सत्येनेच्छन्ते य उ चानृतवादिनः ।। (६.५)

३१. ते राजन्निह विविच्यन्तेऽथा यन्ति त्वामुप । देवा ँ् श्च
ये नमस्यन्ति ब्राह्मणा ँ् श्चापचित्यति ।। (६.५)

३२. एष पुण्यकृतां लोकोनेष मृत्योर्हिरण्मयम् ।
द्यावापृथिव्योर्हिरण्मय ँ् स ँ् श्रित ँ् सुवः ।
स नः सुवः स ँ् शिशाधि ।
आर्द्रं ज्वलति ज्योतिरहमस्मि । ज्योतिर्ज्वलति ब्रह्माहमस्मि ।
योऽहमस्मि ब्रह्माहमस्मि । अहमस्मि ब्रह्माहमस्मि ।
अहमेवाहं माँ जुहोमि स्वाहा ।
अकार्यकार्यवकीर्णी स्तेनो भ्रूणहा गुरुतल्पगः ।
वरुणोऽपामघमषणस्तस्मात्पापात्प्रमुच्यते ।। (१०.१)

३३. तस्माद्वा एतस्मादात्मन आकाशः संभूतः । आकाशाद्वायुः ।
वायोरग्निः । आग्नेरापः अद्भ्यः पृथिवी । पृथिव्या ओषधयः ।
ओषधीभ्योऽन्नम् । अन्नात्पुरुषः स वा एष पुरुषोऽन्नरसमयः ।। (८.१)

३४. सोऽकामयत । बहु स्यां प्रजायेयेति । स तपोऽतप्यत ।
स तपस्तप्त्वा । इद ँ् सर्वमसृजत ।
यदिदं किंच । तत्सृष्ट्वा । तदेवानुप्राविशत् ।
तदनुप्रविश्य । सच्च त्यच्चाभवत् । निरुक्तं चानिरुक्तं च ।
निलयनं चानिलयनं च । विज्ञानं चाविज्ञानं च । सत्यं
चानृतं च सत्यमभवत् ।
यदिदं किंच । तत्सत्यमित्याचक्षते ।। (८.६)

३५. असद्वा इदमग्र आसोत् । ततो वै सदजायत ।
तदात्मान ँ् स्वयमकुरुत । तस्मात् तत् सुकृतमुच्यते ।। (८.७)

तैत्तिरोयारण्यकम्

३६. ऋतं च सत्यं चाभीद्धात्तपसोऽध्यजायत । ततो
रात्रिरजायत ततः समुद्रो अर्णवः । समुद्रादर्णवादधि
संवत्सरो अजायत । अहोरात्राणि विदधद्विश्वस्य
मिषतो वशी । सूर्याचन्द्रमसौ धाता यथापूर्वमकल्पयत् ।
दिवं च पृथिवीं चान्तरिक्षमथो सुवः ॥ (१०.१)

३७. अन्धो मणिमविन्दत् । तमनङ्गुलिरावयत् ।
अग्रीवः प्रत्यमुँचत् तमजिह्वा असश्चत ॥ (१.११)

३८. ऊर्ध्वमूलमवाक्छाखम् । वृक्षं यो वेद संप्रति ।
न स जातु जनः श्रद्दध्यात् । मृत्युर्मा मारयादितिः ।
हसित ँ॒ रुदितं गीतम् । वीणा पणवलासितम् ।
मृतं जीवं च यत्किंचित् । अङ्गानि स्नेव विद्धि तत् ॥ (१.११)

३९. अष्टाचक्रा नवद्वारा । देवानां पूरयोध्या । तस्या ँ॒ हिरण्मयः
कोशः । स्वर्गो लोको ज्योतिषाऽऽवृतः यो वै तां ब्रह्मणो वेद ।
अमृतेनाऽऽवृतां पुरीम् । तस्मै ब्रह्म च ब्रह्मा च । आयुः कीर्ति
प्रजां ददुः । विभ्राजमाना ँ॒ हरिणीम् । यशसा संपरीवृताम् ।
पुर ँ॒ हिरण्मयीं ब्रह्मा । विवेशापराजिता ॥ (१.२७)

४०. यतो वाचो निवर्तन्ते । अप्राप्य मनसा सह ।
आनन्दं ब्रह्मणो विद्वान् । न बिभेति कदाचनेति ॥ (८.४)

४१. दक्षिणोत्तरौ पाणी पादौ कृत्वा सपवित्रावोमिति प्रतिपद्यत
एकद्वै यजुस्त्रयीं विद्यां प्रत्येषा वागेतत्परममक्षरम् ॥ (२.११)

४२. ऋचो अक्षरे परमे व्योमन्यस्मिन्देवा अधि विश्वे निषेदुर्यस्तन्न
वेद किमृचा करिष्यति य इत्तद्विदुस्त इमे समासत इति ॥ (२.११)

४३. ओमिति ब्रह्म । ओमितीद ँ॒ सर्वम् ।
ओमित्येतदनुकृति ह स्म वा अप्यो श्रावयत्याश्रावयन्ति ।
ओमिति सामानि गायन्ति । ओ ँ॒ शोमिति शस्त्राणि
श ँ॒ सन्ति । ओमित्यध्वर्युः प्रतिगरं प्रतिगृणाति ।
ओमिति ब्रह्मा प्रसौति । ओमित्यग्निहोत्रमनुजानाति ।
ओमिति ब्राह्मणः प्रवक्ष्यन्नाह-ब्रह्मोपाप्नवानोति ।
ब्रह्मैवोपाप्नोति ॥ (७.८)

तैत्तिरीयारण्यकम्

४४. भूमिर्माताऽदितिर्नो जनित्रं भ्राताऽन्तरिक्षमभिशस्त
एनः । द्यौर्नः पिता पितृयाच्छं भवासि जामि
मित्वा मा विवित्सि लोकात् ॥ (२.६)

४५. यत्र सुहार्दः सुकृतो मदन्ते विहाय रोगं तन्वा१ ँ स्वायाम् ।
अश्लोणाङ्गैरहुताः स्वर्गे तत्र पश्येम पितरं च पुत्रम् ॥ (२.६)

४६. मृत्योः पदं योपयन्ते यदैम द्राघीय आयुः
पृतरां दधानाः । आप्यायमानाः प्रजया
धनेन शुद्धाः पूता भवथ यज्ञियासः ॥ (६.१०)

४७. हरिः ॐ
शं नो मित्रः शं वरुणः । शं नो भवत्वर्यमा । शं न
इन्द्रो बृहस्पतिः । शं नो विष्णुरुरुक्रमः ।
नमो ब्रह्मणे । नमस्ते वायो । त्वमेव प्रत्यंक्ष
ब्रह्मासि । त्वमेव प्रत्यक्षं ब्रह्म वदिष्यामि । ऋतं
वादिष्याभि । सत्यं वदिष्यामि । तन्मामवतु । तद्वक्तारमवतु ।
अवतु माम् । अवतु बक्तारम् ।
ॐ शान्तिः शान्तिः शान्तिः ॥ (७.१)

४८. ऋतं च स्वाध्यायप्रवचने च । सत्यं च स्वाध्यायप्रवचने च ।
तपश्च स्वाध्यायप्रवने च । दमश्च स्बाध्यायप्रवचने च ।
शमश्च स्वाध्यायप्रबचने च । अग्नयश्च स्वाध्यायप्रवचने च ।
अग्निहोत्रं च स्वाध्यायप्रवचने च । अतिथयश्च स्वाध्याय
प्रवचने च । मानुषं च स्वाध्यायप्रवचने च । प्रजा च स्वाध्याय-
प्रवचने च । प्रजनश्च स्वाध्यायप्रवचने च । प्रजातिश्च स्वाध्याय-
प्रवचने च । सत्यमिति सत्यवचा राथीतरः । तप इति तपोनित्यः
पौरुशिष्टिः । स्वाध्यायप्रवचने एवेति नाको मौद्गल्यः ।
तद्धि तपस्तद्धि तपः ॥ (७.९)

४९. वेदमनूच्याऽऽचार्योऽन्तेवासिनमनुशास्ति ।
सृत्यं बद । धर्मं चर ।
स्वाध्यायान्मा प्रमदः । आचार्याय प्रियं धनमाहृत्य
प्रजातन्तं मा व्यवच्छेत्सीः । सत्यान्न प्रमदितव्यम् ।

तैत्तिरीयारण्यकम्

धर्मान्न प्रमदितव्यम् । कुशलान्न प्रमदितव्यम् । भूत्य न
प्रमदितव्यम् । स्वाध्यायप्रवचनाभ्यां न प्रमदितव्यम् ।
देवपितृकायाभ्यां न प्रमदितव्यम् ।
मातृदेवो भव । पितृदेवो भव । आचार्य देवो भव ।
अतिथिदेवो भव ।
यान्यनवद्यानि कर्मांणि । तानि सेवितव्यानि । नो इतराणि ।
यान्यस्माक ँ् सुचरितानि । तानि त्वयोपास्यानि ।
नो इतराणि ।
ये के चास्मच्छ्रेया ँ् सो ब्राह्मणाः तेषां
त्वयाऽऽसनेन प्रश्वसितव्यम् ।
श्रद्धया देयम् । अश्रद्धयाऽदेयम् । श्रिया देयम् ।
ह्लिया देयम् । भिया देयम् । संविदा देयम् ॥ (७.११)

५०. अथ यदि ते कर्मविचिकित्सा वा वृत्तविचिकित्सा वा स्यात् ।
ये तत्र ब्राह्मणाः संमर्शिनः । युक्ता आयुक्ताः । अलूक्षा
धर्मकामाः स्युः । यथा ते तत्र वर्तेरन् । तथा तत्र वर्तेथाः ।
अथाभ्याख्यातेषु । ये तत्र ब्राह्मणाः संमर्शिनः ।
युक्ता आयुक्तः । अलूक्षा धर्मकामाः स्युः । यथा
ते तेषु वर्तेरन् । तथा तेषु वर्तेथाः ॥ (७.११)

५१. न कंचन वसतौ प्रत्याचक्षीत । तद् व्रतम् ।
तस्माद्यया कया च विधया बह्वन्नं प्राप्नुयात् ।
अराध्यस्मा अन्नमित्याचक्षते ॥
एतद्वै मुखतोऽन्न ँ् राद्धम् । मुखतोऽस्मा अन्न ँ् राध्यते ।
एतद्वै मध्यतोऽन्न ँ् राद्धम् । मध्यतोऽस्मा अन्न ँ् राध्यते ।
एतद्वा अन्ततोऽन्न ँ् राद्धम् । अन्ततोऽस्मा अन्न ँ् राध्यते ॥ (६.१०)

५२. हिरण्यशृङ्गं वरुणं प्रपद्ये तीर्थं मे देहि याचितः ।
यन्मया भुक्तमसाधूनां पापेभ्यश्च प्रतिग्रहः ॥
यन्मे मनसा वाचा कर्मणा वा दुष्कृतं कृतम् ।
तन्न इन्द्रो वरुणो बृहस्पतिः सविता च पुनन्तु पुनः पुनः । (१०.१)

तैत्तिरीयारण्यकम्

५३. अत्याशनादतोपानाद्यच्च उग्रात्प्रतिग्रहात् ।
यन्मे वरुणो राजा पाणिना ह्यवमर्शतु ॥
सोऽहमपापो विरजो निर्मुक्तो मुक्तकिल्विषः ।
नाकस्य पृष्ठमारुह्य गच्छेद् ब्रह्मसलोकताम् । (१०.१)

५४. अकार्यकार्यवकीर्णी स्तेनो भ्रूणहा गुरुतल्पगः ।
वरुणोऽपामघमर्षणस्तस्मात्पापात्प्रमुच्यते ॥ (१०.१)

५५. यतो वाचो निवर्तन्ते ।अप्राप्य मनसा सह । आनन्दं
ब्रह्मणो विद्वान् । न बिभेति कुतश्चनेति ।
एत ँ ह वाव न तपति । किमह ँ साधु
नाकरवम् । किमहं पापमकरवमिति ।
स य एवं विद्वानेते आत्मान ँ स्पृणुते ।
उभे ह्येवैष एते आत्मान ँ स्पृणुते । य एवं वेद ॥ (८.६)

५६. यथा वृक्षस्य संपुष्पितस्य दूराद्गन्धो वात्येवं पुण्यस्य
कर्मणो दूराद्गन्धो वाति यथाऽसिधारां
कर्तेऽवहिताभावक्रामेद्यद्युवे हुवे ह वा विह्वदिष्यामि कर्तं
पतिष्यामीत्येवमनृतादात्मानं जुगुप्सेत् ॥ (१०.६)

५७. विश्वानि देव सवितर्दुरितानि परासुव ।
यद्भद्रं तन्न आसुव ॥ (१०.१०)

५८. अदितिर्देवा गन्धर्वा मनुष्याः पितरोऽसुरास्तेषा ँ
सर्वभूतानां माता मेदिनी महतो मही सावित्री
गायत्री जगत्युर्वी पृथ्वी बहुला विश्वा भूता
कतमा काया सा सत्येत्यमृतेति वसिष्ठः ॥ (१०.२१)

५९. सैषाऽऽनन्दस्य मीमा ँ सा भवति ।
युवा स्यात्साधुयुवाऽध्यायकः । आशिष्ठो दृढिष्ठो बलिष्ठः
तस्येयं पृथिवी सर्वा वित्तस्य पूर्णा स्यात् ।
स एको मानष आनन्दः ।
ते ये शतं मानुषा आनन्दाः । स एको मनुष्यगन्धर्वाणा मानन्दः ।
श्रोत्रियस्य चाकामहतस्य ॥ (८.८)

६०. ऋतं तपः सत्यं तपः श्रुतं तपः शान्तं तपो दानं
तपो यज्ञं तपो भर्भवः सवर्ब्रह्मै तदुपास्स्वैतत् तपः ॥ (१०.८)

CHAPTER
SIX

Personification of Abstract Ideas, Inanimate Objects and Natural Forces to Illustrate the Sacrificial Cult in Taittirīya Āraṇyaka

Pravargya

The fourth Book of the Taittirīya Āraṇyaka contains the verses used in performing the ceremony of Pravargya. The Brāhmaṇical expositions of this ceremony have been embodied in the succeeding Book V. Pravargya is part of Agniṣṭoma Deva-yajña. Majority of the verses used in performance of this ceremony are out of those (with minor variations here and there) as contained regarding Pravargya in the Maitrāyaṇī Saṁhitā (IV.9.1-11) of the Black Yajurveda. Some of these verses are found in the Ṛgveda, Vājasaneyi and other Saṁhitās of the White and Black Yajurvedas and chronologically supervening many other Śrauta Sūtras. An earthenware vessel,[1] one span in height is made, the middle of which is contracted (like a mortar) which has a rim or belt (mekhalā) about three fingers lower down from the top which is a large and deep bowl and has at the end a hole or spout for pouring in liquid. This is called Mahāvīra and it resembles three pots placed on one another. There are two other earthenware vessels (which are also called Mahavīra). The hot milk mixed and contained in the mahāvīra is called "gharma", of which offerings are made to specified deities. With this brief background about the ceremony, it appears worthwhile to examine as to how this Pravargya has been personified in the ceremony detailed out in Books IV and V of this Āraṇyaka :

The very origin of Pravargya is rather supernatural and mysterious. It has been said that the gods held a Sattra (some sacrifice) for attainment of prosperity and glory. In that sacrifice, Vishnu got the glory and bequeathed his colleagues and associates (the gods). From the hands of Vishnu, a bow and a number of arrows were produced. Other deities could not dare to face him. Hence, Vishnu became vainglorious and jeered at other gods. Consequently lustre bade him farewell. Other deities concealed it in Śyāmākā grass. Vishnu followed the deities for wreaking vengeance with stretched bow. On the request of other gods, ants called upadīkās cut one end of the stretched string of the bow. Consequently, the head of Vishnu was blown upwards upto heaven. When it fell down under its own weight, it touched both heaven and earth in turn. Thus, Pravargya came into existence. From its accompanying echo, great virility, carrying away were evolved what are respectively called as "Gharma" "Mahāvīra" and kingship in ritualistic parlance. Thus, the very emergence of the ceremony of Pravargya, its title of kingship, names of Mahāvīra and Gharma are enshrouded in mystery.

The gods performed a sacrifice with the headless body of yajña-puruṣa or Vishnu. They neither obtained any gains nor the heaven from this sacrifice. The gods approached their physicians called Aśvins for re-producing the head of the yajña-puruṣa which the latter did. Performance of sacrifice with this complete body of the srcrificial man bestowed all gains and the heavens. Hence, on account of this inevitable equation between the head of the yajña-puruṣa and the 'Pravargya' ceremony, it is only through prior performance of this ceremony that a sacrificer gains the desired ends as well as heaven. It is because of its importance that the pravargya has been called as the head of the Soma sacrifices. All this unequivocally brings out the supreme importance and exalted place of pravargya in the sacrificial cult. It is on account of this that a prayer has been made in section IV.2. for giving long life, prāṇa, apāna, sense organs, mind, speech, knowledge of the Self and fame both to the priest and the sacrificer (S. 1).

Section V.3 ibid lays down that Mahāvīra should be constructed only within an enclosure if divine glory is to be attained. While laying down the Mahāvīra one should keep his face in another direction so that his out-breathing may not be incident on it. This is essential for saving his life. It has further been said that the sacrificer should not stand in between the Sun and the Pravargya. In case this rule is violated, the sacrificer shall fall a prey to leprosy. Pravargya bas been equated to lustre and as such, it enhances the lustre in the life of its performer. Construction of Mahāvīra is instrumental to the attainment of all the three worlds and valour.

Section V.4 ibid. puts forth that the performer of the ceremony is blessed with lustre, is able to vanquish the demons, lives long, obtains divine glory, food and control over evil persons. He is gifted with the authority of a king and is also blessed with kith and kin. Covering of the Mahāvīra by gold secures heaven for the sacrificer. The sacrificer should encircle around the Mahāvīra four times with the recitation of the prescribed verses. One who does not go round for the fourth time is afflicted with a skin disease. Recitation of certain other prescribed verses bestows the highest heaven on the sacrificer.

The Gharma or Mahāvīra has been stated as one prominent among the deities and hence a prayer to him to protect the gods. He is also vested with the quality of bestowing on us the speech that may be instrumental in the attainment of gods. It has also been assigned the following highly personified epithets and qualities which are rather symptomatic of henotheism[2] :

(*a*) Womb of the gods.
(*b*) Father of the people.
(*c*) Lord of the people.
(*d*) Wisdom of the wise.
(*e*) He is our father and guide.
(*f*) He is lustre.
(*g*) He is heaven.
(*h*) He is upholder of righteousness and may bestow on us the qualities of a learned Brahmin, a warrior and a good business man.

The Mahāvīra has also been stated to be giver of longevity, divine glory, lustre, wealth etc. He has been stated to be even Vaster than the sky.

(*i*) He shines like the sustainer of heaven and the regions of earth (S. 2).

Mahāvīra is prayed to be instrumental for increasing our food-stock, energy, learning, bravery[3] etc. Thus, he is vested with an all enveloping role in management of the lives of all the creatures. The Mahāvīra is also vested with the power of destroying our enemies.[4] The Pravargya is fulfiller of all our desires, remover of all our sins and is also a friend. He is Intelligence-par-excellence, Creator of even the seas, Inducer of happiness[5] etc. He has also been given the epithets of milk of the cows meant for drinking by gods (S. 3), supreme source of light and the essence of entire vegetation (S. 4). Similarly divine epithets are glore for the Pravargya in section IV.19. Pravargya has been specifically assigned the following four epithets during the various stages of the ceremony :

Epithet	*Stage of preparation*
(*a*) Prajāpati	When being prepared as earthenware vessel.
(*b*) Samrāṭ	When fully produced or prepared.
(*c*) Gharma	When it has been cooked.
(*d*) Mahāvīra	When it has been set out.

The Pravargya is of the nature Āditya. It has also been given various names like Vaiśvadeva, Vasus, Māruta, Vāk[6] etc. during its various stages of preparation. Finally, it has been said that it is nothing but an embodiment of Prajāpati himself.

NOTES AND REFERENCES

1. Kane, P.V., The History of Dharamaśāstras, p. 1147.
2. TA., V. 6.
3. *Ibid.*, IV. 10.
4. TA., IV. 10.
5. *Ibid.*, IV. 11.
6. *Ibid.*, V. 11.5.

SOURCES VI

तैत्तिरीयारण्यकम्

१. आयुर्धेहि प्राणं धेहि । अपानं धेहि व्यानं धेहि ।
चक्षुर्धेहि श्रोत्रं धेहि । मनो धेहि वाचं धेहि ।
आत्मानं धेहि प्रतिष्ठां धेहि ।। (४.२)

२. धर्ता दिवो विभासि रजसः । पृथिव्या धर्ता ।
उरोरन्तरिक्षस्य धर्ता । धर्ता देवो देवानाम् ।
अमर्त्यस्तपोजाः ।। (४.७)

३. मह्हीनां पयोऽसि विहितं देवत्रा ।। (४.१२)

४. ज्योतिर्भा असि वनस्पतीनामोषधीना ँ रसः ।। (४.१२)

CHAPTER SEVEN

Myths and Parables Found in Aitareya and Taittirīya Āraṇyakas

A. MYTHS AND PARABLES CONTAINED IN THE AITAREYA ĀRAṆYAKA

The language and style of the Aitareya Āraṇyaka is characteristically Brāhmaṇical. A major portion thereof has been devoted to willy-nilly philosophize the various ritualistic ceremonies performed in the consummation of Mahāvrata. In this process, a good part of the Āraṇyaka has brought out and also rather lucidly explained the paramount importance of prāṇa in the human body. This has been elucidated in the form of certain parables as per supervening details :

(*i*) As narrated in section II.1.4, speech, sight, hearing, mind and breath vied among themselves that each of them was 'uktha' or the most vital organ of the body. With a view to prove the same, they decided that each of them should leave the body one by one and see the effect thereof. First of all, speech went forth; yet the body remained speechless, eating and drinking. Similarly on successive exits of sight, hearing and mind, the body continued to function, though of course, it was shorn of the essential functions of these three organs respectively. Then, the prāṇa went forth and the body instaneously fell. It was decayed.

Despite all this, each of these organs still claimed himself to be 'uktha'. With a view to clench the matter, they decided that each of them may re-enter the body one by one. They did so. On the re-enter of speech, sight, hearing and mind, the body lay still. However, as soon as the breath re-entered, the body arose. Ipso facto, the prāṇa was accepted as the 'uktha' or the most important functionary of the body.

(*ii*) Lord Indra[1] sat down besides the seer Viśvāmitra who was about to recite the hymns of the Mahāvrata day. The latter recited the thousand bṛhatīs and he went to Indra's dear home. Viśvāmitra repeated the recitation of these thousand bṛhatīs thrice. Indra felt exceedingly happy and offered to give a boon to Viśvāmitra. Upon this, the latter asked Indra to reveal his real nature to him. Indra said, "I am breath, thou seer, are breath, all creatures are breath, he that shines is breath. In this form, I pervade all the quarters. Prāṇa is the food and support of all the creatures. I am he that shines."

B. MYTHS AND PARABLES CONTAINED IN THE TAITTIRĪYA ĀRAṆYAKA

Origin of the Ceremony of Pravargya

The Taittirīya Āraṇyaka[2] contains a parable regarding the origin of the ceremony of Pravargya. Speaking about the invincibility of the All gods, this section puts forth that none of the gods including Varuṇa, Agni, Indra or any mortal being can vanquish them. One end of their expansive bow is in the heaven and the other on the earth. Indra disguised himself as white ant and cut the end of the bow of the All gods. The bow of Indra cannot be broken. Similar are the bows of Śaṁyu (son of Bṛhaspati) and Rudra. The heavenly end of the bow of Rudra cut off his head and pounded it. The head so powdered became 'Pravargya'. Thus, a person who performs a sacrifice with 'Pravargya', he rejoins the head of Rudra. The latter, therefore, does no harm or injury to such a sacrificer as well as to a person who knows the significance of the performance of the sacrifice alongwith the ceremony of Pravargya. The narrative made out here is sufficiently different from that contained in Book V of this very Āraṇyaka which is more detailed about the mythological background regarding the origin of the ceremony of Pravargya.

Importance of Wearing the Sacred Cord

Section II.1 opens with a short narrative that both the gods and demons wanted to attain heaven. Both the sects started performing separate sacrifices. The demons thought of winning the heaven by forces and armed themselves for battle. However, the gods continued with their ritual with due observance of celebacy. The demons on account of their foolishness and not knowing as to what was exactly to be done, met with dismay and could not attain heaven. On the contrary, the gods through successful performance of the yajña could attain the heaven. The demons were humiliated on account of unsuccessful progress of their sacrifice. The sacrifice should be performed only by wearing the sacred cord or by putting on a garment made of the skin of black deer. The sacred cord should be worn over the right shoulder and made to hang below the left arm. Wearing in a manner contrary to the above is called Prāchīnāvītam. When the cord is allowed to hang between the two arms (from the neck, of course), than this method is called saṁvītam. It is usually adopted by men.

Secret of Worship of the Sun

The Taittirīya Āraṇyaka[3] contains another short narrative. In the remote past, the demons performed hard penance. They obtained a boon from Prajāpati that the Sun should be their opposing fighter. It is on account of this reason that the Sun has to fight hard against devilish forces right from the moment of its rise till it sets. However, these evil forces are subdued only with water which is surcharged with potent strength by the recitation of Gāyatrī Mantra over it. The narrative goes on to say that it is on account of this reason that the discoursers of sacred texts offer water surcharged with Gāyarī stanza to the Sun in the evening by facing towards the east. The water so offered acts like a potent weapon against these devilish forces and casts them far away. A learned person who, therefore, makes obeisance to the rising and setting Sun, he attains prosperity and happiness. It has authoritatively been asserted here that the Sun itself is the Supreme

Brahman. The person who knows this himself becomes Brahma and ultimately attains the Supreme Being.

Pravargya

In counter distinction to the story contained in section I.5, Book V of the Taittirīya Āraṇyaka opens with another Brāhmaṇical parable. It relates that the gods held a sattra (a soma sacrifice) for the attainment of prosperity and glory. They all felt that they were already fully equipped with glory as deities as a class. However, Vishnu got the glory in that sacrifice. He thought that other deities should be without glory and hence left them. Other gods followed him. From the left and right hands of Vishnu, a bow and a number of arrows respectively were produced. He became vainglorious and jeered at others gods as they could not dare to face him. Hence, Tejas (lustre) bade him farewell. The other deities followed him and made this Tejas enter the vegetation called Śyāmākā. With a view to wreak vengeance, Vishnu followed the deities with fully stretched bow. The latter got one end of the stretched bow cut with the aid of ants called upadīkās. Consequently the head of Vishnu was blown off to heaven. When falling under its own weight; the head touched both heaven and earth in turn. Thus, Pravargya came into existence. From its accompanying echo, great virility and carrying away came into existence Gharma, Mahāvīra and Kingship respectively.

The gods distributed the headless body of the yajña-puruṣa into three parts. Agni, Indra and the All-gods caught hold of the morning, mid-day and evening soma pressings respectively. However, from the sacrifice of this headless body, the sacrificing gods neither got any material gains nor the heaven. Hence, the deities approached the Aśvins, who are physicians of the deities, for re-joining the head of the sacrificial man. They did so after being assured by the gods that they will always get a share in the sacrificial offerings. Hence, performance of the sacrifice with the complete yajña-puruṣa bestowed all gains and the heavens. This head of the sacrifice was the Pravargya. Hence, on account of this inevitable equation between the head of the sacrificial man and the Pravargya ceremony, it is only through prior performance of this ceremony that a sacrificer gains the desired ends as well as heaven.

Second Parable

Section V.10 starts with a Brahmaṇical parable that the gods made Prajāpati as Kāma-dhenu (cow) and milked the bright milk. It could not be sufficient for all the deities. Hence, Agni made it manifold. Different types of milk so produced became Sāmans of the Pravargya ceremony. The milk of cow is the milk of sāmans and that of goats is dear to the gods. By offering such milk, Prajāpati and the gods are satiated. The learned persons who know this importance of Pravargya and perform this ceremony are blessed with full benefits thereof.

NOTES AND REFERENCES

1. AA., II. 2.3.
2. TA., 1.5.
3. TA., II. 2.

CHAPTER

EIGHT

Mystic Words as Found in the Aitareya and Taittirīya Āraṇyakas, their Nature, Significance and Explanation

AITAREYA ĀRAṆYAKA

1. *Mahāvratam*

According to Sanskrit English Dictionary,[1] Mahāvrata means as follows :

(*i*) a great or fundamental duty (5 in number according to the Jaina System);

(*ii*) a great religious observance;

(*iii*) name of a Sāman or Stotra appointed to be sung on the last day but one of the Gavāmayana (applied also to the day itself or its ceremonies);

(*iv*) the religious usages of the Pāśupatas;

(*v*) one who has undertaken solemn religious duties or vows performing a great vow.

Sāyaṇa points out that the Taittirīya Brāhmaṇa has explained the term Mahāvrata in three ways :

(*i*) (the performer) becomes great by performing this ceremony; or

(*ii*) vow undertaken for (pacification) of a great god;

or

(*iii*) that is a big vow (S. 1).

In almost the very opening sentence of the Aitareya Āraṇyaka an altogether different connotation has been given to the ritual known as Mahāvrata. The origin of Mahāvrata[2] has been stated to have followed the episode of the killing of Vṛtra by Indra—When he (Indra) became great, then came into being the Mahāvrata (S. 2). According to this episode, the Indra became great by his rare and heroic act of annihilating his mighty foe, the Vṛtra. Thus, whosoever goes through the ritual of Mahāvrata attains greatness. The ceremony of Mahāvarta, therefore, owes its very name to the gains that rather inevitably accrue or follow suit. There also seems to be symbolical depiction of Indra. The Great, by the word Mahān and resemblance of vocables between Vṛtram and Vratam so as to symbolically represent the heroic deed of Indra by investing the ceremony of Mahāvrata with the capacity of bestowing equally immense worldly gains so as to exalt the sacrificer of this ritual to the status of a 'Very Important Person' in the present day mundane existence.

2. *Viśaḥ*

This word has been translated as folk (Prajāḥ) by Dr. A. B. Keith. It has been correlated with the word 'puṣṭi', which has been translated as 'increase' by Keith. Since folk signifies increase, so the word Puṣṭi accordingly means likewise. However, Sāyaṇa takes the more usual meaning of the word viśaḥ (plural) and explains it as :

> "The businessmen making large earnings through trade also pay heavy taxes. In this way, they increase or support the folk or community." (S. 3).

The word 'Viśa' also means property or wealth. Wealth or the worldly wherewithal is definitely strength giving. Thus, this word has been used in this opening part of the Aitareya Āraṇyaka (I.1.1) quite in a symbolic or rather mystic sense.

Folk also signifies plurality or multiplicity of numbers. Plurality of numbers or individuals, ipso facto, signifies at least physical stregth.

Hence, viśaḥ automatically signifies strength. Therefore, it has been said that a person desirous of increase should use the hymn, "The quest of your folk" (RV, VIII. 74) because folk indeed are increase or strength. Therefore, he becomes strong (S. 4).

3. *Atithi* (*or Guest*)

According to Sanskrit English Dictionary,[3] Atithi is a masculine word from root at, or said to be from a-tithi, 'one who has no fixed day for coming'. It means a guest, a person entitled to hospitality. It is also a name of Agni, of an attendant on Soma and also Suhotra—a king of Ayodhya and grandson of Rāma.

In the Ṛgveda, the epithet of Atithi has been very frequently used for Agni (RV.I. 73.1; II.2.8; III. 2.2; X. 91.2 etc.). This very epithet has also been used for the sun (RV., IV. 40.5). This epithet plausibly seems to have been used for fire as it is a very venerable and rather foremost deity in all the rituals. In fact, Agni has always been accepted as carrier or impeller of other gods to a sacrifice. Ipso facto, no insignificant and much less any derogatory epithet could be used for such a conspicuous deity. Hence, a really significant and meaningful epithet like Atithi was rightly attributed to the lustrous god called Agni.

The name Atithi appears to have been given to the Sun; because, etymologically, the word Atithi is derived from the root at (to go constantly) and the Sun is also, according to the traditional view, not stationary, but something that always moves.

The word Atithi (RV., V. 4.5) in the sense of a guest, has not been analysed in pada-pāṭha, implying that the origin of this word had become obscure by the time pada-pāṭha was developed. Yāska (IV. 5) in his two etymologies of the word, takes it as a non-Bahuvrīhi compound :

(*a*) One who goes to the homes of people[4] (S. 5). This etymology is from the root at, which, with the prefix 'Abhi' meant 'going towards'.

(*b*) He goes to the home of the yajamāna on specific days like Pūrṇimā etc. This derivation was from i+tithi, 'a' of tithi being the relic of a nominal from aya from the verb i, 'to go' (Abhyeti tithiṣu Parakulāniti vā gṛhāṇiti vā). The later popular etymology which supposes the word to be a bahuvrīhi in the negative sense a-tithi, was incompatible with the vedic accent, for according to a well known rule of Pāṇini's Aṣṭādhyāyī (VI. 2.172), a

Bahuvrīhi negative was always finally accented, while atithi is initially accented.

Using the line of thought ingrained in RV, IV. 40.5 and the first etymological break up of atithi given by yāska, the Aitareya Āraṇyaka[5] also, in the first instance, says that a guest is liable to go begging (S. 6), but as a matter of his conviction, the seer of the Āraṇyaka states in unequivocal terms that a guest indeed is one who becomes good and attains excellence. For him, who is not so, men do not deem worthy of hospitality (S. 7). Thus, according to this Āraṇyaka, the 'atithi' is the best out of the best persons. This word has, therefore, obvious mystical significance.

4. *Hiṅkāra*

According to Sāyaṇa, the word hiṅkāra is representative of the chirping of some birds. M. Monier Williams explains it as the lowing sound or cry made by a cow seeking her calf; the sound or cry hiṅ is used in the ritual.

In this section[6] of the Aitareya Āraṇyaka, it has rather been mystically emphasized that the recitation of the mid-day śāstra called Niṣkevalya in the Mahāvrata ceremony should be preceded by the recitation of the word hiṅkāra (translated as him by Keith) because of its mystic importance as detailed below :

(*i*) The word hiṅkāra is Brahman, this day is Brahman and hence the sacrificer begins his day with Brahman.

(*ii*) The word Hiṅkāra is masculine and the ṛks of the śastra are feminine. Hence, beginning of the recitation of śastra with the word hiṅkāra, ipso-facto, represents presence of a couple which is capable of procreation. Hence, the sacrificer who opens recitation of the mid-day śastra with 'hiṅkāra' ensures for himself the blessing of children and cattle (S. 8).

(*iii*) The beginning of recitation of the śastra with hiṅkāra has the efficacy of a shovel (Abhriḥ) in digging out or unraveling the mystries of Brahman.

(*iv*) Pre-recitation of this word also ensures fulfilment of all worldly desires and in fact, the knower of this digs out all these mundane attainments for himself.

(*v*) The word hiṅkāra also constitutes discrimination between the divine and human speech and hence who begins with the utterance of this word, ipso facto, discriminates between divine and human speech or in other words acquires knowledge of such differentiating features.

5. *Nāda*

The Āraṇyaka or the Forest-Text-Books being the immediate successors of the intensively ritualistic Brāhmaṇical literature could not ipso facto, completetly shun some of the apparently whimsical assertions/beliefs of the preceding ritualist cult. So, the forest-texts are also studded with such-like conceptions either in the form of certain superficially unassailable, obscure and abstract statements or certain words only, admitted to be endowed with mystic significance. The Aitareya Āraṇyaka[7] provides a very apt example. The section opens with the statement that ostensibly with a view to arm the verses with greater mystical efficacy, the verses be extended by interpolating the mystically surcharged word 'Nāda' in between the recitation of two verses (RV, X. 120.1 and VIII., 69.2). The word 'Nāda' has been identified with man and hence a person speaking sounds at it were (S.9). Competence or instrumentality of the verses to bestow blessings on the sacrificer is obviously multiplied if the verses are recited by interpolating after each pāda of RV. X. 120.1, the syllables pu, ru, ṣaḥ (of the word puruṣaḥ) followed by one pāda of the hymn Ṛgveda VIII.69.2 so as to make a bṛhatī. Thus, inter-mixture of the verses containing the metaphysically the potent word 'Nāda' and the three syllables of the Puruṣaḥ so as to constitute Bṛhatī metre is considered (though, of course, plausibly under the waning influence of the Brāhmaṇas) to be more effective in bestowing worldly pleasures and wherewithal on the sacrificer and his family.

This is not all about the versatile nature of the word 'Nāda'. It has been identified with 'odatyaḥ' and 'Yoyuvatayaḥ' which, according to this Āraṇyaka, signifies the heavenly and etheral waters. These have further been, rather syllogistically, equated with the watery saliva in the mouth, perspiration flowing down the body of a toiling person, the rain water that impregnates the entire vegetation and the semen that is gifted with the power of procreation. In this way, the word 'Nāda' has been put forth as an indirect agency of all botanical and physiological creation.

TAITTIRĪYA ĀRAṆYAKA

6. *Seven Vyāhṛtis*

The Taittirīya Āraṇyaka catalogues[8] all the traditionally known seven vyāhṛtis or mystic utterance, namely, Bhūḥ, Bhuvaḥ, Suvaḥ, Mahaḥ, Janaḥ, Tapaḥ and Satyam. Earlier,[9] the first four were mentioned in the Āraṇyaka and the fourth (Mahaḥ) was equated with the illustrious Brahman itself. It was given out to be the Self and other gods were stated to be its limbs. It was further made out that the Vyāhṛtis are so-called because they are uttered in various rituals. Four-fold combinations were made out and the different vyāhṛtis were stated to represent the following :

Vyāhṛti	*Phenomenon represented in each of the four combinations by each Vyāhṛti*			
	1	2	3	4
Bhūḥ	This world	Agni	Ṛks	Prāṇa
Bhuvaḥ	Atmosphere	Vāyu	Sāman Chants	Apāna
Svaḥ	Yonder World	Āditya	Yajus Formulae	Vyāna
Mahaḥ	Sun	Moon	Brahman	Food

Bringing out the significance of the above four-fold division of these vyāhṛtis, it has been stated that a knower of the same, comes to acquire the knowledge of the Brahman and all the gods pay tribute to him.

NOTES AND REFERENCES

1. M. Monier Williams, First edition, reprint, 1974.
2. AA., I. 1.1.
3. M. Monier Williams, First edition, reprint, 1974.
4. Verma, Siddeshwar, The Etymologies of Yāska, p. 155.
5. AA., I. 1.1.
6. AA., I. 3.1.
7. AA., I. 3.5.
8. TA., X. 27.
9. *Ibid.*, VII. 5.

SOURCES VIII

१. (क) महान् भवत्यनेन व्रतेन वा

(ख) महतो देवस्य व्रतम् वा

(ग) महच् च तद् व्रतम ।।

ऐतरेयारण्यकम्

२. इन्द्रो वै वृत्रं हत्वा महानभवद्यन्महाव्रतमभवत्तन्महाव्रतस्य महाव्रतत्वम् ।। (१.१.१)

३. वेश्यास्ते हि वाणिज्येन बहुधनमार्जयन्तः करमपि बहुलं प्रयच्छन्ति । अतो विशां पुष्टित्वम् ।। (१.१.१)

४. विशो विशो वो अतिथिमिति पुष्टिकामः ।
पुष्टिर्वै विशः पुष्टिमान्भवतीति ।
(सायणाचार्य की १.१.१ पर टिप्पणी)

५. अभ्यतितो गृहान् भवति ।।

६. ईश्वरोऽतिथिरेव चरतोः ।। (१.१.१)

७. यो वै भवति यः श्रेष्ठताभश्नुते स वा अतिथिर्भवति ।
न वा असन्तमातिथ्यायाऽऽद्रियन्ते ।। (१.१.१)

८. वृषा वै हिंकारो योषर्क्तन्मिथुनं मिथुनमेव तदुक्थमुखे करोति प्रजात्यै, प्रजायते प्रजया पशुभिर्य एवं वेद ।। (१.३.१)

९. ता नदेन विहरति पुरुषो वै नदस्तस्मात्पुरुषो वदन्सर्वः संनदतीव ।। (१.३.५)

CHAPTER

NINE

Conclusions

The foregoing study of the Aitareya and Taittirīya Āraṇyakas from the point of view of mysticism and symbolism has led us to the following conclusions :

1. *Points of Similarity*

Archaic Language : After the Saṁhitās, the priestly class developed a very detailed and complicated system of liturgy. All this naturally gave birth to reaction in the saner elements of the seers. Ipso facto, they once again thought of reverting to the original vedic system of making devoted prayers to the gods and seeking their blessings. With the object of achieving this purpose, they undertook writing of Forest texts or the Āraṇyakas in which the actual performance of the ritual was never undertaken. Because the brāhmaṇical literature had taken sway over the minds of the people at that time, the rishis of the Āraṇyakas were, evidently, well-advised to proceed to the evolution of the real nature of the Supernatural only in stages. They, therefore, purposely did not openly condemn the hollowness and futility of sheer ritualism. They steered clear to their objective of attaining the ultimate Reality without coming into an open conflict with the contemporary powerful sect of ritualism. Ipso facto, they had to retain the substantial part of the methodology and details of ritualism in their writings alongwith the archaic language of the brāhmaṇical scriptures. Thus, both the Aitareya and Taittirīya Āraṇyakas have archaic language because of the inevitable effects of the historical background.

Morally upright life : A glance through both of the Āraṇyakas under study reveals that they essentially reiterate leading of a morally upright life which necessarily entails truthful dealings/earnings, uprighteousness in behaviour etc. In fact, details of morally exalted life as brought out in the Taittirīya Āraṇyaka are much more elaborate. This Āraṇyaka repeatedly reiterates the purity of means of our earnings, honesty in thought, word and deed, upright dealings, removal of sins, healthiness of mind, the study of the Vedas, respect for parents, teachers, guests etc. for adoption in life.

Mystical and Metaphysical Beliefs : Both the Āraṇyakas firmly believed in the immanence and supremacy of the single Godhead. They also established identity between the ātman and brahman. The ātman was believed to be permeating whole of the body right from the nails of the toes upto the hairs of the head. It had also no sex of its own whatsoever. In fact, it was known to have the sex of the body in which it was ensconced. The then Aryans fully believed in the theory of transmigration of soul and its ultimate liberation. The Taittirīya Āraṇyaka in particular lays great stress on the mystical significance of syllable OM. The element of renunciation has been imported into the Taittirīya Āraṇyaka at a very late stage in the last Book which, in fact, constitutes a mere supplement.

Attitude towards enemies : The crude law of nature regarding 'Survival of the fittest' had a positive place at the time of both of these Āraṇyakas. No doubt, the Aitareya Āraṇyaka does not in any way stress on the annihilation and routing of the enemies; but all the same, there are passages which advocate subjugation of the enemy, evil-minded persons and all those who are full of hatred for us. On the other hand, the Taittirīya Āraṇyaka lays great stress on the obliteration of our enemies. It outrightly says that all our enemies may be pounded out of existence and they should flow far away from our lives just as water flows down the slopes.

2. *Points of Contrast*

The Aitareya and Taittirīya Āraṇyakas differ from each other in so many vital aspects. Some of them may pertinently be catalogued below :

Pseudo-mysticism : Aitareya Āraṇyaka primarily deals with the ceremony of Mahāvrata. Barring the Upanishadic portion (II. 4-6), almost whole of the book consisting of five Āraṇyakas has been devoted to either cataloguing of the details of Mahāvrata or giving ill-logical and irrational interpretations or attaching unwarranted significance to the performance of various steps in that ceremony. Such priestly assertions and dogmatism cannot stand on the touch-stone of any logic and rationale. Such type of pseudo-mysticism and brāhmaṇical interpretations are very scanty in the Taittirīya Āraṇyaka except Book V which contains brāhmaṇical details/parables pertaining to the evolution of the ceremony of Pravargya.

Mystical and metaphysical contents : No doubt, certain basic mystical and metaphysical concepts regarding brahman, ātman, transmigration etc., are identical in both of the Āraṇyakas, nevertheless, the philosophy of the Taittirīya Āraṇyaka definitely took a long march ahead over that of the Aitareya Āraṇyaka. The Upanishadic part in the latter is very brief and the longest chapater out of the three devoted to Upanishad primarily deals with the evolution of the universe. What makes the vital difference at the stage of the Taittirīya Āraṇyaka, is the Upanishadic protion thereof. In fact, it is the only Upanishad wherein the theory of the so-called sheaths or bodies of the soul has been given. No doubt, the Nārāyaṇa Upanishad (Book X) is henotheistic about the portrayal of the immense qualities of Nārāyaṇa; but all the same, this book also exhibits a high degree of metaphysical and mystical development. Thus, in short, the peaks of mystical experiences exhibited in the Taittirīya Āraṇyaka are far higher as compared to those in the Aitareya Āraṇyaka. When this is being said, it in no way, underrates the basic and fundamental concepts which had been clearly evolved in the Aitareya Āraṇyaka.

Prayers : A small section of the Aitareya Āraṇyaka does bring out the determination of the speaker to speak the right and the truth; but all the same, the prayers contained in the Taittirīya Āraṇyaka are really much more developed and they unmistakably bring out the yearning of the devotee not only for being bestowed with the wordly wherewithal, pleasures, health, strength, fame etc.; but also seek for panoramic blessings of the Almighty on him.

Importance of study of scriptures and real nature of penance: But for the Upanishadic portion and a few other passages/stanzas, the Aitareya Āraṇyaka is primarily ritualistic in its contents and subject-matter. No doubt, the first six books of the Taittirīya Āraṇyaka are also ritualistic; but they are mostly (except Book V) shorn of any illogical priestly dogmatism. On the contrary, certain portions of these Books very lucidly and emphatically bring out the necessity and basic importance of Svādhyāya (Self-study) in human life. In contrast to the present-day conception of repetition of some name of God or some incarnation thereof, the Taittirīya Āraṇyaka clearly mentions Ṛtam, Satyam, tranquility etc. as the essential itmes constituting austerity. This conception of austerity docs, ipso-facto, take human life to a higher moral pedestal.

Social conceptions : Aitareya Āraṇyaka clearly lays stress on leading of mutually affectionate and interdependent life among the members of a family; but all the same, it does believe in so many odd omens which are rather conspicuous by their absence in the Taittirīya Āraṇyaka. It also does discriminate in the treatment to be given to a brahmin and a non-brahmin even if the lapse comitted by both of them may be of the same nature and gravity. On the contrary, the Aryan culture brought out in the Taittirīya Āraṇyaka shows that the people did not feel irretrievably morose on the death of their kith and kin. They also did not believe in the custom of self-immolation by the widow of the deceased with her husband.

The above points of similarity as well as dissimilarity depicted in the two Āraṇyakas under study do present a panoramic view of the Aryan culture prevailing in that hoary past. In brief, it may be stated that the Aryans constituted a nation of above board and active people who were up and doing in all walks of life and firmly believed in the leading of really purpeseful lives.

Appendices

APPENDIX I

Some Examples of Illogical Statements/Assertions in the Aitareya Āraṇyaka

I. 2.2 (*i*) Following immediately after quotation of a Ṛgvedic hymn (X. 27), there is an abstract statement that "true indeed in this day and perfect its form as endowed with truth." How the day in question assumed the abstract quality of 'truth' has remained blissfully unelucidated.

(*ii*) Then, follows a statement about the composer of the aforementioned hymn (vasukra). his being the Absolute Brahman and ipso facto, the day being Brahman. Thus, the day of recitation of the Marvatīya śastra forthwith transforms its character from "Truth" to "Brahman".

(*iii*) Then, supervenes the statement that the aforesaid hymn having not been specifically attributed to any deity is, ipso facto, attributable to Prajāpati. However, a single reference to the word "Indra" in the hymn, perforce, attributes it to Indra. Thus, the hymn is strangely attributed to the two of the mightiest gods, viz. Prajāpati and Indra. This line of argument sounds basically mundanc because human nature, as it is, attributes all its deliberations either to mighty persons or mighty gods. That is why, perhaps, there follows a eulogy about the word "Mahat" and the day, by dint of this very fact, assumes the character of being "mighty". This is fourth attribute of the day in addition to the earlier three of Truth, Brahman and Indra.

(*iv*) Briefly stated, then follows a discussion about the mystic significance of the hymns composed by Bhardvāja and Viśvāmitra and those known as Kayāśubhīya hymns.

(*v*) Last of all, quite a mystic significance has been worked out between the number of verses in the Marutvatīya śastra, limbs of the human body and span of 100 years of human life full of health strength and glory and the metre of the hymns (Triṣṭubh) despite their variation from hymn to hymn of the śastra.

Section I. 2.3 also brings out similarly odd and apparently irreconciliable reasoning as the following brief survey of section shall clearly establish :

(*i*) This section and the next one pertain to the ceremony of mounting the swing while reciting the Niṣkevalya śastra after having offered the mid-day oblations of Marutvatīya śastra. The section rather characteristically and also with at least apparent mysticism opens why a swing is a swing? He who blows is the swing," is the reply. He swings forward in these worlds and hence is called the swing. A swing cannot possibly vibrate in the ether without any point of sustenance. Hence, ipso facto, it has to vibrate in this material world and nowhere in the so-called invisible worlds. Hence, the very argument adduced in support of its definition apparently does not convey any sense.

(*ii*) Then follows a chain of arguments about the number of planks that should go to make the swing—there should be one plank because the wind blows in one direction and a swing should be like the wind. It should have three or two planks so as to synchronise with the number of three worlds (Heaven, Ether and Earth) or two worlds as the ether does not actually constitute any world. All this argumentation sounds rather fallacious and apparently irrational. In the first instance, wind, no doubt, at one moment, blows in one direction only; but it can change its direction at any time. However, a swing can vibrate within a certain set and specified range only and it entirely lacks both the force and manoeuvrability of the wind. Similarly, there can reasonably be no coherence and much less any identity between the planks of a swing and the number of the worlds. However, the seers of the Forest-Text Book in question do seem to purposely enshroud every step of the ceremony of Mahāvrata in apparently inconceivable mystry.

(*iii*) In the chain of arguments, it is rather vainly philosophized that the planks should be made of Udumbara wood as the same is somehow put forth to represent sap and food and thereby the sacrificer shall win both. Both the planks should be raised in the middle because eating of food is strangely enough asserted to give maximum satisfaction in the middle. This argument blatantly contradicts the present day well-known economic dictum called the "Law of decreasing marginal utility" and is apparently unacceptable because the starting morsels give maximum utility or satisfaction to a hungry person than those taken in the middle of the meals.

(*iv*) Last of all, there is no dearth of philosophizing when it is asserted that even the supporting twin ropes of the swing represent different types of animals and the availability of these ropes ensures supply of both kinds of animals to the sacrificer. The irrationale of this argument can better be understood than being explicitly explained. How can a swing be hung without two ropes and how these inanimate ropes be instrumental in mystically procuring various types of animals for the sacrificer, does not, at least, appeal to any logical person. To further crown this line of fallacious reasoning, it is asserted that the ropes be of 'darbha' grass because of all the plants darbha is free of evil. It is once again a strange authoritarian dictum. How can a particular grass be potent enough to destroy sins ? Besides, it is an admitted fact that it is very difficult to make ropes of darbha grass and even if made, their tenacity to support the swing and the priest is extremely doubtful. In short, when all is said and done, the entire line of argument in this section seems to pile absurdity over absurdities.

APPENDIX II

Stotras and Śastras used in the Performance of the Mahāvrata Ceremony as Detailed out in the Aitareya Āraṇyaka

MORNING LIBATION

There are two ghee offerings :

I.1.1 (i) *Vaiśvadeva Śastra*

In this śastra, the following hymns are recited for achievement of various worldly objectives as mentioned against each :

(*a*) For prosperity	RV.III.13	=	7 verses
(*b*) For increase	RV.VIII.74	=	15 verses
(*c*) For glory	RV.V.1	=	12 verses
(*d*) For children and cattle	RV.II.5	=	8 verses
(*e*) For food	RV.VII.1	=	25 verses
I.1.2 (*f*) For destruction of evil	RV.III.13.1	=	1 verse

I.1.4 (ii) *Prauga Śastra* (*Seven Tristichs*)

(*a*) For readiness of the day for the sacrificer and the gods.	RV.I.2.1-3	=	3 verses
(*b*) For denoting what is well prepared.	RV.I.2.4-6	=	3 verses
(*c*)	RV.I.2.7-9	=	3 verses
(*d*) For gaining food.	RV.I.3.1-3	=	3 verses
(*e*) For invitation to Indra.	RV.I.3.4-6	=	3 verses
(*f*) Invocation to all gods.	RV.I.3.7-9	=	3 verses
(*g*) Invocation to Sarasvati.	RV.I.3.10-12	=	3 verses
		=	89 verses

MID-DAY PRESSING

(i) *Marutvatīya Śastra* (*Two Tristichs*)

(*a*) First Tristich	RV.VIII.68.1-3	=	3 verses
(*b*) Second Tristich	RV.VIII.2.1-3	=	3 verses

(ii) *Pragāthas (part of Marutvatīya Hymn)*

They are	RV.VIII.53.5-6	
	RV.I.40.3	
	RV.I.40.1	Two verses of a Pragātha make a tristich. Hence, these verses constitute six tristichs
	RV.I.40.5	
	RV.III.20.4	
	RV.I.91.2	
	RV.I.64.6	
	RV.I.64.6	
	RV.III.89.3	
	RV.VIII.89.1	
	RV.VII.32.10	
	= 12 verses	

Then are recited all the Pragāthas, all the ukthas, all the Pṛṣṭhas, all the Śastras, all the Praugas, all the pressings of the Soma.

I.2.2 (iii) *General form and specifically Mahāvrata part of the Marutvatīya*

(*a*)	Vasukra Hymn	RV.X.27	= 24 verses
(*b*)	Another Hymn	RV.VI.17	= 15 verses
(*c*)	Kayāśubhīya Hymn	RV.I.165	= 15 verses
(*d*)	Viśwamitra Hymn	RV.III.47	= 5 verses
(*e*)	Janiṣṭhā Ugraḥ	RV.X.73	= 11 verses
			= 97 verses

I.3.7 (iv) *Niskevalya Śastra*

(*a*)	Rājana Sāman	RV.X.120	= 9 verses
(*b*)	Tām Sūte	RV.X.54	= 6 verses
(*c*)	Bhūya idvāvṛdhe	RV.VI.30	= 5 verses
(*d*)	Nṛnām u tvā	RV.III.51.4	= 3 verses

Note : 1. RV.X. 120 1 with ten syllables and 'Nadom vaḥ' (RV. VIII. 69.2, with seven) are extended by addition of pu.

2. He extends the verses by 'Nadam vaḥ' (RV. VIII. 69.2) as per directions in I.3.5 and I.3.8. Next comes Sūdadohas verse (RV. VIII.69.3).

I.4.1 (*v*) *Neck verses* = 3 verses

Next comes Sūdadohas verse

(*vi*) *Head verses or Arkavati verses* RV.I.7.1-9 = 9 verses

Next comes Sūdadohas verse

(*vii*) *Vertebrae verses* = 3 verses

Next comes Sūdadohas verse

Note : Three sets of verses, neck, head and vertebrae are all to be repeated with a pause at the half-verse. This means that there is a pause at the end of the halfverse (and Om at the end of the verse). The other possibilities are (1) pause at each pāda, with Om at half-verse; (2) no pause, Om at end.

I.4.2 (viii) *Right Wing* (*Rathantara Sāman*)

	RV.VII.32.22-23	= 6 verses
	RV.VIII.3.7-8	Four Bṛhatis turned into six verses.
	RV.I.32	= 15 verses
	RV.VII.18	= First 15 verses
	RV.VII.19	= 11 verses
	RV.VII.20	= 10 verses
	RV.VII.23	= 6 verses
	RV.VII.25-29	= 26 verses
Saṁpāta Hymn	RV.IV.20	= 11 verses
		= 100 verses

Then followed by the paṅkti I.80.1.

Next comes Sūdadohas verse.

I.4.2 (*ix*) *Left Wing* (*Bṛhat Sāman*)

RV.VI.46.1-2	= 6 verses
RV.VIII.61.7-8	Four Bṛhatīs turned into six verses
RV.VI.18	= 15 verses
RV.VI.23	= 10 verses

	RV.VI.24	= 10 verses
	RV.VI.25	= 9 verses
	RV.VI.31-38 (5×8)	= 40 verses (Five each hymn)
Saṁpāta Hymn	RV.IV.23	= 11 verses
		= 101 verses

Then followed by the paṅkti I.81.1
Next comes Sūdadohas verse.

(*x*) *Tail verses*

	RV.X.157	= 5 verses
	RV.X.172	= 4 verses
From other Śākhās		= 12 verses
		= 21 verses

Next comes Sūdadohas verse.
Next comes Dhāyyā (additional) verse—X.74.6.
Next comes Sūdadohas verse.

I.4.3 (*xi*) *Tristichs*

(a) Gāyatrī	RV.VIII.6.1-45	= 45 verses
	RV.VIII.78.1-3	= 3 verses
	RV.VIII 2.4-39	= 36 verses
(For verse No. 28.	RV.VIII.80.1 is substituted)	
	RV.VIII.77.1	= 1 verse
	RV.VIII.92.2-33	= 32 verses
	RV.VIII.93.1-33	= 33 verses
	RV.VIII.32	30 verses
	RV.VIII.45	42 verses
	RV.VIII.81	= 9 verses
	RV.VIII.82	= 9 verses
		= 240 verses

Next comes Sūdadohas verse.

V.2.4 (b) Bṛhatī

RV.VIII.1.1-29	=	29 verses
RV.VIII.3.1-6; 9-20	=	18 verses
RV.VIII.4.1-14	=	14 verses
RV.VIII.33.1-15	=	15 verses
RV.VII.32.1-2; 4-21; 24-27	=	24 verses

(For RV. VII.32.10 is substituted RV. VIII.92.1).

6 Vālakhilya Hymns

RV.X.49-54	=	56 verses
RV.VI.46.3-14	=	12 verses
RV.III.44	=	5 verses
RV.III.45	=	5 verses
RV.VIII.61.1-6; 9-18	=	16 verses
RV.VIII.66.1-14	=	14 verses
RV.VIII.70.1-11	=	11 verses
RV.VIII. 88	=	6 verses
RV.VIII. 90	=	6 verses
RV.VIII.97.1-9	=	9 verses
	=	240 verses

Next comes Sūdadohas verse.

V.2.5 (c) (i) Uṣṇih

RV.VIII.12	=	33 stanzas
RV.VIII.13	=	33 stanzas
RV.VIII.15.1-12	=	12 stanzas
RV.VIII.98		12 stanzas
RV.VIII.24.1-27	=	27 stanzas
RV.I.84.7-9	=	3 stanzas
RV.V.40.1-3	=	3 stanzas
RV.VI.43.1-3	=	3 stanzas
	=	126 uṣṇih stanzas

(ii) Then Gāyatrī Stanzas

RV.VIII.14	=	15 stanzas
RV.VIII.16	=	12 stanzas
RV.VIII.17.1-13	=	13 stanzas

RV.III.37.1-10	=	10 stanzas
RV.I.4	=	10 stanzas
RV.I.5	=	10 stanzas
RV.I.6	=	10 stanzas
RV.I.8	=	10 stanzas
RV.I.9	=	10 stanzas
RV.VI.45.1-30	=	30 stanzas
RV.I.30.13-15	=	3 stanzas
	=	133 gāyatrī stanzas or

114 uṣṇih stanzas, making in all 240 uṣṇih.

Next comes Sūdadohas verse.

I.5.1 (xii) Vaśa Hymn

RV.VIII.46	=	20 verses
Sūdadohas serse	=	1 verse
	=	21 verses

The Vaśa verses are recited with the word 'Om', according to metre and according to the manner of occurrence (yathopapādam). Sāyaṇa explains this with reference to the technical rule given by Āśvalāyana Śrauta Sūtra, VI.5.11.12, that dvipadā verses are to be recited with a pause in the middle and 'Om' at the end; while ekapadā verses are to have 'Om' prefixed and suffixed.

(xiii) *Thigh verses*

RV.VIII.40 = 12 verses

Note : A Triṣṭubh is recited at the end. Sāyaṇa holds this to refer to a special mode of recitation by which after the first pāda, there is a pause, and Om follows the second, and so for the third and fourth and which he calls triṣtup samaya. This is from Āśvalāyana Śrauta Sūtra, VI.15.6.

I.5.2 (xiv) *Verses representing other limbs of the Śastra bird*

RV.X.50 = 7 verses

Note : After reciting the fourth verse, the nivid is to be inserted and it is to be 'Indro devaḥ Somam pibtu (or pinvamānaḥ). Nivid is inserted among triṣṭubhs and jagatīs.

	RV.X.29	=	8 verses
Sajaniya Hymn	RV.II.12	=	15 verses

Tārkṣya Hymn	RV.X.178	=	3 verses
Ekpadā verse (Sāmaveda I.456)		=	1 verse
	RV.I.11	=	8 verses

V.3.1.

Note : Additions are made to first 7 verses of RV.I.11. Having recited the first-half stanza of the first stanza of this hymn, he combines the first-half stanza of the second stanza with the second half-stanza (of the first stanza), (joining) quarter stanza with quarter-stanza so as to make anuṣṭubhs. Upto the last stanza, he combines every succeeding half-stanza with the preceding. The rest are done in the usual way.

Virāj verses	RV.VII.23.1-6	=	6 verses
Vasiṣṭha Hymn	RV.VII.24.1-6	=	6 verses
		=	54 verses

Note : The sixth verse of VII.24 is placed after the fourth and the fifth comes at the end.

I.5.3 EVENING PRESSING

(i) *Vaiśvadeva Śastra*

(*a*) Strophe Tristich	RV.V.82.1-3	=	3 verses
(*b*) Anti-strophe Tristich	RV.V.82.4-6	=	3 verses
(*c*) Savitṛ Hymn	RV.IV.53	=	7 verses
(*d*) Dyāvāpṛthivi Hymn	RV.I.185	=	11 verses
(*e*) Ṛbhu Hymn	RV.IV.36	=	9 verses
(*f*) Vaiśvadeva Hymn	RV.I.164.1-41	=	41 verses
(*g*) Vaiśvadeva Hymn	RV,I.89	=	10 verses

Note : After the ninth verse, the insertion (Nivit) is made as follows :

'Viśve devāḥ Somasya matsan.'

(ii) *Agni-Māruta Śastra*

(*a*) Vaiśvanara Hymn	RV.III.2	=	15 verses
(*b*) Mārut Hymn	RV.V.55	=	10 verses
(*c*) Jātavedas Hymn	RV.I.99.1	=	1 verse
(*d*) Jātavedas Hymn	RV.I.94	=	16 verses

APPENDIX III

A Note on Āruṇaketuka Fire as Described in the Taittirīya Āraṇyaka

In the introductory stanzas of section I.1 of the Taittirīya Āraṇyaka, Sāyaṇa refers to five types of Agnis, namely, Sāvitra, Nāciketa, Cāturhotra, Vaiśva-sṛja and Āruṇaketuka. Thereafter, he introduced the Baudhāyana Kalpa Sūtras so as to give out the concept of the watery bricks called 'Abīṣṭakās'. However, the origninal text of the Āraṇyaka does not make mention of any kinds of such fires or the watery bricks upto section I.21. Thus, the commentary of Sāyaṇa upto this section that the watery bricks are to be laid with the recitation of the various stanzas of the Araṇyaka without any corroboration from the original context of this treatise is rather confusing and off the mark till the reader goes through section 22 of Book I. Sāyaṇa could at least very justly give an introduction that the concept of the different types of fires and the watery bricks finds specific mention in as late a section as 22, but on the authority of the subsequent literature known by the name of Kalpa Sūtras; he was prescribing laying of the watery bricks from the very first section. In the introductory stanza to Book II too also, Sāyaṇa rather wrongly states that in the preceding book details of Aruṇketuka Agni have been given; even though a student of this treatise fails to find any mention of this fire in the first twenty one sections of a total of 32 sections of Book I. The commentator could definitely bring in exactitude in his commentry so as to ward off the inescapable confusion to any reader of this text till he reaches section I.22. From the original text, nothing is evident that the first 21 sections anywhere make mention of any of the eight fires and the so-called watery bricks.

The watery bricks find specific mention for the first time in section I. 22. It has been stated that a knee-deep pit should be dug towards the north of the fire-altar. It should then be filled with water upto the ankle level. On this water, then the leaves, stems and flowers of the blue lotus should be made to swim. Upon that, the fire should be kindled right on the water. However, this fire is not firmly established in this world. Hence, all around it, the watery bricks should be arranged. It has been specifically stated that this fire should be kindled in the sacrifices known as Agnihotra, Darśapur-aṇamāsa, Paśu-bandha, Cāturmāsya and in fact all the sacrifices. A branch of seers known by the name of Śaṇḍilās lay down that fires known (in sacrificial parlance) as Satriya, Sāvitra, Nāciketa, Cātur-hotriya, Vaiśva-sṛja, Upānu-vākya and Āruṇaketuka are to be kindled primarily for the attainment of the objectives of longevity, sun, health, Brahman, strong body, happiness in this life and hereafter and over-coming a great calamity respectively.

Detailing out the process of initial creation of the world, it has been stated in section I.23 that in the beginning, it was all water and nothing else. Prajāpati made his appearance on a lotus leaf and thought of creation. He found that the Unmanifest could be instrumental in the creation of the manifest. He brooded over and shook his body. Certain specified categories of seers and a tortoise were created. This tortoise was the Primeval Puruṣa. He acquired to himself numerous heads, eyes and feet. Thereafter, this Puruṣa threw handful of water in various directions on the watery bricks of the Āruṇaketuka fire reciting the verse "*Eva hy ev eti*" (Given in full in section I.20). Thereby, the Fire, Air, Indra, Pūṣan, deities, men, the manes, Gandharvas, fairies, various directions and intermediate regions were created. Whatever drops of water fell outside the fire-altar, from them the demons, Rākṣhasas and Piśāchas were created. Thus, the Āruṇaketuka Agni has its basic significance in the creation of the universe by the Primeval Man; though it has remained unexplained as to how this fire had itself come into existence for the first time. It is from sprinkling of water towards the northern side of the fire-altar of Āruṇaketuka fire that the basic gross element known by the name of fire came into existence. Then, the question naturally arises to how the Āruṇaketuka fire came into being earlier. Perhaps, the seers of this forest text intended to bestow the characteristic of 'Apauruṣeya' on this mysterious fire.

The next section[1] delineates the procedure as to how water is to be collected from four different sources for laying down the watery bricks of the fire-altear of Āruṇaketuka fire. The clouds, lightning, thunder and rain are the representative sources of water. Rain water collected from a sunny place is placed in the eastern direction of the fire-altar. This is instrumental to the attainment of divine glory. Water obtained from a well is to be placed on the southern side. This makes the sacrificer powerful or energetic. Stagnant and flowing waters, after collection from their respective sources, are to be placed on the western and northern sides respectively. They are conducive to the enhancement of the social respect and greater bodily strength respectively of the sacrificer. Water procured from domestic containers is to be placed in the middle of the four directions. It enhances self-respect. Water brought from a pool or pond is to be placed on the bricks lined in the middle. This secures a place for the sacrificer in the heaven. Water is sprinkled in all directions. This bestows abundance of food. This fire was kindled by seers called Aruṇās, Ketus etc. Hence, this was given the name of Āruṇaketuka. One who establishes this fire, his respect or fame is increased multifold.

Section I.25 details out the almost identical process of kindling of an eighth kind of sacrificial fire called Pāñktaḥ.

The supervening section[2] details out the sacrifices and kinds of fires which should be kindled and the materialistic gains accruing therefrom. It has been laid down that in case Sāvitra Agni is kindled alongwith Aruṇaketuka fire, an enemy may injure the testicles of the kindler and he becomes bereft of the power of procreation and his sacrifice shall, ipso facto, be rendered fruitless. From this, Sāyaṇa infers that only Āruṇaketuka Agni should be independently kindled and that too on the northern side of the fire-altar of the sacrifices as specified in section 22 above. This fire should be kindled by one who is desirous of having children, cattle, rain, freedom from disease, bewitching anybody, attacking and slaying the enemy, brilliance, fame, divine glory and attainment of heaven.

There are certain taboos also, One who has kindled the Āruṇaketuka fire should not run while it is raining on him. He should not ease himself or urinate in water. He should neither spit in water nor take bath by being fully naked. This fire is mysterious and all this should be done to avoid being harmed by this fire. Similarly, the sacrificer should also not tread over lotus leaves and gold or ornaments thereof. Likewise, the meat of tortoise and other acquatic animals like fish should not be taken so as to avoid injury or harm by waters.

The supervening section[3] urges the decendants of Bharata to enkindle this Agni by giving up lethargy and with all zeal. Cataloguing the benefits those accrue as a result of worship of Āruṇaketuka fire, it has been said that this fire saves an unmarried woman, a young woman and also a devoted and virtuous wife from the sin each or any one of them might have committed by sexual indulgence with any other man. It also provides a blanket protection from any other sins. Knowers of Indra and this fire need not take resort to any other means for salvation or attainment of heaven irrespective of the fact whether they have steady or unsteady minds or are worshippers or otherwise.

Two verses of the above section do command that all the sinners including women of immoral character, evil born and evil-minded well-born persons should be kept away from the site of the fire-altar of Āruṇaketuka fire.

Last section[4] briefly outlines the procedure and rules which should be adopted before the kindling of the Āruṇaketuka fire. Soma should be pounded thrice daily and before doing so, bath should be taken. Meals should be taken after begging only in the morning and evening. The fuel should be only of Udumbara. Cleaning of the body be done only with clean water stored in utensils and not by going to some stream or tank. Food left over in the begging bowl should not be consumed. A yajña should be performed everyday for appeasement of the Supreme Brahman and the gods like Agni, Air, Sun, Prajāpati etc. and the Rishis like Aruṇas and Kāṇḍas. The rules regarding kindling of Āruṇaketuka fire should be studied only in a hermitage in a forest. The specified verses should be recited. A cow, a utensil of metal and silken or inferior clothes (if silk cannot be afforded) be given as offering to the preceptor after successful learning of these rules.

NOTES AND REFERENCES

1. TA., I. 24.
2. TA., I. 26.
3. TA., I. 27.
4. *Ibid.*, I. 32.

BIBLIOGRAPHY

THE VEDIC SAṀHITĀS

Ṛgveda Saṁhitā with the commentary of Sāyaṇa, 4 Vols. : Vaidika Saṁshodana Maṇḍala (Vedic Research Institute), Poona, 1941.

Ṛgveda Saṁhitā translated by H.H. Wilson, 7 Vols., 1977 : Cosmo Publications, New Delhi.

The Hymns of the Ṛgveda translated by R.T.H. Griffith, 2 Vols. : The Chowkhamba Sanskrit Studies, Vol. XXXV, 1963.

Vājasaneyi-Mādhyandina-Śukla-Yajurveda Saṁhitā with the commentaries of Uvaṭa and Mahīdhara, 1971 : Motilal Banarsidass.

The texts of the White Yajurveda translated by R.T.H. Griffith, 3rd ed. , 1957 : E.J. Lazarus and Co., Medical Hall Press, Benares.

Kāthaka Saṁhitā of Yajurveda, 1943 : Svādhyāya Maṇḍala, Aundha.

Taittirīya Saṁhitā with commentaries of Bhaṭṭa Bhāskara and Sāyaṇa, 2 Vols. : Vedic Research Institute, Poona, 1970.

The Veda of the Black Yajus School entitled Taittirīya Saṁhitā translated by A.B. Keith, 2 Vols, 1967 : Harvard Oriental Series, Vols. 18-19, Motilal Banarsidass, Delhi.

Maitrāyaṇī Saṁhitā of Yajurveda, 1998 BK : Svādhyāya Maṇḍala, Aundha.

Atharvaveda Saṁhitā with commentary of Sāyaṇa. 1960 : Vishveshvaranand Vedic Research Institute, Hoshiarpur, Punjab.

The Hymns of the Atharvaveda translated by R.T.H. Griffith, 2 Vols., 1962 : Master Khelari Lal and Sons, Varanasi.

Atharvaveda Saṁhitā translated by William Dwight Whitney, 2 Vols., 1962 : Motilal Banarsidass, Delhi.

THE BRĀHMAṆAS

Vājasaneyi-Mādhyandina Śatapatha Brāhmaṇa with commentary of Sāyaṇa, 1940 : Laxmi Venkateshwar Steam Press, Kalyan-Bombay.

ĀRAṆYAKAS AND UPANISHADS

The Aitareya Āraṇyaka edited by A.B. Keith, 1909 : The Clarendon Press, Oxford.

The Aitareya Āraṇyaka with commentary of Sāyaṇa : Ānandāśrama Sanskrit Series No. 38, Poona.

The Taittirīya Āraṇyaka with commentary of Sāyaṇa, 2 Vols., 1926-27 : Ānandāśrama Sanskrit Series No. 36, Poona.

The Principal Upanishads by S. Rādhākrishṇan : George Allen and Unwin Ltd., Ruskin House, Museum Street, London, 1953.

The Thirteen Principal Upanishads translated by Robert Ernest Hume, 2nd Edition : Oxford University Press, London, 1931.

The Upanishads by Sri Aurobindo : Sri Aurobindo Āśrama, Pondicherry, 1972.

The Upanishads by M.P. Pandit, 2nd edition : Ganesh and Co. (Madras) Private Ltd., Madras 17, 1968.

The Mahānārāyaṇa Upanishad by Col. G.A. Jacob : Bombay Sanskrit Series.

The Mahānārāyaṇa Upanishad translated into English by Swāmi Vimalānanda : Sri Rāmakrishṇa Math, Mylapore, Madras, 1979.

The Philosophy of the Upanishads by Paul Deussen : Oriental Publishers, Delhi, 1972.

A Constructive Survey of Upanishadic Philosophy by R.D. Ranade. : Bhāratīya Vidyā Bhavan, Chowpatty : Bombay, 1968.

OTHER BOOKS

A History of Indian Literature, Vol. I. by Maurice Winternitz, 2nd ed., 1972 : Munshi Ram, Manohar Lal, Delhi.

History of Dharamaśāstra by P.V. Kane, Vol. II, Part II : Bhandarkar Oriental Research Institute, Poona, 1975.

A Vedic Concordance by Maurice Bloomfield, 2nd ed., 1964 : Harvard Oriental Series, Vol. 10, Motilal Banarsidass, Delhi.

A Concordance to the Principal Upanishads and Bhagvat Gita by Col. G.A. Jacob, reprinted 1971 : Motilal Banarsidass, Delhi.

Encyclopaedia of Religion and Ethics, edited by James Hastings, Vol. IX and XII, 2nd Impression, 1930 : Edinburgh, T & T Clark, 38, George Street.

General Index

The names and subjects of the Bibliography have not been included here. The numbers refer to pages.